Learning from Mistakes
in Clinical Practice

CAROLYN DILLON
Boston University School of Social Work

BROOKS/COLE

™

THOMSON LEARNING

Australia • Canada • Mexico • Singapore • Spain • United Kingdom • United States

BROOKS/COLE

TM

THOMSON LEARNING

Publisher: *Marcus Boggs*
Sponsoring Editor: *Lisa Gebo*
Editorial Assistant: *Sheila Walsh*
Marketing: *Caroline Concilla*
Assistant Editor: *Alma Dea Michelena*
Project Editor: *Kim Svetich-Will*
Production: *Buuji, Inc.*

Manuscript Editor: *Alan DeNiro*
Permissions Editor: *Sue Ewing*
Cover Design: *Denise Davidson*
Print Buyer: *Vena Dyer*
Compositor: *Buuji, Inc.*
Printing and Binding: *Webcom, Inc.*

For more information about this or any other Brooks/Cole product, contact:
BROOKS/COLE
10 Davis Drive
Belmont, CA 94002 USA
www.brookscole.com
1–800–423–0563 (Thomson Learning Academic Resource Center)

Printed in Canada

10   9   8   7   6   5   4   3   2

Library of Congress Cataloging-in-Publication Data
Dillon, Carolyn
   Learning from mistakes in clinical practice / submitted by
Carolyn Dillon.
      p. cm.
   Includes bibliographical references (p.) and index.
   ISBN 0-534-52401-X (alk. paper)
   1. Clinical psychology—Decision making. 2. Critical thinking.
3. Mental health counseling. 4. Counseling. 5. Counselor and
client. I. Title.

RC454.4 .D554 2003
616.89—dc21   2001052462

To the clients, colleagues, and loved ones
who help me see the hidden wisdom in mistakes

Contents

Preface

I wrote this book to affirm that mistakes are great teachers, and they are as inevitable in clinical practice as they are in everyday life. While developing clinicians may think that they alone make and repeat mistakes, those of us who instruct and support them know that human fallibility and systemic complexity ensure that none of us will ever be exempt from error.

Normalizing and universalizing mistake making should help reduce the embarrassment, defensiveness, and lessened esteem that many people manifest when reviewing mistakes aloud with instructors and colleagues. Additionally, when we share our own mistakes as a feature of the mentoring process, we symbolically decrease distance between ourselves and our learners, and demonstrate the importance of remaining humble and open to feedback indefinitely in order to temper any urges we might feel to "perfect" ourselves or our work.

I've also written the book in the belief that being forewarned *is* being forearmed. I believe learners will profit from having a virtual "handbook" of what to look out for, so that awareness of learning phases, challenges, and mistakes prepares them to spot their misconceptions and missteps earlier, reflect on these candidly with instructors and peers, and review productive alternatives. Handily locating dozens of pitfalls, challenges, mistakes, and suggested alternative strategies in one easy-to-read volume should bring long overdue, positive attention to these elements of work as important generators of knowledge and awareness building. Learners can come to appreciate fully how both successes and mistakes enhance knowledge and skill use.

A goal of this book is to help learners identify and rework some classic mistakes frequently observed in counseling work, such as *too many boilerplate responses* ("mmmhmm," "I see," excessive head nodding); *detouring around uncomfortable subjects* like financial practices, sexual activity, and death; *talking intrusively;* often *interrupting the client*; and *asking too many—or irrelevant—questions.* Since mistakes memorably support further reflection on solid practice principles, they can also reveal a need for more theoretical understanding and clarity, and can promote a deepening and broadening of conceptualization—a side benefit of mistake making.

OTHER GOALS OF THE TEXT

Learning from Mistakes in Clinical Practice emphasizes the influence of cultural diversity and theoretical orientation on the interpretation of what constitutes a "mistake," demonstrating how an error in one moment or situation might be just the right strategy with another person or at a different time. It stresses the importance of developing a set of reliable theoretical principles to guide one's stance and work with clients of great diversity. The book also encourages our learning about the cultures we work with *from experience within them,* through social, family, spiritual, or neighborhood bonds and shared activities that increase our knowledge of norms, expressive styles, and beliefs about change and help seeking.

Such learning will be a radical shift from many learners' expectations that we mostly learn about diversity through classroom and conference presentations; or by asking clients about their guiding beliefs, behavioral patterns, and approaches to problem solving. Readers are alerted to the problem of depending on clients to be our major or regular educators about their cultures. While this is certainly helpful for us, it can use up precious client speaking/reflecting/feeling time, and can leave students and workers looking uninformed and uninvolved with communities and their needs, styles, and rights.

The book also frames content in relation to commonly described phases of work with clients: setting a safe and private context for work; engaging clients in relationship, assessment, and contracting; carrying out goal-focused work together; reviewing its course and efficacy; and tapering down to the ending of work. Tasks, challenges, and useful skills in each phase are discussed, followed by review of mistakes common to each phase and suggestions for more productive use of knowledge, skills, and self.

Mistakes are examined multidimensionally, with content elaborating the personal, interpersonal, systemic, and theoretical factors that can produce mistakes, including worker efforts to use a favorite theory to help clients, even though it's visibly a poor fit with their needs and style. Numerous worker-client vignettes illustrate clearly and practically what missteps can look and sound like, as well as illustrating the various effects they may have on the relationship and the work.

The book honors career-long clinical learning with others, emphasizing that clinical work involves interaction and reciprocity, continuously influencing participants and process. This work can't really be learned alone. The text encourages professionals to share mistakes more openly and to learn from each other's mistakes and not just one's own, in order to advance practice conceptualization, and move to more sophisticated levels of mistake making. Workers with only themselves as both supervisor and sounding board run the risk of not knowing what they don't know, and of not being able to see and hear what others might.

The book encourages worker self-care through the intentional creation of healthier lifestyle practices, and renewing connections and activities with nurturing others within and outside work. The less tired, overburdened, isolated, and stressed workers are, the less they are likely to commit errors stimulated by those conditions. We need not be naïve about how long we can last and still work well with clients while under unremitting stress or pressure with little mitigating relief or support.

ABOUT THE BOOK

I designed *Learning from Mistakes in Clinical Practice* for use primarily by people assuming or advancing clinical roles and responsibilities, whether through bachelor's or master's degree programs, or through other educational initiatives that help volunteers, ministers, medical and allied health professionals, business professionals, and attorneys enhance process knowledge and skills. Clinicians with fewer than five years of experience can also use the text to update themselves on practice principles, common sources of mistakes, and alternative strategies for work.

The designations "worker," "clinician," "student," "learner," and "client" are utilized throughout the text to facilitate use of the material by a variety of learners, some of whom may be very interested in recognizing process mistakes and alternatives, even if they're not in formal clinical learning programs or internships. To simplify language, gender designations of workers and clients are alternated in order to avoid a distracting repetition of the words "his or her."

The text is intended to be warmly human and accessible in language, and its principles are frequently illustrated by highly disguised, first-person accounts of commonly observed mistakes and attempted repairs from my own practice and that of many colleagues and students sharing mistakes over the years. Examples and vignettes are multicultural and derived from work in home, residential, school, psychiatric, health, and community-based settings. Although it's oriented around practice with individual clients, collaterals, and service teams, much content is also applicable to our wider roles with families and community groups. While a "mistakes book" makes a good companion for practice texts already in use, it can also act as a stand-alone practice primer because of its elaboration of the phases, principles, strategies, methods, and roles common to sound clinical practice of all kinds.

ORGANIZATION OF THE BOOK

The book is divided into nine chapters, the first of which, "Becoming a Professional," introduces readers to the notion of a clinical learning pathway and some common awakenings and changes that learners experience as they try to move from good-natured, random listening and responding to disciplined, purposeful, and empathically attuned responsiveness that's increasingly theoretically informed. Chapter 2, "Early Successes and Derailments," discusses characteristics of effective clinical work and several means of tracking ourselves and our work in order to maintain purpose and focus. It defines mistakes and some sources and signs of them in addition to identifying general strategies for reworking or avoiding them.

Chapter 3, "Engaging with Clients and Getting Started," and Chapter 4, "Professional Relationships: Steps and Missteps" elaborate the special skills, openness, empathy, sensitivity, and relational capacities needed to engage clients in exploration of their needs and strengths, and to make and maintain working alliances with a wide variety of clients requesting assistance alone or in groups. The chapter emphasizes the need for agencies and workers to represent in inclusive ways the populations they serve, and to accommodate clients' needs and styles insofar as realistically possible. Discussion is informed by a strengths perspective, by multicultural practice theory, and by relational theory from the Wellesley College Stone Center for Service and Research on Women.

Chapter 5, "Assessment and Contracting," delineates the features that distinguish effective from less effective working agreements. This chapter also describes attitudes and techniques helpful with mandated or ambivalent clients. The importance of focused, well-timed questions is stressed, and other techniques of information gathering are detailed. Workers are asked to note how, in being inducted via sympathy and concern into the systems they're evaluating, they may play important change roles in families, and how they can also lose perspective and useful differentiation.

Chapter 6, "The Middle Phase of Work," and Chapter 7, "When the Work Doesn't Work," utilize psychodynamic, cognitive, behavioral, and systems theory to discuss knowledge, skills, and mistakes common to the intervention phase of work. These chapters highlight the importance of motivation in both worker and client, utilization of client strengths and community resources, work with spiritual resources, and complex worker use of self as appreciative listener, witness, model, guide, and persistent "keeper of the flame" of belief that change can happen when people work hard and well towards clear objectives. The chapter encourages workers to be "where the client is," and incorporate a not-knowing perspective. Egregious mistakes and their malign consequences are discussed, with suggestions given regarding action steps to take when these occur.

Chapter 8, "Common Mistakes in Ending," reviews how to plan and effect positive and educational endings that make good use of what has been achieved and learned to date. The chapter discusses strategies for reworking frequent mistakes in ending—for example, premature worker or client disengagement, excessive self-disclosure, and trying to inject too much material into final meetings before closing out contact.

The ninth chapter and epilogue, subtitled "Developing Important Capacities, Allaying Common Concerns," summarizes worker capabilities crucial to clinical work of high quality. The book ends with an appeal to learners not to skip the middle step of development as a clinician—that of seasoning through exposure to new challenges and to continuous learning involving quality feedback that keeps us growing.

Each of the first eight chapters concludes with an Exercises section. These sections constitute a mini–teacher's manual for working with the class within a range of clinical content and experience. The exercises include independent journal reflections by students, in-class small group discussions, large group discussions, and role play demonstrations of practice mistakes and various methods of reworking them. In each chapter's Exercises section, I've included a brief narrative from my own learning and work over the years, and instructors comfortable in doing so can share with their students similar kinds of learning from their own mistakes. The Exercise sections embody the book's central premise that mistakes are great teachers and are as important as successes in educating us to be knowledgeable, self aware, and skilled practitioners.

ACKNOWLEDGMENTS

I would like to express thanks to Lisa Gebo, my Wadsworth editor and an inveterate inspiration and guide in the completion of this project. I'm equally grateful for the important guidance and support of Assistant Editor Alma Dea Michelena, whose responsive collaboration has helped bring this text to fruition.

Special thanks to Mary Collins, Margaret Griffin, Susan Fineran, Cynthia Poindexter, Christine Flynn Saulnier, Joe Spiegel, Lee Staples, and Libby Zimmerman, writing group colleagues at the beginning of the project whose feedback greatly enriched the subsequent work. Many thanks also to Toni Tugenberg for important fine-tuning suggestions and encouragement. I'm also indebted to several outside reviewers who gave me detailed feedback that greatly improved content and organization. Many thanks to Dr. Michael Altekruse, University of North Texas; Sally Alonzo Bell, Azusa Pacific University; Dr. Dana Comstock, St. Mary's University; Dr. Robin Ersing, University of Kentucky; Dr. Jackie Leibsohn, Seattle University; Dr. Russell Miars, Portland State University; and Dr. Bruce Thyer, University of Georgia.

Carolyn Dillon

1

Becoming a Professional

Every clinical role involves a capacity to anticipate situations wisely, relate and listen purposefully, initiate meaningful activity, respond differentially to others based on their unique assets and needs, and have some insight about one's effect on people and process. Development of these important capacities is a tall order and requires lifelong learning. Yet newcomers to clinical learning may expect this formative process to be easy and natural—a mere extension of long-familiar ways of caring and being.

Many people come to clinical education with prior experience as community volunteers, residence advisors in schools, after-hours coverage staffers in psychiatric or residential treatment facilities, and hotline staff. Others transition from careers in business, teaching, law, nursing, or allied health professions such as occupational or speech therapy. Still others, such as ministers or medical residents, may simply want some brief clinical training to improve listening and responding capabilities with clients or patients. Since all have had some experience in helping roles, many may wonder what could be so novel or difficult about caring, listening, and responding well in clinical education and work.

THE DAWNING OF A NEW AWARENESS

It can be very disconcerting to set out eagerly in clinical learning and suddenly find that, while you're doing quite well at some tasks, your instructors begin to identify numerous mistakes in your work with people. Startled—perhaps embarrassed or ashamed—people learning about clinical work can feel and behave defensively at times, justifying responses or perhaps even repeating behaviors to try to prove that they work well after all. Regular reflection on mistakes can be a hard pill to swallow, especially if people have been told repeatedly what good listeners and helpers they are, or if they come from backgrounds where perfection was expected and mistakes were often met with criticism or shaming. It can also take a good deal of trust to believe that instructors, who are at first quite unfamiliar to us, really do have our own and our clients' best interests at heart when they critique our work.

Those new to clinical learning may anticipate that the hard part of a practice education is the immersion in the sad stories and daunting problems of clients, or their involvement in the uphill battle against social injustice. Few of us approached this learning with awareness of a far subtler challenge: the necessity of transforming ourselves from casual conversationalists into disciplined listeners and responders, using skills and selves in purposeful, goal-directed ways. After all, very little detail about the life-changing and style-altering nature of the clinical learning process is to be found in school or agency catalogs.

Learning this new purposefulness initiates us all into the novel process of having our conversations and behaviors closely scrutinized by instructors, program administrators, other students, and colleagues. Although seasoned colleagues will provide support, instruction, and validation of our personhood, knowledge, and skills, they will also provide us with continuous feedback about perceived missteps. Tolerating—and then actually seeking out—such scrutiny and feedback requires a strong commitment to a rigorous course of learning. This is a course frequently focused on building an awareness of personal comfort , skill levels, and rough spots observed in our work with clients and others.

For some, this increased self-awareness and deliberate use of self in clinical learning and work engenders a kind of culture shock. This shock is especially painful if family, culture, friends, and prior educational settings haven't encouraged focus on self as central to success in the workplace. For some people asked to focus so much on self in order to enhance work with others, this can feel grandiose and self-serving on the one hand, and intrusive on the other.

ADDITIONAL COMPLICATIONS
IN CLINICAL ROLES

Initiates into any clinical learning program confront a mind-boggling array of new people, myriad practice domains and theories, competing community organizations and agendas, and various surrounding systems of sociopolitical influence. Arriving at busy practice sites, learners assume case responsibilities right away, with little time for orientation, observation of colleagues at work with clients, or rehearsal of skills. Considering the complexity of clinical learning and the heavy demands that work and learning environments place on learners, it's no surprise that mistakes occur repeatedly over the course of everyone's professional development. Much comes at us, and much comes out of us. Mistakes are inevitable under such circumstances.

Actually, experience teaches us that mistakes are inevitable under *any* circumstances. As human beings, we remain subject to the subtle influences of shifting dynamics within and between us, events or stimuli of the moment, and the swirl of wider world circumstances and events. There is no way to bring so many complexities and reciprocal influences together without making mistakes. Years of study, practice, and personal work can alter the number and kind of mistakes we make, but not their inevitability. Often we can learn as much from our mistakes as we can from our successes, since both kinds of experience highlight growth edges—things to preserve and things to discard or use differently (Kottler & Blau, 1989). Once we accept mistakes as a human given, and not just as personal flaws or too-daunting challenges, we can begin to normalize mistake-making as part of a developmental learning curve in the clinical professions.

THE PROFESSIONAL LEARNING CURVE

Within the first few months of study, recognition dawns that the process of acquiring and refining clinical knowledge and skills will be a complex one involving a number of phases.

Initial Idealization and Excitement

Students usually gravitate towards instructors and senior workers whose poise, values, knowledge, and technical acumen they admire. They hear experienced colleagues and instructors discussing the years of course work, supervision, reading, and personal work they've undertaken to get where they are today. It's quite normal for newcomers to experience an initial exuberance and readiness to tackle assignments, to log the experience and learning needed to achieve the practice competency levels of advanced senior practitioners and thinkers. As a comfort in this initial phase, remember that while you are inevitably making mistakes, your hopeful outlook and positive spirit are very refreshing for educators, clients, and colleagues alike, and your undiluted eagerness to reach out to and help others will very often distinguish your work.

Saari (1989) observes that during this initial phase of excitement and hopefulness, clinical learners tend to operate from a belief that "caring" itself is the major force that brings about human change. This assumption may explain in part strong impulses to try to rescue clients instead of thinking of ways to empower them, and to use excessive reassurance, praise, and sympathy as predominant techniques of helping while in the process of developing a more complex and realistic understanding of client/system strengths and problems.

Bafflement and Blues

As the realities and demands of complex new learning and difficult case assignments set in, learners often find that their zest starts to be peppered with bursts of anxiety related to new understanding, heightened self awareness, and self-focus stimulated by supervisory feedback, course work, and discussions with colleagues and peers. Previously confident people can begin to feel somewhat inept, deskilled, and self-conscious when they trip up in interviews or have the bottom fall out of work plans and initiatives, despite tremendous caring and effort. Saari notes that periodic crises of confidence can move learners toward a belief that theoretical understanding is what really works in helping people. This new faith in transformative ideas is still too unidimensional, yet is on the right track toward the development of greater complexity in conceptualizing the assessment and change process.

When a learner realizes that initial ideas about "what works" are too simplistic, he or she can plummet into an overly serious, rather blue period of self-doubt and confusion about what really does help people. In their research on theoretical models guiding therapeutic practice, psychologists Prochaska, Norcross, and DiClemente (1994) identify over four hundred systems of psychotherapy (p. 22), each with its own epistemology for interpreting and responding to human needs and problems. Little wonder that clinical learners routinely express exasperation about the lack of one clear, memorizable "answer" or "way" to resolve human problems. Faced with a variety of ideas that often conflict with one another, anyone can get caught up in a quiet internal debate about the goodness of fit between oneself and the clinical disciplines, which become perceived as complicated, full of imperfect people and seemingly insurmountable client problems, and fraught with confusing theoretical ambiguities and clashes. Gardner (1995) and Reynolds (1942) speak of learners' acute needs for instructional empathy and support during these periods of confusion and doubt, to help learners deal with understandable frustrations and insecurities.

Upwards—or Onwards

On the positive side of change, greater perspective on clinical practice's potentials and limitations reflects a newcomer's appreciation of the need for personal stretching through continued learning. Sometimes formal learning is augmented by personal therapy as learners elect to work on blind spots, sensitive issues, relational conflicts, or personal reactions that visibly intrude upon personal and professional development. Holman and Freed (1987) note that

> . . . [t]he process of achieving a professional identity and increasing self-awareness and control over reaction is full of anxiety and uneven accomplishments. Clients confront . . . workers with developmental conflicts which may resonate within the student. Thus, related developmental issues may be revived in the student worker and may bring about either regressive manifestations or further growth and resolution of the conflict (p. 7).

There also comes greater awareness of the opportunities and frustrations of working within impinging larger systems, and of the wide range of assets and problems within people and their environments. For example, in reminiscing about his experiences as a fledgling counselor, Kottler (1997) describes his unsettling surprise (familiar to many of us) when he realized how much time he would be spending alone as a counselor. Here he was, a counselor with others, and always surrounded by others—yet part of a group of colleagues usually too busy with tasks to come together for support and relaxation.

Corey and Corey (1998) suggest many motives that can both propel people towards clinical practice careers and later take them in other directions. These motives include needs for money, prestige, and status; self-help and gratitude while helping others; and to be in control and provide answers to problems (pp. 4–8). Some newcomers turn away from the professions if they become overwhelmed or turned off by complexity, frustration, disillusionment, or lack of social recognition and status in work hierarchies. Those who stay with the extensive learning process usually emerge with greatly increased knowledge, skills, comfort, and good feelings about their more realistically perceived roles within the huge universe of helping resources.

A student recently compared her own intense learning experiences at a cancer treatment center for young children with the experiences of many people living with cancer:

> I have always been very exacting on myself. If you drew out a pathway, there are just two steps. Step 1 is "Beginning" and Step 2 is "Perfection." There's no middle. I can see now that what I'm learning here is the middle step. It really threw me at first, but I think I'm back on my feet now. Some patients go through a lot of the same awakening. Step 1 is diagnosis, and they think Step 2 is death, but often it isn't. Step 2 is a long, bumpy middle where nothing is certain, and you just do your best and get the very best help you can.

AT ONE WITH CLIENTS, YET DIFFERENT FROM CLIENTS

One of the reasons clients say they seek out counseling is to get new or different ideas to aid in problem-solving, or fresh perspectives from someone not too deeply immersed in their situation or worldview. A continuing challenge for developing clinicians is figuring out how to join with clients through empathy and identification, while maintaining enough differentiation and perspective to be able to assess and respond helpfully.

Such challenges pitch the learner into a continuing professional debate in which some colleagues discuss ways to reduce the distance, formality, and air of superiority that once suffused the role and mystique of the clinician (Miller & Stiver, 1997), while others believe that clients within some non-Western cultures may expect or prefer their counselors to be experts demonstrating a special knowledge and power not found in ordinary members of the community

(Gutierrez, Parsons, & Cox, 2000; Kleinman, 1988; Lee & Armstrong, 1995; Lum, 2000).

As you bring your own fresh eyes to clinical education, you may readily spot another paradox. While clinicians speak of "leveling the playing field" between ourselves and our clients (implying an unfavorable power-over mentality in practitioners), we also acknowledge that our professional knowledge and skill base, and clients' special expertise about their own lives and coping skills, can separate us in ways that spark both creativity and conflict. You will also see that clients, communities, and workers sometimes stratify by differing economic realities and opportunities and by unresolved tensions around class, color, ethnicity, religion, gender, sexual orientation, age, ability, and language use.

Eventually you are likely to discover that through enriching life and community experiences, course work, case consultation with many instructors, and diligent personal work, you can feel "like" and "with" clients sometimes, and at other times experience the worth and importance of participants being and feeling different and unique. At the same time, you have the opportunity to work within communities to reduce social distance and barriers to social equality.

CRISES AROUND LEARNING
TO BE DELIBERATE

Starting out in the helping professions, few of us realize how much we are going to need to learn about relationships and grow in our relational skills. We learn to establish purposeful, goal-directed relationships in which we tailor responsiveness to the unique assets, needs, and styles of each client or situation. We learn to be quieter and more witnessing with some clients, more interactive and encouraging with others; more personally disclosing in some situations, while more restrained in others. With some people we can bring in humor and a light touch; with others, we might work in a more businesslike manner out of respect for client styles and preferences.

Using ourselves differently with different people can feel at first like playacting or becoming a chameleon. What is being asked instead is that we *start and be where the client is*—that we relate in ways that help clients with many different backgrounds and styles feel more at ease with us. Feedback from clients, instructors, colleagues, and allies in the community about cultural beliefs, values, and practices assists in the development of appropriately flexible relational behaviors. In addition, relational work involves an informed, disciplined use of self, rather than just being and doing randomly according to our own personal feelings and impulses at any given moment. What we learn about our style and skills in relating to others through respectful and frank exchanges makes us more self-aware and responsible in our processing. At practice sites we also get to see how different colleagues handle themselves in professional roles of various kinds, allowing us to compare our ways of interacting and try out new ideas or styles.

At first you may worry that you are becoming so acutely self-aware in action that at times you're almost paralyzed by self-consciousness and fumbling.

While beginning to understand and produce effective responses in client sessions, you may feel much less natural, spontaneous, and effective than you did before coming for specialized education or training. In her pioneering work on the stages of learning in social work practice, Reynolds (1942) refers to this phase of clinical learning as "understanding the situation without power to control one's own activity in it" (p. 79). Worries in this stage often signal that you have begun to appreciate your effect on clients and process, the effects of clients and process on you, and your need to deepen and firm up guiding knowledge and practice principles.

Here newcomers begin to experience a necessary internal shakeup in which they realize that they truly do need to grow and change in identified ways in order to be more effective in professional relationships and work. You will likely find yourself beginning to blend naturalness and deliberateness much more easily and pleasurably as you integrate advanced understanding of yourself and of practice principles into your "natural" self. During this transition, however, loved ones may plead, "Please don't look at me like that" (with somber, analyzing gazes) or "Please don't 'therapize' me," as you bring your increasingly intentional style and tone of voice into private relationships without thinking twice about it.

Once you begin to notice and purposely alter your use of self through reflection with and feedback from others (including clients and loved ones), you can begin to experience the satisfactions of a disciplined use of self. You begin to see the benefit of helping clients focus conversations purposefully on goal-related material in order to make maximum use of the client's and agency's time and resources. Sometimes your clients will begin to replicate some of the things you say and do with them with people in their own lives, and you can see and appreciate how growth ripples outward and not simply inward.

TENDING, NOT JUST HAVING, RELATIONSHIPS

Just as their mentors have done with them, clinical learners can begin tentatively to give voice to problems arising in clinical relationships, instead of pretending that such problems don't exist. This work forwards direct discussion closer to the time when problems occur. The client gains encouragement to respond to the worker's initiative—for example, a worker expressing an unusual angry edge toward the client at the moment. Honest acknowledgment of in-the-moment process events can be unique for both workers and clients, as many have been taught to skirt around interpersonal tensions or blunders should they arise in social conversation (Miller & Stiver, 1999). Purposeful authenticity is refreshing in its encouragement of participants to use the working relationship itself as a laboratory for learning more about how relationships can unfold and develop differently when consciously nurtured together. Such efforts are part of a process of relational tending that can be experienced by both workers and clients as empowering and edifying (Jordan, 1993; Miller et al. 1991).

YOU, TOO?

Your relationships with frank, supportive, nonjudgmental supervisors will act to support authentic examination of both your work with clients and your personal reactions within that work (Kaufman, 1996). Seeing how supervisors talk comfortably and openly about their own dilemmas and mistakes provides wonderful lessons and insights towards skill building, as well as enormous relief from secret fears that frequent mistakes make us inherently unsuited for clinical practice. Corrective understanding and self-acceptance are also fostered when clinical presentations and texts such as this one share mistakes openly as teaching examples that can guide both reconceptualizations of clinical problems and worker responses to them. Eventually you may want to join study or supervision groups in which both successes and mistakes are shared and reviewed together to enrich insight, practice knowledge, and skills.

NOTING AND MAKING USE OF PARALLELS

One of the great common epiphanies among interns and new workers is the realization that we all go through a lot of the same things our clients and supervisors do as we all start to do work together around the client's presenting concerns and needs. Clients, clinicians, and supervisors are usually somewhat nervous getting started with a new set of challenges, and may have similar anxieties concerning whether they'll perform well and whether vulnerabilities will be exposed in the work together, ending in a loss of mutual respect. All want to be respected and valued, and to make useful contributions to problem resolution. All know some things that the others may need to learn from them, and all are in various states of not understanding some things that will hopefully become clearer as the work proceeds. All realize that nothing is certain, and will shortly be reminded that there is still no magic or cure available in human service work. All will feel motivated and energized at times and dispirited and detached—from the sheer time commitment and complexity of the work—at other times. Appreciation of these parallels can help you relax a bit more and feel increased empathy and identification with clients, mentors, and colleagues. Eventually you'll learn how and when to examine some parallel experience with supervisors and clients, to help normalize and validate common human experiences.

RECONCILING WITH STRENGTHS

AND LIMITATIONS

Clinical learning will importantly involve a growing capacity to recognize, elicit, honor, and utilize strengths in clients, in self, and in the larger systems in which work and learning occur. A pride of affiliation will grow as you begin to feel that you're a part of—and can make a difference within—historically rooted professions with noble values, traditions, and goals. As a worker hones, tests, and formally measures his or her knowledge and skills, self-respect and competence grow. The worker *can be seen to contribute* to small changes in people and systems. A sense of mattering grows as you use professional membership groups to advocate for and win small enhancements in rights and in social conditions, enriching the quality of life for clients and fellow citizens. Some workers will go on to take leadership roles in local, state, or national government, or other organizations affecting the quality of life for many. Others will become clinical instructors in class and field, and contribute to the research base of human behavior and practice knowledge guiding the work of many disciplines. These positive experiences sustain professionals over the course of long and meaningful careers that include, but may not be limited to, clinical work.

Those who decide to remain in clinical work also have to reconcile themselves with a number of limitations in systems and people, including ourselves. There will be flaws and limitations in the helping systems of which we're a part, including inadequate funding; cumbersome procedures; long waiting lists; preferential treatment of some and not others; and shabby or unhealthy work spaces. To our dismay, we also encounter many people with no interest whatsoever in thinking about, providing, or paying for human services. This realization can be a deflating wake-up call for those still idealizing people, human nature, and helping processes. You'll also encounter some unanticipated limitations in populations served, including entrenched personal and family problems; client schedules with little room for clinical work; ambivalent motivation, insufficient determination, or outright refusal to work towards needed change; and other factors that sometimes make consistent, relationship-based work very difficult.

Our work with many people and situations over time eventually leads us to a reconciliation with some of our own limitations as well. These are perhaps the last limitations we identify accurately and acknowledge aloud, since we, our instructors, and our therapists may keep trying to perfect ourselves while affirming that no one need be perfect!

We may experience instances of racism, intolerance, resentment, hopelessness, and judgment coming out of ourselves towards clients—if not in words, then in looks, actions, or attitudes. We may come to see that we can't work with some clients because of our own deeply rooted qualities of fear, bias, or lack of empathy around some people, issues, and situations. We may hide personal problems in ourselves or loved ones, a process likely to affect our work with clients or colleagues at some point. At times we may simply prove too uncomfortable to be able to work helpfully with certain people or problems, or in certain settings.

An advisee said that after a successful summer as a camp counselor, a friend and fellow counselor at the camp invited her to come interview with him at a kids' treatment center in Chicago where she could work the next summer as a counselor of teens, since she'd done so well with them at the camp. She went with her friend to interview there, and was shocked when the interviewer told her at the end of their meeting that he found her too tense and serious to work with the particular teens in his program. He said the kids would be cruel to her about her inability to relax under stress, and would "chew her up and spit her out." He thought she had a lot of talents but needed to lighten up, and he said so, kindly. While stunned, she told me this was not the first time she had been told that she comes across as uptight. She was considering getting some therapy in order to look into why this might happen sometimes but not all the time. She remembered that particular interviewer gratefully for his kind honesty.

MOVING FROM SMART TO WISE

Egan (1998) aptly describes the way clinical learning moves us "from smart to wise" (p. 17) by helping us to transmute accrued information and experience into an humbling yet empowering blend of reflective wisdom, common sense, and compassionate action. An inextricable part of any eventual wisdom is that of *being aware of ourselves as we act and interact*—developing a capacity for self/other/systems process observations that will constitute a continuous aspect of clinical evaluation.

The development of informed and accurate observational capacity moves us from simplistic notions of individuals as both the primary cause and outcome of their inner and outer lives, towards understanding human behavior in the context of the many larger systems in which it's inevitably embedded and to which it is responsive. Holman and Freed (1987) note that cognitive and attitudinal changes in learners are prerequisites for skill learning and application, since deliberate application of guiding principles isn't possible until those principles have been learned and owned over time.

Becoming wise also requires the development of critical thinking—an evaluative process to which many newcomers to clinical learning may not be accustomed. Mumm and Kersting (1997) describe critical thinking as involving the development and application of criteria for evaluating the many theories in which practice is grounded. Rather than just swallowing elegant or compelling theories wholesale, practitioners learn to divide theories into their component concepts, assumptions, and hypotheses, trying to understand the history and context of these constructs and to evaluate their strengths, weaknesses, and practice implications. Critical thinking and formal measurement procedures come to be valued as crucial aids in evaluating the effectiveness of methods and programs, at the same time as the clinician's ease and skill with clients contribute to more effective evaluative process (Gambrill, 1997).

In addition to impressive anecdotal reports of success from clients and clinicians, research validation (or invalidation) of methods and programs can help lend credence and confidence to our work with people and systems. Learners come to appreciate that evaluation of practice and program efficacy isn't simply for the purpose of defending one's discipline and role, but also contributes importantly to our efforts to ensure that clients receive the best possible services we can devise for them.

WILL ANYTHING RULE ME OUT?

Students of clinical practice realize early on that our work is inherently *other-centered* in its mission, values, ethics, attitudes, focus, knowledge base, and techniques. It becomes reasonably easy to spot colleagues who don't seem to fit in with missions and values, are hard to be around due to temperament or inappropriate behaviors, or who frequently dismiss or violate professional standards, using work to gratify personal needs (Cobb & Jordan, 1989; Egan, 1998; MacCluskie & Ingersoll, 2001). The privacy of sessions and the confidentiality of process may delay detection of inappropriateness in a colleague's thinking, comments, or behaviors, but clients, relatives, or other observers often begin to voice concerns until at last problems are revealed in all their unhappy detail.

A disillusionment you may confront personally in a clinical profession stems from the identification of colleagues—sometimes close associates or admired figures in the field—who are not ethical or safe in their work with people, yet still practice due to legal loopholes or the lack of power or will in colleagues and regulatory bodies.

> *One of my most highly regarded instructors lost his license to practice due to sexual involvement with adolescent girls referred to him because he was very understanding and helpful in his public presentations on the problems and needs of these girls. That was quite a blow for me, and for some time I wondered how one could really tell which colleagues were trustworthy. I was very aware from reading and discussion that very few clients ever complain about their therapists, instead blaming themselves for problems or fearing they won't be believed. It upset me even more when I heard that, after this psychiatrist lost his medical license, he simply moved to a distant state and continued to see clients, newly billing himself as a "counselor."*

Fortunately, very talented, ethical, and inspiring colleagues abound in the clinical disciplines, far outnumbering those who negatively impact clients, colleagues, the professions, and the community. An important part of professional mentoring is learning how to intervene with and assist colleagues in trouble, as well as how to restrain those who prove unable or unwilling to alter harmful attitudes and behaviors.

CONCLUSION

Memmott and Brennan (1998) believe that becoming an effective clinical worker involves the development of a solid capacity "to view oneself 'as if' from some external vantage point" (pp. 90–91)—that is, to assume a "metaposition" in relation to oneself, in order to evaluate and modify one's learning and working style in response to new understanding, perspective, and feedback.

When we use the words "problem-solving work" as one definition of clinical practice, these words have applicability for workers as well as clients. Through work together, clients hopefully resolve some presenting problems while strengthening their inner and outer resource base. At the same time, clinicians work to resolve problems in their interviewing skills and style; their attitudes and biases towards clients, colleagues, and communities; reactions to clients' material and feelings during the work; and in carrying out a wide range of responsibilities with a shifting cast of players while still new to roles and procedures. All learn and grow together—quite visibly so.

It's important that you clarify early on your motivations for becoming a clinical worker, so that your hopes and actions can be tied increasingly to realistic goals, supports, and rewards that will nourish your self during inevitable periods of stress and perplexity.

EXERCISES

1. *Reflection.* In your journal, reflect on what you expected clinical training would involve in terms of changing yourself and the way you are with other people. Compare that with actual expectations. What have been your biggest discoveries or surprises regarding what it takes to be an effective practitioner? Which of your own strengths are being confirmed and utilized well?

2. *Small Group Discussion.* In groups of four or five, discuss whether you experienced the initial excitement of the newcomer to clinical work discussed in this chapter. Then discuss any frustrations or disillusionments you've felt as you've worked with complex problems and systems and a wide variety of theories about "what works" to bring about positive change. Where are you now in the acculturation process of becoming a professional?

3. *Class Discussion.* Muse together regarding what is meant by a "professional culture" in the clinical disciplines. Can you observe any language, dress, rituals, or other artifacts of such a culture in your educational program or workplace? Are there any changes that you would like to help make within this culture as you gain more comfort and authority in it? Who has an easier time being accepted into your profession's culture? Who has a harder time? What does it seem to require to become a leader or icon in one's disciplinary culture?

4. *Instructor Activity.* Share some of your own developmental experiences as a clinician and instructor of practice. What have you liked and not liked about being in clinical work? Do you represent or possess artifacts of a professional culture? Do you resist any aspects of such a culture? Who and what are the icons of the professional culture of which you're a member? What knowledge, talents, or contributions do they possess?

5. *Author Sharing for Further Discussion.* Heading for my very first interview in my first clinical social work practicum, I was nervous and walking too fast, not paying attention. I caught the high heel of my shoe on the stair and tumbled down four or five steps, landing where clients were waiting for workers like me to pick them up for their appointments. It took me a few seconds to collect my wits, suppress tears, and try to scramble up. I

was so shaken that I couldn't really get up alone. Everything about this entrance was so wrong that I just didn't want to face the group of clients seated right in front of me. My skirt was pushed up by the fall, my under-things were showing, my stockings were ripped and two bleeding scrapes were evident on my legs and arms. I didn't feel at all like a professional, and I could only imagine what my supervisor would say when I had to tell her what had happened on my first outing as a "helper." (Notice that my first thoughts were not about my client's reactions, but about my supervisor's.)

My client, a farmer in jeans who'd been described in the record as "depressed and barely able to function," rushed right over to help me up, having heard me call out his name as I approached. I wanted more than anything to evaporate—go home, fix my cuts, and have a good cry for myself. My client asked if I were okay, and supported me to the point where I could get back on my feet. I said I was sorry for being such a mess, and he answered with a wise smile, "You know, I'm a pretty big mess myself . . . we might make quite a team." This made me laugh and feel okay again, something I had thought I was going to do for *him*! We ultimately made it to the office and had a more relaxed first session than I ever expected. We proceeded to do some good work together over many months, and I've remembered him fondly as a good teacher of what really matters between people.

For Class Discussion. From this example, what different things can you observe and discuss about becoming a worker? What made the inter-view above more relaxed than the worker had expected? Share with each other some of your own ups and downs on the professional learning curve. How accepting are you of your own and others' mistakes at this point, and what is helping you with the acceptance process?

RECOMMENDED READING

Corey, G. (1996). The counselor: Person and professional. In *Theory and practice of counsel-ing and psychotherapy* (pp. 14–49). Pacific Grove, CA: Brooks/Cole.

Cormier, S., & Cormier, B. (1998). Knowing yourself as a counselor. In *Interviewing strate-gies for helpers* (pp. 11–34). Pacific Grove, CA: Brooks/Cole.

Delgado, M. (1999). Reflections on collaborative practice. In *Social work practice in nontra-ditional urban settings* (pp. 212–221). New York: Oxford.

Kottler, J. A. (Ed.). (1997). *Finding your way as a counselor.* Alexandria, VA: American Counseling Association.

Mumm, A. M., & Kersting, R. C. (1997). Teaching critical thinking in social work prac-tice courses. *Journal of social work education, 33*(1), 75–84.

Ram Dass, & Gorman, P. (1985). Who's helping?. In *How can I help?* (pp. 18–50). New York: Knopf.

Sussman, M. (Ed.). (1995). *A perilous calling: The hazards of psychotherapy practice.* New York: Wiley & Sons.

2

Early Successes
and Derailments

L ike the new driver with a banged-up fender or a gas tank suddenly empty
due to misjudgments, inexperienced clinicians err in ways that are all too
familiar to colleagues further down the road. New to professional self-
discipline and purposeful dialogue, you may lack relevant knowledge and experience, and may be anxious at times due to pressure from new people, situations,
and roles. It's understandable that you might try to solve new problems by falling
back on preprofessional thinking and behaviors and in doing so, make mistakes.

Many people come to clinical learning primed with the familiar directive,
"Don't just sit there, *do* something"—a great source of subsequent mistakes in
work with people. Earlier in development and education, action may have been
highly touted as a panacea. Pausing to contemplate implications, choices, and
costs of behaviors may not have been widely encouraged or modeled by others.
Uncertain about what to do at a given moment, newcomers often count on
habitual actions and reactions if these have been of use in the past. Some strategies tried may actually work by accident, without theoretical underpinnings.
Other strategies are mistakes that can derail plans and process in various ways.

DEFINING AND IDENTIFYING MISTAKES

A mistake in clinical practice may be defined as an attitude, behavior, feeling
response, communication, contextual arrangement, or strategy for work that
undermines the stated purpose or specific intent of a given intervention.

Mistakes are the things we do, often unwittingly, that subvert our own conscious goals and plans with clients.

For example, a worker might have the intention of helping a woman give voice to her own ideas and feelings more frequently. Yet on reviewing the videotape of a session, she realizes that she's often led or coached the client, putting her own words into the client's mouth ("His arrest for assault must have made you pretty glad you divorced him"), instead of asking her to express her own thoughts. You might want to help a group of HIV-affected men heighten their own interrelatedness. Yet your group co-leader points out that when a member asks a question about something going on in the group, you often answer instead of turning the question back to the group members. I might have the hope of working with an African American family in a culturally knowledgeable and responsive way, but then I forget to ask the family what it's like for them to be seeing me, a white person, when they'd specifically asked to work with someone African American if possible.

Mistakes like these are common, and often represent good intentions not yet linked usefully to an internalized professional knowledge base. They remind us that it takes much new learning and experience to translate a wish to help into effective clinical practice.

HOW CAN WE TELL WHEN CLINICAL WORK IS ON TRACK?

In order to detect and repair mistakes, we first have to learn how clinical work looks when it's on track. Then we can develop a baseline of knowledge and expectations against which to measure subsequent theory-based hypotheses, experience, and intuitions about what's happening at any given moment in the work. In addition to using formal measurement protocols, one very productive way to tell if work is working is to examine worker-client process in some detail through direct observation, as well as through use of written process recordings and video or audiocassette tapes of client sessions.

USEFULNESS OF RECORDINGS

As we watch and listen to the back-and-forth between worker and client, recordings reveal a great deal about the direction, focus, tenor, and balance of client-worker conversation and activity. From recordings and direct observation, we gather important information and impressions that help to plan and guide further learning and skill development. In a classic article defending the importance of process recording, Urdang (1979) asserts that process recording often suffers from bad press and lack of appreciation. She describes its crucial role in clinical learning as it allows examination of student progress in:

1. Development of the therapeutic dialogue
2. Awareness of interactional aspects of interviews
3. Learning how to utilize and develop cognitive skills in clients
4. Dealing with affective and latent aspects of communication
5. Developing ability in diagnosis and treatment analysis (p. 3)

Observation and review of work helps protect clients by tracking the nature, extent, and quality of services rendered. They also provide informative, ongoing snapshots of the following important interviewing parameters:

- Timeliness and helpfulness of session openings and closings
- The extent of purposeful focus on goals, as opposed to numerous topics randomly introduced in a superficial fashion
- Client and worker comfort and participation levels
- How often the client is leading in the session instead of just following the worker's lead
- Whether the worker's strategies and techniques appear to be the most advisable ones for achieving desired ends
- Signs of movement towards goal attainment or person-situation improvements
- Unanticipated bumps in the road that throw the worker and merit further discussion and strategizing
- Mistakes the supervisor thinks the worker made, flagged for review in order to develop alternative thinking or strategy
- Clarity between worker and client about "where to go from here" at end of meeting
- Accuracy of worker's later observations about "where the client is," missteps and achievements in the session; and client signals or feedback about the session or the overall work

Clinical instruction often focuses on these parameters and how they develop differently for each learner. So much depends on each individual's unique makeup and capacity to learn and perform. Development is also contingent upon past learning and experience in the field; the present learning environment and access to excellent instruction, learning materials, and experiences; and work with numerous, varied, and challenging enough case assignments to support continuous advancement of knowledge and skill.

GENERAL CHARACTERISTICS
OF EFFECTIVE WORK

We generally look for some tried-and-true signs of effective relating and work. Keeping an eye out for these signs can help workers stay on track, notice nuanced movements in the work, and maintain a sense of the possible with clients in spite of expectable bumps along the road.

1. *The worker and client focus conversation on agreed upon work goals and topics most of the time.* Process review and direct observation reveal that the worker and client are talking most of the time about subjects directly related to goals they'd agreed to work on, like finding a better paying job or using meditation and walking to control stress. At the same time, when an interview drifts off-focus, the worker begins to notice the drift more quickly, moving to reestablish focus. If the client wonders about the change of subject, the worker can explain with increasing simplicity and clarity why staying on topic is important to goal attainment.

2. *The clinician's demeanor begins to gradually increase the ease of the client within the relationship and the work.* The clinician's use of self, pacing, and techniques also contribute to this easing. In response to empathy, caring, and nonjudgmentalism, the client gradually relaxes more, settles into a working style and collaboration, and doesn't seem so tentative, challenging, or defensive as he or she may have seemed at the outset of contact. This settling in may require days, weeks, or months, and like a good soup, cannot be rushed. As evidence of settling in, there may be more warmth and spontaneity shown by workers and clients alike.

Feeling understood and respected can activate a kind of thawing out in the client, verbally and bodily, from the frozenness of old habits, defenses, and mindsets. The worker tries not to push for too much information, understanding, or feeling too soon, trying instead to align and follow well, asking questions attuned to the client's needs, pace, and style. Calm demeanor and purposefulness act as a holding environment to help soothe and contain as needed. These developments tend to occur more frequently with the passage of time and the growth in both parties of understanding and comfort.

3. *The client takes more responsibility for the focus, and initiates more work on issues, meanings, and feelings both within and beyond meetings with the worker.* Clients begin to express themselves with more focus and depth, showing interest in why things happened as they did and how they can be changed or maintained, rather than just reciting a chain of events as though describing a movie of someone else's life. Feelings may begin to arise and be tolerated and explored more comfortably. Clients begin to stop themselves when getting off track, redirecting themselves without prompting from the worker. They may begin to tell trusted others about counseling and the challenges and benefits of the process.

4. *There is a mutual deepening of understanding of the client's primary relationships and other assets, dynamics, aspirations, and surrounding systemic influences.* The client begins to differentiate individuals and resources rather than just lumping people and events together simplistically as "good" or "bad." Examples of small successes begin to be mentioned spontaneously without the worker digging for them, and the client can take pride in these. The client, in collaboration with the work, exercises and validates his or her strengths as much as possible, encouraged to build or renew some community linkages in order to increase meaningful support and outside activities.

The client no longer expects the clinician always to be the director of conversation, and may now even seem a bit impatient when they spend time on worker talk rather than on client talk. At the same time, as trust builds, clients occasionally ask the worker more personal questions, wanting to know more about this unusually understanding, accepting, and helpful person. Workers often want to share a little more of themselves as well, once they've assessed the client as able to hear a bit more about them without feeling upset or overwhelmed by what they learn.

5. *The client begins to rehearse problem-solving strategies in counseling sessions and then try these out afterwards, bringing them back in for review and further tinkering.* Although there may be frustration for both worker and client when things don't happen as quickly as each might like, both worker and client begin to understand that the change process is complex, requiring persistence, patience, and the slow harnessing together of many unpredictable forces and allies.

Worker and client now work together more as a team, developing strategies, trying them out, then discarding and replacing those that turn out to be less useful. Some problems move towards resolution, others may diminish in intensity over time, while still others may need to be accepted as unchangeable for now. Even though growth and accomplishment usually involve two steps forward and one step back, worker and client begin to appreciate and feel good about the two steps forward, rather than being so discouraged by the one step back. Until we ourselves can appreciate the importance of small gains made step by step, we'll have a hard time encouraging clients to maintain hope when frustrated.

6. *Both the client and the worker feel more competent as the work works.* Both take pride in step-by-step achievements, look forward to further work, realize they enjoy meeting around the work, and may spontaneously comment on some or all of these elements of the process. The client's new good feelings leave the worker proud and satisfied with self and work. It feels good to have learned enough to actually be able to help activate another person's hope, intentions, and efforts. Each may express gratitude to the other for persistence and hard work.

Many clients get comfortable enough to mention worker mistakes directly and describe the effects of these mistakes on them.

> *James said that when the worker teased him in front of the other kids in the summer work program, it made him feel ridiculous, and he didn't want to talk with him any more. But then the director had explained that the worker was just trying to ease him up from overdoing his piece of the work, so James was going to give the worker another chance.*

> *Bobbi said her counselor was very rushed today, and it was making her feel like she was in the way. She said it was okay if the counselor needed to be someplace else; if the counselor just said so, they could stop and reschedule for another time.*

As the work develops, workers begin to discuss blunders with instructors more comfortably, and slowly begin to appreciate mistakes as learning opportunities rather than as evidence of ineptitude. Once able to do that, they are readier to help clients be more accepting of their own pratfalls and misjudgments and see these as opportunities for growth.

7. *Others comment on the work.* Responses to effective work can be favorable or unfavorable, so positive comments, while welcome, are not the only or best signs that effective clinical work is reaping gains. For example, sixteen months of counseling aimed at reuniting a mother with her latency-aged daughter in foster care may bring great happiness to the mother, uncertainty from a child who's seen many comings and goings, and worried calls to the worker from the foster parents about the fitness of the mother to manage all the tasks of making a healthy home for the child they love. Each of these responses would be appropriate, given each person's experience and perspective. Workers often use group or family meetings to inform decision making about functional levels and readiness for change, and then carry out follow-up calls or meetings, to see whether perceived strengths, readiness, and alliances hold up over time.

Interns and new workers come to learn that negative comments and conflicts in the work can signal growth, and are highly productive foci for exploration. Often critical remarks signal sensed threats to established patterns in the client's life, indicating that change is afoot but will require further exploration and encouragement. For example, a call from an irate parent threatening to have the worker fired "for messing up my kid's head by saying I have problems" could be an indirect cry for help by behaving in a way that validates the child's complaints regarding parental rage and use of force.

8. *Step by step, some goals start to be reached, while others may be added or redesigned more realistically.* Goal-focused work begins to pay off in small gains. When work works, there is often a quiet spiraling of developments in self, knowledge, skills, and relationships with others. People new to clinical work can miss the forest for the trees, looking for dramatic changes or powerful "aha!" moments that indicate that the work has worked. In reality, a lot of change is incremental, frequently trial-and-error in nature, and manifested in very ordinary ways. That's why change can go for a time unnoticed by the worker and unappreciated by the client.

For example, one morning a homebound person might suddenly walk to the corner store to get a paper and a coffee, when the counselor is waiting for the woman to go to her first meeting at the Senior Center three miles away. Another client might say to an intern that friends disagree with advice the intern gave the client earlier. If the intern reacts defensively, she may miss important points: that the client *talked with friends* about the work, and can actually *convey their differences of opinion directly* to the intern. For a previously passive client, both of these are growth steps that deserve notice, exploration, and validation.

> I've been working for a long time with a shy and easily overwhelmed woman in our day treatment program. One goal is just to help her get up the courage to take the bus to downtown by herself. This would open up a whole new set of prospects for her when the center is closed. Monday morning she came in pleased as punch with herself, announcing in group that she'd taken the bus all by herself and ridden about ten stops before getting off, crossing the street,

and waiting for the return bus. She was too scared to have a destination, so she just rode. We all broke into a spontaneous round of applause. Then she said with excitement that later in the week she is going to try riding as far as the Farmers' Market in order to see what that's like.

DISCERNING OUR MISTAKES

By contrast with indicators that the work is working, mistakes often trigger palpable shifts in the level or direction of the work, or in the feeling tone or experience of the participants. These shifts can manifest in a number of different ways, depending on the professional's own developmental levels and personal style.

Noticing Client Behavioral Signals

Sometimes clients directly signal us about a mistake, and we can readily see and repair it on the spot. For example, in the middle of a colloquy to a female client about something he wants to get across, the worker notices that the woman has stopped attending. While nodding mechanically and with a polite, fixed smile, she also keeps looking at her watch. Realizing that his speech is falling flat, the worker can use this behavioral signal from her to ask what's going on for her at the moment. He could also apologize for taking up so much of her air time by talking, noting her response to either of these strategies. He might also say that, with all the talking he's doing, perhaps he's acting a bit like her mother, a woman the client has often described as talking *at* her, not with her. These efforts are designed to try to bring the worker back into closer alignment with the client's perspective and needs, with the goal of helping the client strengthen her own participation rather than witnessing that of others.

Sometimes, though, a mistake is recognized only in hindsight, after a client's behaviors (like looking aghast, gazing off, or abruptly changing the subject) bring the worker to a full pause of surprised awareness of an intention gone wrong. A client's signaling behaviors—the red flags of clinical work—teach us a great deal and can be used as memorable guides for future practice. They help us to become more informed and attuned to pace and nuance in work with others. Each culture will have its own signals for when things don't feel right in collaboration with others around personal matters, and these signals are important for workers to learn through relationships and study with cultural insiders.

Using the Clinical Radar Screen

In order to read client signaling behaviors more quickly and accurately, we have to develop a good grasp of each client's baseline functioning (average behaviors on his or her best days during the past several months). We notice and remember the client's usual relating and speaking style, demeanor, verbal and nonverbal patterns of communication, and responses to various levels of worker exploration and comment around presenting concerns and requests.

Such a baseline constitutes a kind of clinical radar screen that can register periodic blips signaling client distress and worker mistakes in progress. While many things having nothing to do with you may cause a blip on your clinical radar, it's good practice to remain alert to the possibility that you might have said or done something to contribute to a sudden shift in the focus, the tone, or the experience of the relationship. As we become more relaxed, attuned, and self-aware monitors of ourselves and our clients, more often than not it gets easier to tell whether we've fumbled or whether something in the client or the surround has triggered a change.

Common Client Signals of Mistakes in Progress

1. *The worker says something far afield of where the client is, and the client does not even seem to register it. It's as though the worker's statement is a nonevent.* The client steers right by the worker's offering and just keeps on talking on whatever subject is at hand. The worker's statement is but a momentary disruption and is talked right through. If we asked this client what the worker just said, she probably couldn't remember because it was so misaligned with her needs and comfort level at the time. For example, you might ask an elderly homemaker whether it's safe for her to drive, given her increasingly poor vision. To this the homemaker responds, "So, like I said, are you coming every week like the last girl did?"

2. *A "huh?" response.* The client is baffled, either by an idea itself or the language used to frame it. For example, a mental health clinic worker tells his client that he looks "pretty Parkinsonian today," and the client responds, "Huh?"—having no idea what "Parkinsonian" means. A Spanish-speaking intern translates for an Ecuadoran mother that the team doctor says her daughter's diagnosis is "Borderline," and the mother murmurs "What?" and looks puzzled and frightened.

3. *The client corrects the worker, expecting him or her to change.* "No, that's not what I meant," and "You just don't get it" are frequent signals of tension and differences around material or feelings at hand. Often the comment is testy, or has a critical edge to it. In a softer version, the client may say something like, "Let me see how I can put this so it's clearer to you," or "I don't explain things very well." In the latter instance, the worker has to make sure to clarify with the client that it may well be the worker's not understanding, and not the client's way of expressing, that's creating the problem at the moment.

4. *The client suddenly shifts emotional contact or focus following a worker offering.* The client may look down or out of the window nervously, might ask to be excused to refresh herself, may want to get up and pace or leave early. He or she may want to change the subject, or suddenly focus on bodily pain—"I'm starting to get a bad headache, could I have an aspirin?" While this movement may illustrate some aspect of a client's conflicts or coping style, it's a move away from the current conversational point rather than a move more deeply into it.

A client having an anxiety attack about joining a yoga group, with eventual hopes of reducing isolation, might say, "If you insist that we talk about that, I'll just go away one way or another."

5. *The client suddenly questions the worker's competence.* Questions may abruptly emerge about the worker's age, experience, certifications, or expertise: "I'd really hoped to see a doctor . . . I wonder why I wasn't assigned to one." Such statements can be withering for newcomers doing their best to be helpful, as the client's tone may be critical, belittling, or dismissive. Client musings aloud or challenges of this kind may signal that while well intentioned, this particular worker may seem to the client too naïve or inadequately trained to handle the tasks and challenges ahead. Some clients still equate hierarchical status or titles with worth and superior ability, feeling that the clinician's rank reflects on their own specialness.

Questioning the helper's competence can also occur when the worker has simply done the right thing at the wrong time, such as asking a widow to explore her grief in relation to her partner's accidental death before she can deal with the subject. She may shout out unexpectedly, "Are you totally insensitive? Have you never had someone precious die? Have you any idea what you're doing to me?"—leaving the worker feeling incompetent and guilty.

6. *The client suddenly becomes more superficial or mechanical in presentation.* The client may move from deeper feelings to no or more controlled feelings, or to describing feelings without having them. The conversation narrows or flattens out, moving from a deeper to a more superficial level. A teen mom might suddenly move from revealing her worry that she'll be an abusive mom like her own mom, to talking about how cute and innocent girl babies are, to exclaiming how hard it is to find a babysitter, and how there's a run on formula at the market.

Such a shift can reveal the need for a pause or an easing up of probing—a need to transition from worried intensity to easier talk of learning life skills in her high school. It's not that this shift is bad or unproductive. Rather, it's a noticeable shift away from the topic of abuse, and bears remembering by the worker for possible reintroduction at a more comfortable time.

7. *The client, a faithful attender, suddenly no-shows, cancels, or comes very late.* The client puts some unexpected space between himself and the worker or the topic at hand. For example, he or she may actually want to act on an impulse instead of delaying or controlling it, and so doesn't want to see the worker or focus on the problem until further down the line. People who've been shamed or punished a great deal may stay away from workers whenever they feel they've done something that will bring on the worker's criticism or rejection. Other clients have experienced so many breaks in early relationships that they don't have an inner model of constancy in relationships, and so come and go in the same way their early models did.

8. *The client suddenly brings someone else to the meeting, and that person's activity or presence affects the work in progress.* Sometimes clients dilute intensity by introducing new people who distract from ongoing discussions. They might want the worker to give emergency help to another person in need, rather than just focusing on them so much; or they can't get child care on a certain day and

therefore bring a daughter in who plays in the meeting room while the adults attempt to converse. At other times, they may want friends to come in and look the worker and the program over, to see if they seem up to par to an outsider.

In some cultures, elders may want to sit in, help make judgments and decisions, and demand certain actions or remedies. Worker failure to respond empathically to these developments can sometimes lead to a rupture in contact if people feel disrespected or invalidated in their historic roles as family leaders and decision-makers.

9. *The client suddenly seems distant or cold towards the worker.* The worker may have hurt or offended the client, who now wants to be very careful to avoid further wounding. The worker can see the client wordlessly turn inward or away, or can feel the atmosphere of the meeting turn chilly. These things can also happen if a client feels that staff in a meeting are allying with each other in a solid front against the client, or if he or she senses some other kind of betrayal at the hands of the worker.

10. *The client abruptly discontinues work permanently, permitting no further discussion.* Serious mistakes, while rare enough, can cause permanent rifts and exits by clients wishing nothing further to do with the worker. For example, the teasing of James in front of his peers discussed earlier in this chapter, was a technique that backfired and humiliated the sensitive boy, nearly causing a permanent breach in the relationship. That faux pas is a good example of behavior that has the potential to end the work altogether and leave the worker memorably more informed.

When clients feel uncared about, reduced, shamed, excluded, treated unfairly, or continuously misunderstood, we can understand that if conversation does not speedily resolve complaints (as when the program director interceded with James), there would be no reason for clients to continue in work that feels so bad. Permanent rifts can also occur when a vulnerable client feels overwhelmed by an intense counseling focus that undermines brittle defenses. Unable to find words for what's wrong, she feels internally dismantled by the work and drops out.

COMMON WORKER SIGNALS
OF MISTAKES IN PROGRESS

Part of good clinical education is to get to know and own our own responses to mistakes, and to be alert to these responses so as to catch mistakes more quickly when they arise. This learning requires open and comfortable feedback and heightened self awareness, because it can be hard at times for empathic people to tell whether they're registering their own or their client's signals. Often when we think we've made a mistake, we have. A frequent signal of such awareness is the internal question, "Did I blow it just then?" in response to something we just saw change in the client's demeanor or behavior. Sometimes a mistake will haunt our thinking for a time, even when we're not at work, as though it keeps knocking at the door of understanding.

Worker knowledge and comfort levels have everything to do with how we respond to and utilize our own signals around mistakes. Signals can be conscious or unconscious, and involve body functions and movements as well as any of the senses. They can be noticed and dealt with close to events that trigger them, or be denied or put out of awareness, even though clients, colleagues, and instructors may spot and think about our signals immediately. The following are common worker signals around mistakes in progress, and they reveal the diversity of responses through which we express a sense of having erred.

1. *The worker has an immediate uneasy or queasy "gut feeling" following something she said or did.* This gut feeling—distress in somatic form—usually indicates some awareness that an action or statement was less than helpful. The clinician may not know exactly what was wrong, but she knows that something was, cued by some change in the client and the simultaneous "blip" of anxiety in her center.

2. *The worker recognizes from his own developing fund of knowledge that he has just blundered.* The worker sees the mistake as it comes out of him, and wonders why it happened like it did, when he "knows better than that." The error could be a little thing, like coaching the client rather than asking an open-ended question, but it throws the worker—trying to become more open in his interviewing style—for a loop. He can't believe he just led the client again. For a moment, preoccupation with the anatomy of the misstep might make him lose track of the conversation.

If the client suddenly stopped and asked, "Now, where *were* we?", this worker might not know, due to fretting about the mistake and whether or not to do anything about it now. The second error—fretting about skill mastery rather than continuing to follow closely the client's story—compounds the first one. It helps to realize that undoing well-ingrained habits takes time for us just as it does for clients. Often our mistakes don't cause huge derailments in the work, but rather, delay a bit the client's development in the work.

3. *The worker directly observes a clearly upset expression on the client's face, and then has matching feelings of distress, but can't tell whether the client's expression is due to something the worker did or something else not yet identified.* Rather than exploring aloud the expression on the client's face, the worker tries to figure out alone what's transpiring. This mind reading is a very poor substitute for asking the client what's happening at the moment. It would be preferable either to mention the change in expression and explore it, or to simply keep following closely rather than entering into prolonged intellectual speculation that only the client can really validate. Mind reading fails to engage the client's capacity to perceive self experience and explore its meanings. It also undercuts continuing development of worker and client as a mutually observant and responsive team.

4. *The worker can't get an event or a conversation with the client out of his mind and is preoccupied for some time with the worry that he hurt or failed the client in some major way. He's certain that the client is going to ask the agency for a more knowledgeable worker.* The worker's dread may signal an actual serious misstep with the client, or simply an overestimation of the power of the worker's words and deeds in a client's life. Sometimes we also underestimate clients' abilities to

accept and cope with our mistakes so long as these aren't seriously damaging and are not characteristic of our ongoing efforts to help. Thankfully, most clients give many second chances to workers who they feel are sincerely caring and genuinely trying to help.

5. *The worker tries a technique she learned in a recent workshop. It comes out of her awkwardly, and she is more self-conscious and awkward with the client for the rest of the meeting, feeling silly and ashamed.* She's working beyond her comfortable competence level, experimenting on the client without adequate knowledge and preparation. We can understand why some inexperienced colleagues do this: initial field education is full of instances when, as beginners, they're asked to take on new kinds of clients and work for which they're relatively unprepared. It might make sense to them that since they can try new things with new people sometimes, surely it's okay to try their own new ideas with other people at other times.

A difference between these situations is supervisory orientation of workers and interns to new assignments and related working strategies, and the availability of supervisory backup if a new client situation presents issues or complications that arise unexpectedly. New ideas and techniques that a learner introduces into client work without supervisory awareness or support can blow up during the session, and the supervisor may not have the relevant expertise to provide properly informed backup when consulted.

6. *The worker detours around a topic about which his supervisor asked him to get more information. He simply isn't comfortable exploring the material, and therefore doesn't do so.* If the worker initially hesitates to discuss his block with his supervisor, he needs to find another seasoned advisor to sort things out with. A consultant might help the worker resolve his difficulty, redirecting him back to his supervisor for more trusting and frank participation together. In matters like court hearings or investigations of possible abuse of vulnerable others, clients could be seriously affected by a worker's continuing inability to carry out timely and thorough assessments on which to base planning and next moves. Outside consultation can also help the worker discuss aspects of his balking that might have to do with problems in the supervisor or the supervisory style, or problems in his own past stirred up by the content.

7. *For some time, the worker doesn't mention a client in supervision, to avoid revealing mistakes.* This mistake can occur when interns and workers are ashamed of some aspect of their performance and don't trust their supervisors to react supportively rather than critically. It's good to remember that while some supervisors *can* be unsupportive or critical at times, often it's the newcomer's own internal judges that shame the worker and predict dire consequences.

Sometimes, though, inexperienced workers don't bring up clients in supervision because they're doing things with them that a supervisor wouldn't approve of, and they don't want to relinquish these behaviors yet. They may be giving certain clients less time in session because they don't like them, but don't want the supervisor to know this. They may be seeing clients who occasionally come in high, out of fear of losing the client if too many rules are imposed, when agency policy specifically forbids that kind of contact for good reasons. These behaviors are serious mistakes, but the workers involved don't perceive that yet, defining themselves instead as justified mutineers.

8. *The worker forgets a client appointment.* The uncharacteristic forgetting of a client meeting can signal a mistake in progress that the worker isn't yet ready to face. For example, a worker may have planned in the next client session to apologize for an embarrassing mistake made with that person. The worker has been urged to do this by his or her supervisor, before feeling comfortable enough to follow through. So, for the first time, he or she "forgets" to write the client's appointment in the schedule book, and is later shocked on returning from an outside meeting to learn from the secretary that he missed the client's appointment. What's more, the client waited around for some time before leaving—a further source of distress.

9. *The worker constantly asks the client how he feels about the work, and often asks him to let her know if something doesn't feel right or needs to be changed.* Excessive checking-in behaviors can arise during periods when newcomers are making a lot of mistakes in the process of learning and applying theory. Workers worry that their mistakes are going to set clients back, so they double and triple check for impact, eventually calling attention to their own insecurities about what is happening. Checking and rechecking can cause a client to wonder if perhaps there *is* something to worry about. And as in all human enterprise, the more we expect things to go wrong in our work, the likelier they are to do just that.

FREQUENT SOURCES OF DERAILMENT

There are many well-known ways to get off track in clinical work. Since mistakes will be a feature of our human service work for the rest of our careers, it's useful to start identifying common sources of mistakes early on so that we understand right away that we're not bad people or inherently unsuited for counseling roles just because we trip up with regularity. Awareness of the following common sources of mistakes can enhance the process of unembarrassed learning with colleagues encountering similar challenges.

Being Too New to Know

Insufficient knowledge is a primary source of missteps, and can be the bane of the learner's daily existence. People can't know what they haven't learned yet, but newer workers are often very hard on themselves anyway for mistakes caused by not knowing yet.

For example, when asked by a child client not to tell anyone else the important family secret just divulged in a treatment session in a school setting, typically beginners will say, "I won't" (thinking primarily of confidentiality standards for adults) unless they've been thoroughly apprised beforehand of parental rights and team responsibilities in the treatment of minors.

Similarly, it's the most natural of human impulses to want to give a mental health day treatment client a ride in a personal vehicle when it's snowing outside and the worker and client are heading in the same general direction. The good-hearted worker may never think twice (as the legally responsible supervisor would) about the possibility of an accident en route that could injure the client and render the agency liable.

Sometimes colleagues describe the behaviors of less experienced workers as "naïve," when it often turns out upon review that their settings have not prepared them adequately for situations that may be commonplace events for the seasoned staff, but not for someone just starting out. For example, many interns and new employees know where and how to turn for help when a client appears suicidal, but they may have never been told what to do if a client suddenly goes into a diabetic coma, seizure, heart attack, or panic attack during a session. Newcomers are often left frantically guessing or relying on an experienced secretary for advice.

Mismatched Intentions

Mistakes are predictable when clients' and clinicians' expectations of the work are greatly at odds. Clarifying and agreeing on the purpose of meetings is crucial to effective work together, for without a common purpose, there is no real working agreement or viable focus for the meetings together (Shulman, 1999).

A client comes to counseling mandated by the court to attend, in order to "move beyond" drinking and driving. While driving drunk, he injured a teen on a bike, and has now been sober for about eight months, attending the clinic's Out From Under program. His intention is to understand why he drinks to excess. The worker's intent is to focus on sobriety work. She believes their struggle over the focus of the sessions is resistance to sobriety, and becomes irritated with the client. The latter has experienced other people's irritation so often when drinking that he asks the program to replace the worker with someone "more agreeable."

Lack of Supervisory Advice When Needed

Newcomers left on their own hook in situations brand new to them can understandably fumble while trying to do the best they can with what they know. This situation happens often when supervisors and their backups get too busy to respond when phoned or beeped, and no one else senior can be found to consult with.

Ronnie, very upset, called his practice instructor out of the blue one lunch time. He'd been left all alone to cover the storefront crisis center while his supervisor ran to a briefing at the police station and the other intern went to the nearby pizza shop to get them all some lunch. An eleven-year-old client had come in to say that unless he could get $400 by nighttime, a drug dealer blaming him for that amount of missing funds was going to hurt his mom. Having no one else to ask, Ronnie called his teacher to ask what he should do in a situation like this—should he lend the boy the money in order to

protect the mom? He disclosed that, in order to calm the boy down, he'd said
he would see if the center or someone else could lend him the money.

Ronnie's responses are so human and so representative of the caring impulses
that bring many people into the counseling professions. For the very reason
that he and other beginners don't know how to proceed in such a novel and
anxiety provoking situation, people starting out in clinical work are not
expected to function in settings without skilled, approved backup. Yet in the
real world of too many crises and too few supervisors spread across many
responsibilities, they're sometimes left alone briefly out of necessity, with the
hope that nothing beyond their competence will happen.

In this situation, Ronnie knows it's beyond his competence to decide how
to help the child pleading for assistance. In good faith he calls his course
instructor, the only other person he can think to turn to. This is a wise move,
because it affords an opportunity to at least ventilate and think things over with
someone who can calm and reassure him, helping him wait until the supervisor returns before taking any action.

Unhelpful Advice from Mentors

Unhelpful advice from mentors can certainly lead to mistakes by newcomers,
especially when the latter don't have enough experience yet to judge what
helps and what doesn't in situations brand new to them. For example, a supervisor may favor expectant silence over lively interchange with clients, and
advise this approach in work with a new client.

The client, though, describes a childhood and adolescence devoid of
warmth and interaction. Early on, both parents were killed in a train crash and
an alcoholic grandmother reluctantly took the client in and raised her in a
household of much silence and separateness. Not wishing to shape or intrude
upon the story, a worker might nod sympathetically and say little, following
the supervisor's recommendation. The client, though, doesn't return a second
time, the initial meeting having chilled her with its unresponsiveness in the
same way her grandmother often did.

Not Paying Close Attention
to the Client's Story

Egan (1998) speaks of "inadequate listening," in which workers are preoccupied with their own thoughts or problems, or are thinking about what they'll
say next instead of truly following the story closely. It's also possible that we
listen well to those clients we like and identify with, and pay less attention to
those who don't engage us as much, for whatever reasons.

Not following the story closely sets the worker up to make mistakes when
trying to follow up on its details, layers, or nuances. In order to appreciate the
importance of good following, we need only remember times when we ourselves have been sharing a heartfelt story, only to look over and notice that the

other person is somewhere else in their thinking, not with us. It's hard not to feel disrespected at such moments, for the sharing of intimate stories is one of the hardest things for people to do. Experiencing the other as not following well dampens most people's enthusiasm for trying to share intimate material again in future.

Personal Distractions

Pressing circumstances—a child's illness, a secret affair, a serious health problem, or pressing unpaid bills—can certainly lead to inattention. Tiredness, stress, physical pain, hunger, and worrying about upcoming events or meetings can also distract. It's very hard to explain to a client, in any way that makes real sense or seems caring, why we drifted off while they shared important things with us.

Situational Distractions

Phones ringing, beepers going off, noisy foot traffic outside the interview room, hospital bedside interruptions to take fluid samples—all of these things can intrude upon listening and focusing, and can throw both worker and client off-track. Busy workplaces, noisy neighborhoods, bustling restaurants, and home visits full of TV and phone interruptions demonstrate all too well how intrusions can derail plans and focus with clients.

Few things are more annoying to clients than to have the worker's and their own attention broken time after time. The client is then forced to shut down, wait, observe, then start up again. That kind of on-again, off-again cycle can repeat for many people in a living situation in which others always seem more important, or can interrupt anything at any time. Repeating these patterns within the professional relationship is very detrimental to it, and gives the wrong message about the client's value to us.

Larger Systems Pressures and Dynamics

Fast-paced, understaffed settings can put unrealistic expectations and daunting workloads on workers and interns alike. Pressure to work with many people quickly contributes to many mistakes as staff move hastily from one pressing responsibility to another, with little time for reflection before moving ahead.

A worker pushed by his agency director to bring in more funds felt obliged to use a client's air time to discuss her long overdue payment for services. This was just when she was about to reconcile with distant parents after a lengthy separation, and wanted to rehearse potential conversations she might have with them. She sensed that the worker was pretty removed from her own concerns today, and also felt guilty for using money on her trip home instead of paying for her counseling. Mistaking the client's unhappy silence for resistance, the worker added solemnly that the agency might have to close unless clients paid their small portion of what it cost to provide services.

Agency and interagency infighting over clients, policies, and funding resources can also contribute to intern and worker errors, as can layoffs, downsizing, and sales of agencies that can leave workers too anxious to concentrate or focus on work well. Workers may be asked by administrators not to discuss their imminent terminations in order to delay bad publicity regarding agency closings or staff layoffs. If clients hear from other sources about the pending loss of their workers, the breach in their confidence and trust can have long-term effects on future help seeking.

The mission, work patterns, and roles within particular domains of practice can also contribute to mistakes. Medical hierarchies in health settings can leave workers feeling low on the totem pole, overlooked and undervalued when patient care plans are under development. Time and space may be so limited in some settings that conversations have to held at the bedside or out in hallways with others seated close by. Pressure to abbreviate assessments and relationships with health and mental health clients can lead teams to overlook or underrate the importance of emotional, sociocultural, and systems barriers to improved functioning and problem resolution. As a result, too little worker activity may be directed towards family involvement and the construction of an adequate resource base for long-term well-being, so that ongoing problems persist unabated, involving cyclical readmissions for inpatient care.

Influence of Personal and Interpersonal Dynamics

Dynamics refer to the push–pull currents and conflicts at work within and between people, as well as between them and the larger systems in which they're embedded. Sometimes workers and clients evoke warm, collaborative impulses and feelings in each other, and at other times they may evoke anxiety, conflict, and even passing wishes to end the contact. At such times, worker missteps can occur easily because the current worker-client experience is being shaped as much by unconscious replays of old unresolved relational scenarios as by current realities.

> *Before sitting down, Julio always hung his coat on top of the worker's jacket, on the one door hook available. The worker told her supervision group that she felt that Julio was flirting with her by putting his coat on top of hers, as though he were embracing her. The group suggested she test this assumption out by getting a coat rack with several hooks, and seeing how the client behaved then. They also asked if the worker had any attraction to Julio. One member wondered if she might be stereotyping a Latino man as seductive.*

Workers' Own Psychological Difficulties

Without realizing it, some people enter the clinical practice field in order to get help for themselves, and their unresolved personal issues and problems can contribute to mistakes in practice (Mordecai, 1991; Sherman, 1996). Boundary problems, for example, can lead to inappropriate behaviors or relationships with clients or family members. Authority problems can lead to difficulties accepting guidance or limits from instructors or agency administrators.

Depression and low self-esteem can affect work relationships, energy available for learning, and the ability to focus on client needs and bring zest and hopefulness to the work. Impulsivity can cause learners to act rashly, saying and doing things that disappoint or confuse clients and colleagues. Problems with alcohol and other addictions can impair judgment, thinking, and professional behavior with clients and colleagues.

> *Lori needed periodic inpatient hospitalization during her first year in a graduate clinical education program because she had been subjected to severe abuse as a child and had developed what she believed was dissociative identity disorder as a result. She had not explained her problems to the program during the admissions process, and thought it cruel and unfair that she was now being asked to leave the program, even though she was experiencing dissociative episodes and occasional psychotic thinking while sitting with clients. She was not able to think about the effects on her clients of her change in functioning while sitting with them, or of the treatment interruptions caused by her hospitalizations for stabilization on medications. Her inpatient therapist hoped that the school would keep her in the program because its structure was so helpful to her, and having to leave would be a blow to her esteem. She was asked to leave anyway due to her inability to stay client-focused and her serious need for intensive personal help.*

Lori, while much less able to function consistently than most applicants to professional schools, is by no means unique in looking to a professional clinical program to help her with her own recovery. Chapter 7 discusses the growing problem of "wounded healers" and the ways in which we can take good care of our own mental and physical health while caring for the health and well being of others.

Lack of Cross-Cultural Experience and Knowledge

Little exposure to or exchange with neighbors, clients, and fellow professionals from diverse backgrounds leaves many interns and workers at an enormous disadvantage when trying to establish working relationships and goals. It's easy to misinterpret what we see and hear, and to be disrespectful out of ignorance, or due to the habits of privilege.

A "here's what we'll be doing together" approach communicates an attitude of superior authority to clients, as well as an expectation that they accommodate to agency or professional custom whether it makes any sense to them or not. Sue, Ivey, and Pedersen (1996) remind that the appellations *counselor and client* and *therapist and patient* inherently imply a hierarchy, and that a more respectful co-construction of the helping process is only possible when we have dealt with issues of dominance and power in our lives, professions, relationships, and theories (p. 17).

> *In carrying out a home investigation in a child custody dispute, Rona found that the Japanese-American grandfather had stepped in as the natural guardian when his daughter-in-law was hospitalized for severe depression and her*

husband, an unemployed musician, went on a bender and couldn't be located. When Rona told the grandfather that the court would decide where the children would be living, the proud man began shouting that this was his family, and that as a Japanese elder, he was in charge. He alone would decide, and no girl must ever threaten him again. He shouted her to the door and told her never to come back.

As so often happens when we believe mistakenly that our agency's authority gives us the absolute power to step in and alter lives without consulting those involved and affected, the grandfather, who has gone through so much loss and stress already, reminds the worker that this is his family, and he will have to be dealt with on his own terms. Acutely aware of her nonrelational approach to this family, Rona returned later to apologize to the grandfather for her rudeness, and to show concern for his experience of loss and crisis in the family. By the third short visit, he offered her a seat and some tea, and they began to strategize together about what should be done. She later told her supervisor that she'd had an image of Asian men as dominant, and that she would need to "show strength" in order to be heard at all. After further reflection, she mentioned that domination of women by men was an even older theme for her, harking back to her own family of origin.

Similarity, Overidentification, and Idealization

Things can go wrong when worker and client share many similarities and become too closely identified with each other in their minds. They mention often their similarities, and can begin to make sweeping assumptions about what each other thinks and feels without exploring for information that would reveal differences. Because of the distortions of a resulting halo effect, workers who overidentify with clients can fail to carry out appropriately detailed assessments with them, missing issues or conflicts that need attention and care.

Miguel assumed that the fact that he and his client, Rigoberto, were both gay Latino counselors in different New York high schools would make the work on Rigoberto's partnership problems easier. He suggested that part of their problem might lie in his client remaining closeted while his partner was out. Miguel disclosed how much coming out had freed up his own life and the lives of many other folks. After this discussion, Rigoberto stopped counseling, afraid that he would lose his job if he came out, and fearful of disappointing Miguel if he didn't.

Attractions to Clients

Attractions offer opportunities for self-reflection and personal stretching that can help refocus us onto the problem solving work the client originally contracted to do with us. Schamess (1999) mentions the notable absence in professional literature of focus on how to discuss attractions with trusted supervisors instead of suppressing them, denying them, or acting them out with clients. Attractions can be observed by clients in the worker's frequent blushing, or complimenting the client excessively, mentioning the client's looks or clothing a lot, giving the client special treatment or expensive gifts, or arranging ambiguous meetings outside the customary setting.

Human feelings are a cherished core element of human service work, so long as we can experience and understand them as information about ourselves and our work, rather than simply act them out. Workers who continue to experience heightened romantic or sensual feelings in the presence of a certain client but not others need to discuss these feelings openly with a trusted mentor, friend, or therapist. Many factors can contribute to such arousal; for example, a recent separation, divorce, other loss, or a diminishment in self-esteem. Most such feelings subside eventually as we better understand the dynamics of transference (Bridges, 1993). They can be transformed into sustaining mutual regard, an important engine for the hard work that we do together.

Dislike of Clients

Interpersonal aversions involve some of the thorniest matters to talk about in professional education, without learners feeling like bad people because they don't like a client who's been assigned to them (Mehlman & Glickauf-Hughes, 1994). Because of the historic emphasis in the human services on nonjudgmental acceptance of all people, workers are loath to talk out these situations with supervisors for fear of being judged negatively or found unsuited for clinical practice work.

When aversive reactions go unidentified or unresolved, a client can be left with a clinician who may never come to appreciate and really like him or her—a terrible fix for the client. It helps to remember that we can all be hard to like sometimes, and yet we can find ways to work with each other so long as we stay focused on the goals of work—goals around which we can mobilize good will and motivation. Professional ethics ask that workers provide service to all people equally and faithfully, working aversions through rather than acting them out.

Breakthrough of Personal Style

A learner's personal style and preferences can suddenly break through newly forming professional bearing, impinging on the moment in the form of mistakes.

A worker who likes to be comforted by touch understands intellectually that many clients may not like or feel safe with touch because of having known harmful touch in the past from someone regarded as a helper or protector. But without thinking, and moved by his new female client's grief over her recently deceased mother, he instinctively reaches out and touches her hand in order to comfort her. The client has a yet undisclosed rape trauma history and can't bear the physical touch of a man. She looks alarmed and pulls her hand back the moment the counselor touches it. Seeing this, he pulls back as abruptly as he initially came forward to comfort. In the awkward silence that follows, the counselor realizes that the focus must now switch from the woman's grief to his own action. His behavior also leaves the client wondering whether he, too, will be just another man who touches her for his own sake.

Working Beyond One's Level of Competence

Working beyond our competence is specifically prohibited by ethical codes, in order to protect both consumers and workers from organizational pressures to provide some clients with less qualified service, rather than no service at all. Allowing it can occur when there are waiting lists and an administrator decides that it's okay for an inexperienced person to gather new clients together into treatment groups, or to work with families without any prior training in these modalities. Working out of one's depth is unwise unless supervisory backup is readily available for instruction and problem-solving on an ongoing basis.

One reality of clinical education is that, though guided by the principle of not working beyond competence, students are routinely plunged into work beyond their initial capability and knowledge base because they have to start somewhere. Some very fine training sites have few "easy" cases for beginners to start learning with; at the same time these sites offer wonderful opportunities to learn. Consequently, there's not much reaction to this practice, just as there isn't when nurses and doctors understandably have to begin practicing on "whoever comes in the door," and not just the easy patients. Training sites expect students to wear badges, identifying themselves as such so that consumers have a say as to who works with them.

Resistance to New Learning

We all have gone through periods of not wanting to read and think theoretically for a time, and of tuning out during course discussions or supervisory sessions. Sometimes it's a question of tiredness due to jobs, study, and private life pressures. At other times people may feel they are tired of mental work and "just want to work with people." You may find yourself balking at doing process recordings or forgetting supervision meetings from time to time, even though you've learned to count on these processes for support and guidance.

Ambivalence about whether to experiment some with practice theories, rather than just assimilating the prevailing ideas of instructors, is not unusual. If not eventually resolved, though, the struggle around "what works" can leave learners far behind their peers in developing a secure knowledge base and effective practice skills. It's wise to remember that the problem may not rest entirely in learners, since some instructors may be so inadequately informed, and learning environments so deficient or oppressive, that what looks like resistance to learning might actually be a student's healthy attempt to oppose or change conditions antithetical to good learning.

Hubris

Hubris—excessive self-confidence, pride, and arrogance—can be a part of a resistance to formal learning, and can greatly contribute to mistakes. Some interns and workers who work well with a given population take this success to mean that they can do as well with any client they choose to work with, in any modality. With hubris comes lack of both humility and realistic sense of place on the learning pathway.

People can become as stuck on themselves in the human services as they can in any other profession. It can become more important to them that they personally deliver a given service, rather than ensuring that the service is the most helpful available for a particular client. It's not unusual for such interns and workers to inflate their experience levels or boast of their special achievements.

> *Vonda told her single moms group that she could probably get them into public housing more quickly than their case managers because she had been a school aide before starting her social work program, and had connections at City Hall. When a group member mentioned this to her case manager, the manager called the student's supervisor to complain about the student's undermining of her role with the client. The case manager also mentioned the risks of bragging about connections at City Hall, as federal funds were involved, and there would be a great deal of oversight to ensure equal access and fairness of procedures.*

Sometimes, self-aggrandizing workers will blame others for their own mistakes or problems, or want to give an assignment to someone else because they judge that it offers few opportunities to have their own sensed specialness validated. Others decide they are ready to act on their own in very complex situations, guided solely by good intentions and the past positive responses of friends and family. They reason that, at worst, they can muddle through anything, even though they may never have had experiences like those they now confront.

> *Marjann, an intern at a prison for sexually dangerous men, decided on her own that an elderly "lifer" assigned to her for supportive conversation deserved a walk out in fresh air, since he'd been isolated for so long as a repeat offender. The intern felt she had a good relationship with him and that she could tell that he'd never do anything to harm her because he was always so kind to her, holding the doors open for her, bringing her pictures he'd drawn, and so on. Without staff permission, she took him to the cafeteria with her to get coffee. The guards, used to Marjann coming in and out with prisoners, assumed her supervisor approved this. On the way to the cafeteria the client started to mumble obscenities and tried to touch Marjann inappropriately, so that she had to call out for help from a passing administrator.*

Trying to Counsel a Friend or Family Member

Inexperienced workers may believe incorrectly that the knowledge they already have of a close individual or situation will be an advantage to problem resolution when loved ones confide a need for urgent help or advice. It's very hard to develop and enunciate clearly a balanced perspective when we're part of the landscape we're trying to assess fully and fairly.

> *Bertille's friend Linzey called to ask if she could see a friend just to do an assessment of an adolescent-parent crisis that could possibly trigger a heart attack in a vulnerable parent. Bertille had been swimming at the referred woman's pool, and told Linzey she didn't like to mix socializing and work. Linzey said because the husband in the situation was a local judge, they were embarrassed to seek out help from unknown providers, worried about the family's reputation. Linzey hoped they might speak to someone they'd met, and whose discretion they could rely on. She also thought the referred woman drank too much but wanted someone else to take a look. Bertille reluctantly agreed to see the woman, and invited her to meet in her living room, where she often consulted with clients from the village. Linzey's friend arrived very charged up and bearing a half gallon of gin, asking if she could make drinks for the two of them to have while talking. Bertille didn't know what to do except decline, at which point the woman made herself a drink and spelled out her troubles in very slurred speech. As the woman related the family story of drinking and mental illness, Bertille mostly listened, not wanting to make Linzey or her friend uncomfortable.*

A wise adage affirms that the doctor who treats himself has a fool for a patient, as she won't be able to assess and respond to problems with sufficient detachment. This adage can act as a similar caution for workers who take on people and situations with whom it would be impossible to behave in a disinterested way, particularly if there is pressure towards a particular outcome.

The Need to Please and to Be Liked

Hepworth, Rooney, and Larsen (1997, p. 138) mention the need to please others as a frequent source of worker failure to set limits, decline inappropriate client requests, and be sufficiently assertive when worker action is called for to get things moving. Needing to be liked can also undermine useful efforts to confront problem behaviors directly and to express controversial opinions when these may expand the work into new areas or depth.

In the example of Bertille and Linzey previously noted, a need to be liked by powerful local people was very likely involved in Bertille's agreement to assess a casual acquaintance and permit her to discuss her problems with a drink in hand—one of her central problems!—without any reference to the drinking. The client would also have been driving drunk both to and from the meeting, with nothing said by the worker about her condition or risk to self and others on the road, and without driving the client home to prevent an accident. This is a powerful example of how the need to please can often derail us at key points in the work.

CONCLUSION

Learning to identify and work on personal, relational, and systemic sources of derailments is a career-long process. Realizing this can help learners relax perfectionistic expectations of getting it all right within a very short time, and of always knowing how best to understand and respond to a mistake in progress. Every new client, supervisor, instructor, and setting offers fresh and exciting opportunities to gain new perspectives, find new things to appreciate about people, and realize how forgiving people are if they see that we mean well and are trying hard in their behalf. Patience, openness to trying new ideas, and perseverance when flustered are very sustaining qualities during this learning.

EXERCISES

1. *Reflection.* In your journal, recall some mistakes friends or family have made in listening or responding to you while you were talking (for example, glancing at a watch, or looking away). Remember the impact on you when people were not following you closely, or when your story was interrupted somehow. Are there people you avoid talking with because of the way they respond while you're talking?

2. *Small Group Discussion.* Break up into groups of four and discuss how you feel about making mistakes in practice. How can each of you tell when a mistake is in progress? What personal reactions flag a mistake for you?

3. *Class Discussion.* Share examples of how different clients have signaled you about a mistake in progress. How comfortable are you at this point in noting and discussing a mistake with your supervisor or in class? With clients? Do you find that there are some mistakes that are harder to own than others? Discuss together.

4. *Instructor Activity.* Share with the class some of your own sources of derailment in work with clients, and the ways clients have signaled you about your mistakes in progress. Discuss how different clients have reacted differentially to your mistakes, and how you yourself reacted when clients brought up a mistake you made with them? How does someone learning to interview more effectively judge whether to stop, note, own, and apologize for a mistake, or just to let it go and move on?

5. *Author Sharing for Further Discussion.* Starting out, I always thought that if the client looked away or down or out the window, or changed the subject suddenly, it must be something I said or did wrong. As time passed, I was helped to understand that sometimes factors within the client cause those same behaviors to emerge in the conversation, and that I shouldn't automatically personalize the process between us. One of my supervisors taught me

to first ask clients what was happening for them at the moment. Now if I see a signal of disconnection, I first watch to see if the client will say something about it. If not, then I usually ask what just happened when she pulled back, encouraging her to explore and muse aloud about the shift. Many times she'll say that the conversation has begun to touch on uncomfortable material, and that she can feel herself want to get away from it emotionally. Appreciating this, though, doesn't in any way diminish my need to stay alert for my own gaffes and the way they can cause clients to withdraw or shift participation. When I explore a possible blunder without appearing threatened, clients often agree with my assessment, although frequently denying any impact on them.

For Class Discussion. What can lead interns and workers to blame themselves so readily for derailments or sudden changes in process with clients? Can you share instances from practicum work and supervision in which you blamed yourself and then learned about another perspective you might take on events?

RECOMMENDED READING

Goldenberg, I., & Goldenberg, H. (1991). *My self in family context: A personal journal.* Pacific Grove, CA: Brooks/Cole.

Kadushin, A., & Kadushin, G. (1997). The competent interviewer. In *The social work interview: A guide for human service professionals* (pp. 389–405). New York: Columbia University Press.

Kottler, J. A., & Blau, D. S. (1989). *The imperfect therapist: Learning from failure in therapeutic practice.* San Francisco: Jossey-Bass.

Madsen, W. C. (1999). Working with multi-stressed families: From technique to attitude. In *Collaborative therapy with multi-stressed families: From old problems to new futures* (pp. 9–44). New York: Guilford.

Okun, B. (1997). Issues affecting helping. In *Effective helping: Interviewing and counseling techniques* (pp. 250–284). Pacific Grove, CA: Brooks/Cole.

3

Engaging with Clients and Getting Started

E ngagement can be thought of as a phase of work, a hope and goal, an ongoing process, and an outcome of work together. It's the initial *phase* of work in which both workers and clients must become involved in a problem-solving process together. Prominent worker *goals* of this initial phase are to bond with clients and, through exploration of identified assets, problems, and requests, to engage them in relationships and further work.

We and our clients then *hope* that the relationship will be a productive one and that goals will be accomplished through effective use of knowledge, collaborative skills, and focused work.

Clients also hope that *we* will be engaged by their situations and will prove helpful in securing desired resources and change in their lives. Aware that we are people too, with many other assignments and responsibilities, clients hope that we'll care about them, particularly so as to be there when needed and to work hard in their best interest.

The *ongoing process* of engagement involves several steps that strengthen trustful and purposeful bonding. These include:

- working with fairness, energy, and nonjudgmental acceptance
- orienting clients to the expectations, responsibilities, process, rights, and procedural aspects of the helping process
- accurately identifying problems and prospects to be worked with
- responding quickly and helpfully to emergency conditions and needs

- taking turns listening and responding
- cushioning the work through empathy, support, and checking in
- timing exploration and activities so that they feel sensible and helpful
- keeping agreements and following through on plans and promises
- working with other colleagues, services, and systems on the client's behalf

When an anchoring bond has been established (which can happen quickly or take a long time) engagement can be regarded as an *outcome* of all of these efforts, a reliable buffer during the ups and downs of the work, and an adhesive for patching relational breaks should they occur.

TRUE ENGAGEMENT IS HARD WORK

Some clients and workers can "tune out and turn off" when things get rough, so the important work of *remaining* engaged within the supports and demands of the work deserves special emphasis. In professional life as in ordinary life, real engagement involves caring enough about each other to form and maintain a reliable alliance that is mutually respectful and purposeful, one that can weather the stresses and disappointments that can occur in any human relationship now and then.

It's tempting to think that if we are warm, respectful, professional, and interested, then clients will be, too, and will immediately settle in, feel grateful, tell their stories, get the help they need, and move on with their lives. It's important to understand, though, that sharing one's story with a stranger is hard and requires trust. Paradoxically, trust can't really develop very deeply without first sharing one's story and seeing how the worker responds to the story. Engagement is a circular process, not a linear one. Rather than A (trust) leading to B (disclosure of strengths and needs), A and B have a mutually influencing and synergistic effect on each other. Sharing in an atmosphere of validation and acceptance often increases trust; increased trust often leads to more sharing; and so on. The wise worker remembers that while all relationships require time and work, because of the emotional intensity and compelling content of many clients' stories, a sense of relationship and meaningful work can seem to take hold much more quickly than it actually is on a deeper level.

For example, one of the hard common experiences for workers is that of seeing clients drop out of the work together without warning after sharing too much, too soon. These clients might feel too overwhelmed or embarrassed by their revelations to return. The worker may have believed mistakenly that depth and intensity of conversation meant that a solid relationship was in place when it was not, or that in a good relationship, no one ever wants to disengage. Engagement issues can keep popping up after weeks and months of work, surprising workers who mistakenly think that a client's faithful attendance means that both the relationship and the work are invulnerable to shifts.

INITIAL CHALLENGES AND PITFALLS

The beginning phase is a very focused and energized period of work. Because client and worker are usually new to each other and are a bit uncertain about what will come of the meeting, it's easy to fumble despite good intentions and preparation.

Anticipating One Another

Clients and workers commonly try to imagine each other, as well as imagine what meeting together will be like. Interestingly, workers and clients often have many similar startup anxieties and questions about what is about to happen:

- How long will this take?
- Will this be a good match?
- If the other person isn't from my culture, religion, or general background, will I be understood and accepted?
- Will I say and do the right things? Will I be found wanting?
- Can I trust the other person to cut me some slack if I blunder?
- Will I get the information and resources I need for this to work out well?
- Am I suited for this work, and is it suited for me?

Murphy and Dillon (1998) suggest that speculations and fantasies about each other before meeting are often shaped by cultural and family experiences, values, and biases. Both workers and clients may have strong feelings based on past experiences, and may wish they didn't have to work with certain kinds or groups of people. Some workers might try to avoid work with the elderly because they themselves fear aging or haven't ever been close to an older person. Others might avoid work with people with persistent mental illness because they fear them unreasonably due to media stereotypes of the "dangerous psychotic person" who scares or harms others. Some colleagues like group work for its mutual aid and support aspects, but feel threatened by the potential emotional triggering within family meetings. Some may prefer gay people to straight, Latino to Bosnian, Seventh Day Adventist to Catholic, and so on. Misunderstandings and preferences can leak over into initial contacts with clients without our noticing it, and can cause both workers and clients to want to disconnect. It would be a mistake to come into the clinical professions thinking that we can pick and choose whom to like and whom to serve, as our ethical codes require that we extend to all people nonjudgmental acceptance, respect, equality, and justice.

Clients, too, may have been subjected to classism, racism, heterosexism, gender bias, and other forms of oppression that have left them worried that helping professionals may be oppressive, too. The worker's honest attempts to greet them with good will and helpfulness may be met with caution, skepticism, or even contempt or anger. Historically, it has proved all too easy for clinicians to misinterpret client standoffishness as a personality problem, rather than understanding it as a healthy adaptive stance in a world of many oppressions.

Overpreparing

Prior imaginings and review of available information about clients help workers develop a capacity to "tune in" (Shulman, 1999)—to imagine or feel one's way into the client's experiences and feelings (p. 44). Social workers have long described a process of trying throughout the helping process to be *where the client is* (to attune to and align with the client in the moment). The preparatory work that Shulman describes gets us started in that direction even before meeting the client, and certainly from that moment forward.

It's possible, though, to overprepare. You can unwittingly approach new clients overloaded with personal hunches and the prior impressions and formulations of other providers. These ideas can skew thinking and thwart important new first impressions. Especially if prior evaluators are senior to you or have special status or authority, you may mistakenly spend initial visits verifying senior staff's hunches by confining discussion to those issues and concerns already identified.

Another mistake at this point would be to ask yourself, "What can *I* possibly add to what my supervisor or consulting psychiatrist has already found?"

It's important to remember that different people elicit different content and experience from each other, and that sometimes newcomers bring an important fresh perspective to the tasks of listening, exploring, and evaluating. It's useful to acquaint yourself with the findings of others, but to retain informed openness, always holding out the possibility that the client still has more to be, say, and do than is yet known. Openness to the unexpected and the unknown lends an air of hopeful expectation to the initial meetings, without the client having to repeat everything already recounted to other providers.

Cultural Issues Affect Engagement

North America is increasingly rich in cultural diversity. Many immigrants and temporary workers no longer wish to be absorbed into the vaunted North American "melting pot," having observed or directly experienced efforts by dominant whites around the world to eradicate or devalue their most cherished traditions, including religious, cultural, linguistic, and family forms.

Sadly, there continues to be less diversity in North American helping professions than there is in the world itself (Malgady & Zayas, 2001). Often it's only in specialized programs developed to attract and train colleagues of color that we find appropriate representation of population demographics generally, as well as those of the particular clients we work with. One implication of this situation for many clients is that in a large number of human service agencies, they won't be working with many clinicians like themselves who are intimately familiar with their cultures, languages and expressive styles, spiritual and health beliefs, or patterns of everyday life. It follows that few clients may be able to imagine clinical work as an occupation open to them personally, since there's so little evidence of multicultural representation in the human service agencies with which they're familiar—a big mistake.

Clients can also spend more time than they should trying to educate providers about how things work within their cultural and geographic world—both geographic and cultural. These are areas often unfrequented by workers. As today's "minorities" become tomorrow's dominant populations—anticipated by midcentury (Gutierrez, Parsons, & Cox, 2000; Malgady & Zayas, 2001)—imbalances are expected to decrease. At present, we compensate by trying to learn as much as we can about the special norms, styles, customs, and languages of the individuals, families, and groups we serve. We then *demonstrate responsiveness in role* by adapting services, staffing patterns, and procedures to be more representative and inclusive of local people and cultures, in order that clients from many different backgrounds feel welcome, respected, safe, and well served when among human service workers.

Cultural responsiveness and responsibility also involve not approaching or lumping together clients in a one-dimensional way, conceptualized and responded to as interchangeable beings (Cook-Nobles, as cited in Jordan, 1997) by virtue of some shared characteristic like color, sexual orientation, poverty, size, prison record, or abuse history. The principle of regarding people as unique (in spite of some shared characteristics) applies to the way we treat fellow workers as well as to the way we treat clients.

> Dr. B., an honored African American professor of social work, received a phone call from a student she'd never met, asking if she'd be a research subject in a study of stress among female academics. She agreed and invited the student to meet with her in her home in an affluent suburb of a large Northeastern city. When the student rang the doorbell and Dr. B. answered, the student asked if Dr. B. were home, assuming that Dr. B. was the maid—for no other reason than her color in the context of an affluent, predominantly white neighborhood.

Efforts to be more culturally knowledgeable and responsive require that we *participate in* diverse community life, learning new languages and customs and participating in neighborhood building and advocacy projects, in order to make it easier for clients to experience more mutuality in our presence (Devore & Schlesinger, 1996; Lum, 2000; Sue, Ivey, & Pedersen, 1996). As more agencies locate in urban neighborhoods and work more in homes, group residences, churches, storefronts, and shelters, chances increase for more integration of shared values and work with people—*if* we make use of these opportunities to reduce some of the historic distance between us and our clients.

> A friend and I were recalling what it was like for two naïve, white, newly minted social workers to be kicked out of the black community when Martin Luther King was assassinated. We had looked so forward to helping in the inner city when we finished social work school, and seemed to be well received by African American clients and colleagues as we did outreach counseling and case management with poor families. We didn't realize how patronizing it was of us to think we could live well-nurtured, middle-class lives miles away from where we worked, migrating each day between vastly

different circumstances. After King's death, white workers were asked to stay out of the black community for a while. The community would decide if we were needed further, and if so, how and when. Indigenous leaders helped us see that we had framed the community as recipients of our wisdom and help rather than as leaders in a struggle for justice and resources. Added to that, as we looked around our large family agency, there was only one MSW of color in a staff of about 50 workers in six districts, and no supervisors or administrators of color. We were talking the talk without walking the walk, blind to what the community could see clearly.

STARTUP CONVERSATION
AND EXPLORATION

In initial visits, workers usually begin by greeting clients and settling into the designated meeting space. It's okay to point out your own preferred seat and then invite participants to seat themselves as they choose, exchanging warm-up talk while attendees settle in: "How was parking?", "Is it still as cold out as it was earlier?", "Is everyone here who's coming?", or "Let me just tell the secretary not to ring us while we're meeting." Such informal chat usually settles both the worker and client down from the "startup nerves" we all can experience when setting out in a clinical encounter.

Initial conversations are like an orientation—of the worker to the client's situation and story, and of the client to the worker's interest, concern, purpose, knowledge, and skills in identifying the reasons for the visits and useful foci for exploration and work. This orientation sets the tone, purpose, agenda items, and agreements about how the conversation and work together will proceed. It's a cameo of what is to come, although initial nervousness in all attendees may detract a bit from the comfort you'll probably feel as work proceeds.

Topics to be covered in the initial visit usually include:

- who is present and why
- reasons for the visit and participant hopes and goals
- any rules, roles, focal points, and the time available for the visit
- how talking and leadership will be shared
- elaboration and exploration of the client's story
- summary of impressions at ending, and future plans
- reactions of participants to what's happened so far

Clarifying What Others Will Know

While some clients feel better served when major members of a service team know their story, it can be especially hard for clients to have to repeat traumatic or upsetting material (for example, about rape, death, upsetting medical findings, a battering partner) to several unfamiliar staff people in a row. It may seem to them that no one cares enough to fill colleagues in on relevant aspects of client conversation pertinent to staff planning. People can also feel tricked or misled if they share material without understanding from the worker or staff that its details are going to be passed on to people they have never met and whose functions they know nothing about.

To avoid confusion and further distress, the first person to work with a client should clarify whether he or she will continue to work with the client or whether someone else will be assigned. The worker should also clarify early on any need to involve others in further discussion or work (for legal, medical, or safety reasons), or any need to report highlights of their conversation to other team members, parents, or guardians. These clarifications give clients a chance to decide how much they want to share with whom, and in what order—and whether to wait until family, guardians, or legal counsel are present to help with decision making.

There's No Such Thing as a Captive Audience

Workers can mistakenly assume that mandated clients are going to come for help and stay with the process because of the sanctions awaiting them if they don't. In reality, clients can—and sometimes do—decide that they would rather do jail time, community service, or flee than reveal themselves to unfamiliar authority figures.

We can often increase the likelihood of engagement by focusing on what clinical work can and can't offer, and then respectfully elicit the client's own expectations and reluctances around the help-seeking process. This emphasizes both their freedom to choose and the consequences over time of participating or not. It often helps to share our real concern about the impact not attending is likely to have on the client's stated future goals for self or loved ones (Rooney, 1992). It's important to leave plenty of time to discuss implications and possibilities. The concern, clarity, and resolve of the worker can sometimes engage the client in a piece of work he or she can identify as useful "since I have to do this anyway."

An intake client of mine, referred by the court for evaluation following a public episode of violence, did not want to talk with me or anyone, although it was clear from his mother's report that he had just suffered a number of important losses and was actually expressing grief through this violence. I spelled out this hunch to him, and he just stared into space. He was returned to court, did brief community service to cover damages, and disappeared. Three or four months later, I got a phone call from a policeman in another town north of the city. The man had been found lying in a mall there, with nothing on him to identify him except a card from our clinic with my name scrawled on it. He was briefly hospitalized for depression and then discharged to his mother's, where he called me about getting some counseling.

Aligning Communication with Client Needs and Styles

It's a mistake to use language or constructs that are either too complicated, specialized, or simplistic for a particular client or group of people. Kadushin and Kadushin (1997) remind clinicians that words that seem obvious to professionals can mean different things to clients and often need clarifying in order to move understanding from the general to the precise. They note that English contains about 600,000 words, and that the 500 most used words relate to 14,000 dictionary definitions with both general and special meanings for people (p. 39).

Jargon and intellectualizing aren't helpful, and neither is talking down to people, which is patronizing and offensive. In her work with traumatized refugee families, Chambon (1989) noted complaints from families that "human service language seems to be based upon a rational, problem-solving terminology, as illustrated by phrases like 'What are your goals? What do you plan to do?' or alternatively, on the expression of feelings" (p. 12). Chambon regards these modes of communication as culturally biased and uncomfortable for many clients. Additionally, clients don't like being addressed in the high-pitched, sing-songy speech usually reserved for infants or young children, although this tone is often inappropriately utilized with the elderly, with non-English speakers, and with persons with disabilities.

Part of good engagement is developing a sense of clients' intellectual capacity; educational level; facility with language, ideas, and conversation; motivation to participate; and social comfort. Taken together, these capacities tell us something about how to align ourselves properly with them in choice and use of language and concepts. Often it's a lack of confidence or understanding that drives interns and workers to miss the boat in choice of tone, style, words or ideas, forgetting that the best communications are simple, direct, and inclusive.

Example of an Orienting Conversation that Misses the Boat

Judah, I'm Nick Loftus, the court social worker assigned by the judge to follow your community service work to make sure you're participating fully and getting good help at the halfway house. I'll come to see you here each Friday and meet with you in the counseling room for thirty minutes or so, if that's okay. I'd like to hear your point of view and feelings about what's happening each week. We could also talk about what lies ahead if you want. I share with the court and the team here the highlights of our talks, so we don't work at cross purposes. Now, that's a mouthful . . . what are your reactions to what I said?

Here, Nick is clear, but he needs to work on not sounding so much like a cassette recording that could simply be distributed for all clients to listen to before meeting with their social workers. He is communicating the court's authority through his person, and this renders the client a passive witness to his communication. He doesn't leave room for Judah to ask questions, make comments, or raise issues that might differentiate his needs from those of others like himself. Only at the end is the client invited to participate.

Our initial behaviors and words with clients clearly transmit our beliefs about relationship, power sharing, and communication; and clients usually pick these transmissions up right away and react to them with understandable caution and irritation. Nick uses a style that informs without engaging. Sometimes clinicians behave this way when they want the client to be clear about who is in charge. By the time they invite a client response, so many issues have been covered that it would be hard to remember what to say or ask.

It's much more productive to ask clients what it's like for them to be getting started with a new person, and what they've heard and thought about the worker, the program, or the agenda, in order to invite their participation and ideas respectfully from the first moments.

OTHER ORIENTATION TOPICS

It's important to orient clients to the space and time available for meetings; the extent of worker and backup team availability between meetings; and the form future meetings may take (e.g., "I'll be asking you more about yourself and your situation, and inviting you to add anything you think will help me understand things better"). The worker also discusses payment or coverage arrangements, starting or stopping on time, and the need to notify each other and try to reschedule if sessions can't be kept.

Although the importance of these issues seems obvious, some interns and workers "forget," minimize, or postpone discussion of them with clients, especially the issue of payment for services (Trachtman, 1999). Some interns and workers dislike the businesslike aspects of the helping process, interpreting it as poorly aligned with the distress clients feel in initial interviews. Some workers may not feel confident enough in role or valued enough in skills and status to clarify straightforwardly the obligations and expectations of clients seeking services from them (Wolfson, 1999), and at some level may feel ambivalent about these expectations.

In the engagement phase of work, if there are any special benefits or complications in working with the particular agency or clinician, these should be mentioned and discussed. For example, it helps clients to know when and where there are translators available in many different languages, or that there are lesbian, gay, bisexual, and transgendered workers on staff to assist them, or that a hospital has a safe program nearby for battered spouses. Clients are also apprised of whether home visits are possible or not, and whether there is on-site child care to help while mothers are in session. It's also important to let clients know whether and how, if they want to, they can be linked with others who share similar issues and might provide renewing opportunities for mutual aid and social contact. Briar-Lawson (1998) notes that some 25 million people in the United States participate annually in mutual aid groups from which they obtain much benefit.

HESITATING TO DISCUSS
WORKER–CLIENT DIFFERENCES

Some workers believe that it's preferable for clients, not workers, to initiate any startup discussion of concerns about similarities or differences between them, since clients may not be comfortable enough to respond to direct questions about the worker–client fit until they have trust-building experience with the worker and the process. Clients may fear that raising questions about differences in age, sexual orientation, race, color, ethnicity, or religion directly will alienate or irritate workers on whom they will be depending for important services.

Worker silence on the issue of differences, however, may convey that he or she is unappreciative of, or uncomfortable with, the issue or its importance (Daniel, 2000). Our detouring around the issue of differences can discourage clients from introducing these and other difficult matters. Egan (1998) refers to the "diversity-related blind spots that can lead to inept interactions and interventions during the helping process" (p. 48). Jordan (1990) notes that "exploration of difference offers the possibility of integrative change for both people in an interaction." She believes that "without the capacity to bear conflict, an individual is in danger of being defined by another or taken over by another's reality"(p. 4). Openness to conversation about shared qualities and interests as well as differences invites clients to have greater voice and influence in shaping agenda and process with another person.

OVERLOOKING FUNDAMENTAL
HUMAN RESOURCES

Sometimes busy workers forget how important culture, heritage, spiritual practice, and family can be as fundamental resources for managing daily life and thinking hopefully of future prospects. This is especially true for workers who lack positive connections, experience, or memory in these important areas of functioning.

> When first seen at the homeless shelter referral desk, Manton said he only wanted to talk with another Buddhist. Jamie told him there weren't any, and that he could talk with other Buddhists later at the Buddhist Center in town. For now, he had to concentrate on finding day work, because people had to leave the shelter every morning after breakfast. Manton said that Buddhists were usually calmer than shelter workers, who seemed to be rushing, talking on the phone, and meeting with each other more than with residents. Jamie, exasperated, said, "I'm sorry you feel that way," and moved away to use the phone to try to locate some day work for Manton.

Here the worker concentrates on a task rather than on a very important client request that's apparently brushed off as a deluded or trivial matter when compared with the requirements of shelter living. The worker doesn't even bother to ask Manton if he knows any local Buddhists or resources that could be of help in his efforts to resettle. Manton may feel "worked for" (or worked over!) but not really cared about in any truly personal way. As clients often do, he bravely tries a second time to signal Jamie about what the problem is: that workers rush around and spend too much time with each other, with paper-work, or with tasks, when clients need more personal attention. It's doubtful that Manton would confide further in Jamie now, in spite of having reached out to him earlier with a legitimate request. It's possible, too, that connection with the local Buddhist community could help Manton find some day work nearby more quickly than this worker can.

PROBLEMS WITH TECHNIQUE
IN ENGAGING AND STARTING UP

The techniques of engagement that follow are designed to:

- establish confidence and trust in the worker and the work
- elicit comprehensive information about problems and resources
- develop working hunches about the nature and dynamics of strengths and stresses
- check in with clients about timing and dosage of exploration
- involve other people and resources as necessary

When techniques are used deliberately, sensitively, and skillfully, they go a long way towards promoting understanding of the situation, trust building, and sensible planning for further work if indicated.

ASKING QUESTIONS CLOSELY ALIGNED
WITH WHERE THE CLIENT IS

Good questions elicit relevant information, as well as client observations and feelings, as the conversation proceeds. We stay as close as we can to the client's statements or reactions to what is emerging in the work of the moment. We try to ask one clear question at a time and stay on the subject at hand until we learn as much about it as we can without pushing beyond a client's observed comfort level.

A classic mistake is to move too quickly from one topic to another, leaving the client confused about the purpose of the meeting and what's important to talk about, and leaving the worker with very scattered and superficial information to sort through later for meaning, direction, and implications.

Example of Going Off Topic Too Rapidly

Teen: I'd like to get away for a while . . . see the world.

Worker: There's a lot out there to see. Do your folks know you're thinking this?

Teen: No, they'd freak.

Replay, Closely Following Until Worker Gains More Understanding

Teen: I'd like to get away for awhile . . . see the world.

Worker: You'd like to get away for awhile . . . can you say more about that?

Teen: Well . . . my father's new girlfriend is so critical and bossy.

Worker: That can be rough. I'd like to hear more about what's happening.

In the first example, the worker jumps from the teen's fantasy to the parents' reactions, before she explores why or where the teen imagines going at this time. Jumping to see if his parents know of his wish is an abrupt worker transition that could leave this boy sensing that the worker is more concerned with the parents' feelings than with his own. It's far more important to stay with the central theme of the boy so that he feels noticed, heard, and cared about at this time. Giving him a chance to elaborate his thoughts and feelings provides an opportunity for him to sort things out with a sympathetic listener, as in the second example, where the worker stays with the teen's words and explores closely for his detailed meaning.

AVOIDING RAPID-FIRE QUESTIONS

Rapid-fire questions are easy for interns and new workers to ask in initial contacts with a new client, as there is so much we want and need to learn, and often a very short time in which to get what we need for important decision making. The temptation is thus to ask several things at once, not paying good attention to the details of or reactions to any one subject.

Example of Rapid-Fire Questions That Delay Understanding in Depth

Worker: How long have you been in the States?

Client: Just fourteen months now.

Worker: Do you know many people here?

Client: Only family, really.

Worker: Did you know many people back in your home country?

Client: Not too many . . . I worked long, long hours.

Worker: How far did you get in school there?

Client: Primary grades only.

Worker: That won't get in your way here . . . there are lots of jobs now.

This example points up the frequent mistake of not realizing that, although there are many individual bits of data emerging, the conversation isn't really leading anywhere, but simply ranges over a number of topics without an apparent direction. The client has to wait for the worker to ask her things simply because of the lack of clear purpose that would allow the client to offer material instead of waiting for the worker to decide on the lead. The more subjects introduced in a meeting, the less time there will be for depth in any one of them.

USING OPEN-ENDED QUESTIONS

In the initial phase of work, it's especially important to avoid leading and coaching ("Her bossiness must make you angry"), which involves guessing or suggesting rather than asking the client to fill in the blanks. Open-ended questions allow clients more freedom and room to tell their stories in the order, style, and intensity they feel comfortable with. Such questions also demonstrate that the worker respects clients' capacities to lead and narrate conversation with a minimum of worker coaching and shaping of interchange.

When clients are encouraged to initiate ideas, search within for their own experience and viewpoints, and puzzle their own reactions out, these activities develop and refine their reflecting, interpreting, and speaking skills—very strengthening experiences that can be derailed by clinicians' needs to talk or to demonstrate knowledge. People can feel hemmed in and even silenced early on by a worker's frequent guessing or mind reading about their inner lives and thoughts, since they know that a worker who doesn't know them yet doesn't have any real basis for guesswork.

Example of Leading

Worker: When you said a lot of people are counting on you to support them, did you mean wife and kids?

Client: I did mean kids, but not wife . . . I'm gay. My partner has just been laid off and we have two boys and a girl under 10.

Replay, Using Open-Ended Questions

Worker: When you said a lot of people are counting on you to support them, who were you thinking of?

ASKING RATHER THAN ASSUMING

It's easy when meeting new people to make assumptions based on their familiarity with other people we know who appear like them. The worker above assumed she was meeting with a heterosexual man when she wasn't. We might wrongly assume that all newcomers to the United States come with, or into, large support networks, when some are very isolated. We may assume that men will have a hard time expressing feelings and vulnerabilities, when many don't.

Crucial in the engagement phase is the appreciation and valuing of every individual's or family's uniqueness, as well as every person's need to be asked about their stories rather than told about them. In an individualizing approach, emphasis is put on what clients can elaborate about themselves, rather than what we can guess correctly—which is usually very little. Beginning a sentence with "I assume" or "I presume" is always risky business, as in: "I assume the doctor told you to see me because of a reaction to a diagnosis, am I correct?"

LEAVING TIME TO REFLECT
AFTER EACH SEGMENT OF DISCUSSION

Unless people are panicky or seriously disorganized at the moment, conversations tend to unfold in verbal paragraphs—small blocks of thought-feelings around a topic at hand, with little pauses for an acknowledgement or a breath. Startup conversation is an excellent place in which to model pausing after a block of talking, to encourage clients to take a moment in which to reflect on or feel something about what's been said and done so far, and to have more time to think about the next direction the conversation could take. Too often workers feel they must direct the work. With some initial gentle guidance about how clinical conversations work, clients can often make good decisions about subject matter, but not if the worker talks each time the client stops talking.

PURPOSEFUL FOCUSING

Clinical conversation has main roads (central focal points important to achieving goals) and side roads (oblique tangents that are less important to achieving goals). In the engagement phase, the main roads are those that elicit information and increase understanding of participants, patterns, dynamics, and resources. Side roads may be purposefully used to dilute some of the intensity of exploratory work between relative strangers, but for the most part, workers help clients focus on topics that illuminate reasons for requesting assistance, and describe in useful detail the people, problems, and resources to be worked with.

When we start at ground zero with clients, there's so much we need to find out that deciding what to ask about and then focus on can be hard at first. Missteps are common, and initial wandering about in search of a focus is not unusual. Good focusing techniques can help get things going more meaningfully. They include:

- selecting topics to discuss ("Could you tell me more about your accident.")
- offering a choice of two possible foci ("You said that both child care and training are complicated right now. Why don't you pick the one you want to focus on first?")
- pointing out drift ("We're off you and onto me right now . . . is that where we most need to be in this last five minutes?")
- changing the subject back to main concerns ("Getting back to Lionel's drug use . . . ")
- questioning for detail ("Where were you living before that?")

- repeating what was just said ("She's jealous at times.")
- underlining for emphasis ("So he *did* call back?")
- prioritizing ("Since we have to stop early to meet with the team, let's choose the important things to cover before then.")
- prefacing with regret ("I'm sorry to have to ask about something so painful, but I do need to know more about your baby's death before we talk about your volunteering to help new moms in your town.")
- explaining the need to discuss something further ("Before we finish today, I need to know what will happen if the police are called again, because that's going to affect your safety.")

APPROPRIATE TIMING AND DOSAGE

Knowing when to ask what, of whom, in what detail, is a skill refined over time with each client. When starting out as an interviewer, judgment about timing and dosage can be uneven—good at times and poorer at others—due to lack of interviewing experience and old personal habits or style. We have to begin purposefully to discipline ourselves to track time, content themes, participants' reactions, our own comfort levels, and any need for rest, validation, or respectful tapering down.

A poorly balanced interviewing style can also cause problems. Forgetting that conversations have a beginning, developmental middle, and tapering-to-ending, workers may engage in so much warm-up talk that they end up rushing through exploration and development of new information, and must also eliminate most reflective pauses between statements. In the same way, workers can jump right into exploration of painful feelings and memories without allowing enough preparatory experience together at the outset, or enough tapering down before ending and planning for client's feeling management once the meeting has ended.

CAREFULLY WORKING
FROM THE OUTSIDE IN

The purposes of exploration need to be explained at the outset, with intermittent check-ins with clients about how they are faring as they reveal themselves and are asked many questions about their personal lives and functioning. Most will signal when enough is enough, through grimaces, tiredness, emotional withdrawal, or irritable questions about the nature and rationale for so many questions.

Early questions are purposefully more factual unless the client begins the meeting with strong expression of feelings, as when a couple in the emergency room enter the worker's office crying because a beloved relative just died during an emergency procedure. Calm questioning provides a measured, step by step evolution of the conversation and fact-gathering that gives both clients and workers a chance to get used to each other, the material, and comfort levels before reaching deeper for more.

Initial questions often touch on the client's presenting situation and problems and begin to fill in information about living arrangements, sources of support, income and employment status, and any pressing concerns that require immediate attention. This initial process has been compared with the peeling of an orange in its careful moving from the factual outside of conversation to the more detailed and feeling-toned inner aspects of intimate sharing.

Random poking around in clients' information and emotional lives has, on the other hand, been compared to surgery without anesthesia, because of the likelihood of evoking too much information and feeling to be shared all at once with a stranger. Workers are thus careful to keep an eye on clients' reactions to initial process, and to validate how hard, and yet how relieving as well, it can feel to open up with someone we don't know well. Clients can also be given some choices as to the use of time and priorities; for example: "We've got about fifteen minutes left—how do you think we ought to use that time today?"

OVERPROTECTING CLIENTS

A problem arises when workers fail to explore for information or feelings because they feel it's too intrusive to do so, or too hurtful or embarrassing for the client. Often it's ourselves we're protecting when we hold back in this way, and it can signal clients that we're unprepared to discuss frankly subjects of concern to them, such as sex, finances, concerns about color or culture, religious matters, or domestic violence.

If you have a question as to whether a client can bear exploration of certain topics, don't forget to ask the expert—the client. Asking at least signals that you value client input and respect human sensitivities. We often overprotect people from matters that don't trouble them nearly as much as they trouble us.

PREJUDICE AND IGNORANCE IN ACTION

Prejudice and lack of knowledge can cause workers to treat people well where affinity is strong, and to avoid, distance, or less fully engage with others less well-known or respected. Sometimes biases aren't spoken, but are acted out in differential behaviors towards preferred and less preferred clients. Clients of color, for example, are sometimes kept waiting longer for services, assigned more severe DSM diagnoses than white counterparts, and provided with fewer options for treatment (Garretson, 1993; Okazaki, 2000; Rollock & Gordon, 2000).

Workers need to be ready to listen empathically to, and then respond to, the anger of clients and colleagues experiencing discrimination, misunderstandings, and racist structures and procedures in action. Devore and Schlesinger (1996) note that "the fear of racist or prejudiced orientations is never far from the minds of most minority or other disadvantaged people" (p. 198). For example, an agency might decide it's okay to have gay and lesbian staff to serve those clients who self identify as gay, yet feel that such staff shouldn't be routinely "out" because that might make other clients and some community board members uncomfortable.

Biases are usually most obvious to those on the receiving end of them, and are often not processed aloud due to workers' fears of resulting conflict. Until we're able to work with conflict as a normal and generative aspect of sound relationships, and until we can change our own behaviors in response to feedback, we can't really hope to model ways in which clients can alter their own.

> *An African American counseling intern said she was working with a white teen who would bring in pictures of her family and friends to show the intern and ask what she thought of them, clearly seeking approval of them. One day the teen brought in magazine shots of African American hip-hop artists she liked, and also of two or three friends of color she hangs out with from her church group. The intern first said to her supervisor that she thought the teen was trying to show how politically correct she was. Digging deeper, though, she said she really hadn't expected a white teen to admire her, or to have friends of color she was truly proud of. She thought her negative expectations of white people got in the way of her realizing that this teen admired her personally and was trying to show this through the latest pictures, probably hoping that the intern liked and admired her, too.*

Now—if she wants to—the intern can go back and review with the teen how she missed the boat around the pictures of people of color, honoring the girl's efforts to feel similarity and pride with the intern, who never expected this could happen in an interracial relationship. That movement into more authenticity and risk-taking would be a good example of the difference between real engagement and unexamined chatting.

CLASS DIFFERENCES AND CLASSIST BEHAVIORS CAN AFFECT ENGAGEMENT

We rarely talk aloud about the class differences between ourselves and our clients, although clients can certainly spot these differences in the way we dress, speak, relate, move about, and feel familiar and at ease or not. Professionals—even indebted ones—have often accumulated more education, material goods, higher priced clothing, and personal and office accessories than many clients for whom poverty and lack of opportunity may be depressing daily realities.

Just as we wouldn't feast in front of someone unable to afford food, it would be a mistake to wear expensive clothes and jewelry in meetings with clients who are barely making it financially and can't afford the basics for their families.

Adaptability, respect, and thoughtfulness are key in engaging with others. This doesn't mean that we all have to match, but simply that good judgment is called for from situation to situation. There may in fact be times when the accomplishments and possessions of a provider might make some clients proud to be associated with that person, who may represent what might be hoped for or possible in a more open and just society. A balance needs to be struck in demeanor and dress that is suitable to work in many settings and with people from many kinds of backgrounds.

A reverse situation can occur when workers are assigned VIP clients and then experience anxiety or loss of usual confidence due to a status difference between themselves and their clients. You may find yourself feeling inadequate in contacts with a wealthy or important person, while feeling much more at ease with poor or working class clients. Some workers may try to impress important people by bending rules or procedures for them in ways they wouldn't do with less privileged clients—sometimes in ways that aren't really good for them or others.

> Yvette, a wealthy woman, was dying of lung cancer on a unit that caters to rich people from all over the world. One day she confided sadly that the nurses allowed the married patient in the next room to party and have sex with her husband late into the night. At first she had thought this was funny, but she could hear the sexual activity through the walls, and this left her increasingly sad about what would soon no longer be possible for her. She didn't want to complain to the nurses because she feared they might not respond to her needs as actively if she criticized things.

Treating VIPs like human beings often affords them an unusual opportunity to express underlying worries and needs for understanding and consolation—a degree of honesty many around them may not expect or encourage. Like other people, they may not want to work with someone who seems too far removed from their own experience and lifestyle, or who lacks empathy for them because of a big difference in resources and status.

ATTITUDE TAINTS ENGAGEMENT

A respectful and hopeful attitude towards people and work is a vital quality in human service work, as it communicates to clients, colleagues, and community an appreciation of the concept of positive regard and a belief in the human capacity to change things for the better. However, *negative diagnostic spin* ("She's a bad borderline"); *pejorative remarks* ("Big Trouble is back and he's assigned to you"); *stereotyping* ("Older women never want to do anything but complain about their aches and pains"); and *racism* ("That teen looks like a gang member to me, he should see a man") may swirl around you, especially in highly stressed settings. As new people on the block, you may feel that in order to belong and prosper, you must keep silent or join in.

When individuals or work groups make a practice of demeaning fellow staff and clients, negativism can be catching and can subtly leak over into staff members' anticipatory outlook and behaviors. Clients can begin to feel to staff like burdens, and be described dismissively or resentfully. Workers may begin to give them less attention, respect, and caring, and may be observed discussing intimate information with clients in public areas where all can hear, or meeting with them in spaces that are noisy, cluttered, or run down. They may give longer sessions to clients who are "good" (compliant, nondemanding) and abbreviate meetings in which clients challenge worker status or competence. They may come late to meetings, take nonemergency calls during session, or actually tune out or doze off while the client is talking. These are all mistakes that none of us ever think we'll be involved in—until we are. While the aforementioned behaviors are often attributed to staff burnout, it can also happen that some staff simply abuse power once they get it, and others come to clinical work with diminished empathy, respect, acceptance, and patience, changing very little over the years in spite of others' efforts to help them grow.

SHIFTING MEETING TIMES
CREATES BAD FEELINGS

Appointment time is held to be largely inviolable, since a meeting with a clinician should be one of the special occasions in which clients can expect consistency, reliability, and predictability on the part of other people and institutions. It's a big mistake to switch clients' appointment times around frequently, a practice that can lead rapidly to client feelings of not mattering within a system. It can be especially hard for highly stressed clients to hear that these moves are made to "make things easier" for another client or staff person.

EMERGENCY INTERRUPTIONS CAN DERAIL
BONDING AND WORK

We need to inform clients early on when we have to be on call for emergencies during some of their appointments, and discuss with them the effects that obligation may have on the work together. It's a mistake just to wait to see if anything occurs, hoping that nothing will. If something does, clients will realize that the worker was knowingly on double duty without informing them—a real violation of trust that undermines bonding. Clients should be reassured that they will be promptly rescheduled, and apologies tendered. If worker on-call becomes a fixed requirement of the agency, then a frank discussion with clients is necessary, so that they can decide whether they want to continue in a situation that may involve numerous interruptions over time.

EMOTIONAL OVERBOOKING IS VISIBLE

Clients can usually tell when workers are emotionally overbooked—carrying too many responsibilities—by the way we hurry around, tense up, seem preoccupied, keep more obvious track of watch or clock time, and are less available for between-meeting calls. Some clients who've been primary caretakers in their families of origin may begin, out of habit, to try to take care of our needs also, bringing in food or beverage treats, and asking if we need a break before the session or need to end early. These concerns may be personal to an individual client, but could also signal that a worker is looking tired or in need of more support, putting the onus on the client to provide it.

MISSTEPS AROUND CONFIDENTIALITY AND PRIVACY

Workers usually try to talk with clients about confidentiality and its exceptions early in their opening conversation. Understanding right away that the majority of their conversations and disclosures will be held in confidence enhances initial client comfort in discussing problems and concerns with someone they don't know. It's a mistake to put confidentiality off out of politeness, or out of a wish that the client be free right away to be spontaneous. Clients can come in mistakenly believing that everything they say is confidential, and then blurt out material that falls within the exceptions of a particular state's confidentiality laws, resulting in the worker's needing to report what's been shared to authorities. If former clients return to you for further work, it's equally important that you update them regarding any new laws or requirements concerning the work.

BREACHES OF CONFIDENTIALITY

It's a grave error not to learn and be concerned about the details of your state's governing confidentiality laws, since both workers and clients can be hurt by missteps in this area. A very common additional faux pas is to violate confidentiality by talking about client case material or events in washrooms, cafeterias, elevators, or on public transportation where others can hear. Breaches of confidentiality can occur when workers are stressed, scared, or angry and need to ventilate, but are using friends instead of supervisors or consultants for support.

> *Over dinner one night, a colleague was nervous and said she needed to share something with me. She confided that a fellow clinician she was seeing in treatment had developed a crush on her that she tried to help him see as transference. He'd called her and threatened to shoot her and himself, too, if he*

couldn't have her. She called the police and he was taken to an emergency room for further evaluation. She simply spilled all this to me and I didn't know what to do, because I felt sympathy for her, but knew I shouldn't have heard all this confidential stuff.

Sometimes workers violate confidentiality by disclosing the name of an important person—a "trophy client"—they're seeing in therapy (perhaps one reason why important figures are reluctant to see a clinician unless a friend has identified a therapist who's both excellent and "leakproof").

Once while I was in hospital work, a nurse told me in a tone of intrigue that "the gunshot wound" in Room X was a "Mafia soldier" under police protection while healing due to his upcoming trial testimony. I could barely restrain myself from having a look. Another colleague of mine told me that his cousin had worked in the hospital where Elvis Presley was brought following his death, and that other professionals offered him money for locks of hair or other relics of the singer.

INFLEXIBILITY REGARDING CONFIDENTIALITY

It's good to remember that while privacy is an important consideration in engaging with clients, we try not to sacrifice opportunities to connect with people in need of service simply because there is inconsistent privacy in particular situations. Since legal privilege belongs to the client and not the worker, the client is an important arbiter in these matters. It's the worker's job not to be too rigid and insistent on conditions of confidentiality that will likely never be met. For example, in cultures centered in family and community life, clients often want to introduce different family or community members into discussions, since privacy and confidentiality may feel less important than mutual aid and group participation. If a worker worried aloud too much here about individual confidentiality when meeting together, he or she could be viewed as terribly out of sync with family and community values and process.

Many poor communities set aside counseling space in churches, public buildings, club rooms, or schools whenever these are not fully booked. These are very desirable sites by virtue of their proximity to many people needing services and to high-density destinations like supermarkets, bus stations, parks, and ball fields. People can thus reach and use services more easily and with less risk of stigma, since counseling services are often discreetly located within multipurpose facilities. You will want to take every advantage of these sites as great opportunities to engage and work with many underserved clients. Delgado (1999) describes the lengthy and careful relationship building with indigenous community and spiritual leadership that must occur prior to collaborative development of services in community host settings.

Responding to Special Needs

Prior to initial meetings, clients should be asked whether they or loved ones have special needs that can be arranged for in advance, and whether adapted space needs to be arranged for if the agency lacks ramps and adapted doors and toilets. If clients react uncomfortably to any aspect of the space you've arranged, discuss these reactions and try to take any realistic step that may increase client comfort or service accessibility.

Early in her first meeting with her child's school guidance counselor, Martha began to cough, have runny eyes, and request some water. She explained apologetically that she had an allergy to perfume and that the counselor's scent had triggered a reaction like asthma. The counselor had never thought to ask about such a thing before they met in a closed space set aside for parent meetings.

It would be a mistake simply to tell clients they can't receive service at a given locale because of special needs. The expanded role of workers includes allying with other local providers to make things happen in behalf of clients. Licensed federal and state agencies have a responsibility to help develop neighborhood and family-oriented services at alternative sites if their main offices are not fully accessible and adapted.

Janet wrote to the town council about her need for space in which to run a group for wheelchair-bound women who had had strokes and could live at home, but were limited in their socializing. She was invited to talk further about her request at the next council meeting, and some weeks later, was notified that a room in the small town library would be available one afternoon a week. The library had a ramp and the available space was on the first floor. With her group's permission, Janet wrote the new group up in her church newsletter. The Senior Apartments manager saw the piece and invited the women to come to their center by free senior transport following their meeting, so they could enjoy the weekly movie and mixer each Wednesday if they wanted to.

Work Involving Pets

An increasing number of health, day treatment, and residential settings allow pets and pet therapists to be brought in to cheer isolated or depressed residents and patients or people unable to return home for some time. Pets can also afford a safe responsive relationship to people who are shy or fearful in human relationships (Sable, 1995). Due to health laws, allergies, and some people's fear of animals, it would be a mistake simply to arrive on-site with a pet without getting prior permission with authorities, thinking that others will be cheered by the animal just because you are. In addition to health laws and allergy concerns, some staff and clients have actually felt jealous of the attention and warmth that animals receive compared with what they themselves receive in the setting or work.

Be honest with clients about any fears or allergies of your own that may make the presence of their pets problematic in meetings with you. If you home-visit a small apartment where the pet has no place to go, think together about whether there is somewhere else you can meet, or whether the situation requires the assignment of another worker. Clients are usually very accommodating to reasonable worker needs, so long as we are flexible, too. If you use a seeing eye dog yourself, inquire of new clients whether they have allergies to dog fur. If so, arrange for someone else to work with the client or for your dog to remain in safe space nearby for the duration of the meeting, to minimize effects on the client. This work is a good example of putting the needs of the client before the needs of the worker.

Emergency Assistance and Case Management Services

Sometimes, clients come for emergency help and the focus of engagement and assessment is the emergency, the needs and complications it may have given rise to, and immediate joint efforts at problem resolution and resource mobilization. At other times, emergencies arise in the lives of clients after they have begun seeing a professional for other concerns such as parenting, employment, or relationship problems. Part of early engagement work is to inform clients of the extent and range of services available so that they know whether concrete emergency assistance can be part of the working agenda or whether only counseling work is provided.

It's a huge mistake to disdain case management roles as inappropriate for clinicians, since case management functions sustain and empower clients invaluably. By helping to resolve very real crises of survival and adaptation, we demonstrate our understanding of life's priorities and our readiness to respond immediately and practically when destabilizing events strike and preoccupy people.

Determining a Good Fit

During early meetings with clients, participants have to determine if the agency's mission and resources are a good fit with clients' needs and requests for services. If not, it's easier on clients to refer them speedily to more appropriate agencies and not keep them because the agency caseload is low or because interns need case experience. People may come to an agency out of desperation to talk or to receive concrete assistance without much knowledge of the particular services or specialties of that agency. Busy staff can overlook clients' desperation and ask a secretary to point them in the direction of another agency known to provide the services they need. Further exploration by a worker might elicit more information about these applicants' coping capacities, safety in continuing to manage urgent needs, and their ability even to make it to another agency. If clients *are* able to go elsewhere, workers help by communicating respect for the other agency, ensuring that clients get there safely, and by making a referral call in advance that can speed clients' entry into the other system.

Identifying People and Problems with Whom
We Don't Want to Work

Sometimes in the engagement phase, interns and workers realize they don't like or respect a new client they see and don't want to go any further with him or her because of very strong feelings about some aspect of the client's persona or lifestyle. Some people are put off by very poor hygiene, or an insistently flirtatious manner, or by hostility shown towards worker and agency throughout an initial meeting. Presenting problems may awaken aspects of our own histories that are still toxic for us, so that resulting discomfort interferes with bonding and being fully open to client experience and feelings.

Not every agency can afford to relieve workers of assignments that feel untenable for them, but it's important that you raise with your supervisor any instances in which you feel yourself to be a poor match for your client's story or needs. Sometimes the perception of poor fit can be resolved by personal review and work on self, but sometimes it can't, since working through of our own problems may take longer than the client will be with the agency.

While committed to serving all people with unqualified acceptance, workers, supervisors, and agencies also understand the importance of mutual investment in counseling work, and may be able to reach some accommodation or decide on a transfer of the client to someone else after the completion of the assessment process. Sometimes workers are encouraged to keep an assignment in order to do some necessary growing around the challenges it poses. At other times we may wish to give the client a fresh start with a worker who will experience less personalization and reactivity in the presence of the client's issues or style.

Asking for Help When You Don't Know What to Do

There's no way to predict who will appear at an agency, how work with clients will develop, what may suddenly occur in an interview, or what crises may beset a client or an agency at any time. An initial meeting may be going smoothly when suddenly, something novel occurs, calling for responses not yet in a worker's repertory.

Sometimes we can call for help by voice, a call button on the desk, or stepping outside to ask a secretary or team member for assistance or a second opinion. Sometimes we do our best to complete a meeting, consulting afterwards with a supervisor about what happened, following up by phone or a home visit if different or urgent action needs to be taken. But sometimes we simply do things out of habit, such as exclaiming, "Get a hold of yourself!" or "Hey, you can't do that here!"—as though we're in another time and place. These are real responses from real people trying to cope with the unfamiliar the best way they know how. We can learn a lot about our strengths and our growth edges in such moments.

Cora, a client easily angered when frustrated, came in for a session with Marta, her health clinic social worker. When Marta checked in with her about her smoking levels for the week, Cora became furious, got up, moved towards Marta, then stopped short, punching a hole in the wall about four feet from her worker. Marta exclaimed, "Don't you dare lay a finger on me!" Frantic, Cora fled the room, too ashamed to stay or to return the next week. Marta had to do a lot of reaching out to get her back in, at which time each apologized for her reaction. Supervision relieved Marta's guilt and helped her find words for an apology.

The ability to ask for help when needed is a must for every worker's learning agenda. It's developed through solid orientation to setting procedures, clinical backup, and behaviors expected in role. It also develops through steady ongoing supervision that reviews potential risks and suggests step-by-step responses to these. Serious incidents can occur in first contacts with clients, so it's wise to be as prepared as possible through consultation before entering what appear to be risky first meetings. Workers should never be too proud to ask for help, no matter how long they've been working in human services.

Dealing with Dire Predictions

Knowing in advance from other staff that a client may be difficult to sit with due to aggression, threats, rudeness to staff, or a general dislike of counselors can leave workers feeling nervous before they even meet with the client and see for themselves. Because different staff evoke different responses from clients, we need to give each client the benefit of a fresh appraisal, in case previous workers might have been biased in their assessments of particular people. It's impossible to predict when a new relationship may click with someone who then opens up more freely because of the caring and considerateness shown.

If unacceptable levels of disrespect, threats, or verbal abuse occur, workers can end a meeting, modeling carefulness and self-respect by explaining that visits can resume at any time the client can control demeaning behaviors or language and focus on meaningful activity together. If there is any risk that violence could erupt in a home visit, a thorough review with supervisors may determine that a visit should not be made until hostilities are clarified and resolved by phone or in an agency meeting. We can also arrange for another professional or a law enforcement officer to accompany us on home visits if risk is present, but a visit needs to be made to determine the safety of people in the home.

Engagement in the Electronic Age

Engagement can also be initiated and supported by letter, phone, fax, and Internet, but workers need to remind clients of the lack of security in communicating via these media. Since there are likely to be many therapy offerings on the Internet, clients should be alerted that anyone online can call himself or herself a therapist and can post false credentials or someone else's resume.

At all times, clients should carefully evaluate with the worker or other trusted allies any advice received from sources on the Web whose credentials cannot be researched and validated. Importantly, child and adolescent clients should be asked early on to discuss with parents and workers any unusual individual outreaches to them by Web visitors attempting to solicit meetings, phone calls, pictures, or letter exchanges.

Many people now use the Internet productively to locate health and mental health information, services, and referrals. In journal fashion, clients can also e-mail workers between sessions, reflecting further on thoughts and reactions they've had since meeting. Again, there needs to be an understanding by the client that these communications can never be regarded as secure, since both authorities and random hackers have demonstrated the capacity to enter, track, and exploit communication systems (Gelman, Pollack, & Weiner, 1999). We'll also need to let clients know whether we'll be responding or not to client e-mails of a journaling nature, since busy schedules or individual preference may limit responding.

> *Zach's worker, Ed, told him he could e-mail his thoughts from prison if that would help calm him at times when confinement made him antsy. But he alerted Zach that anyone could access the e-mails without either of them knowing about it, and that Zach could decide what to e-mail and what to reserve for face-to-face visits.*

The proliferation of Internet therapies prompts examination of a number of pros and cons. On the positive side, people who may feel too shy, exposed, or stigmatized to seek out face-to-face counseling may feel safer revealing themselves to a stranger electronically, particularly if they are used to chat room interaction. Others may be able to locate a particular kind of clinician more easily on the Internet than they could in their particular country, region, village, or neighborhood.

The Internet also offers more anonymity and distance, which for some people may be a relief and for others, a complication in trust. Internet anonymity permits people with varying qualifications and motivations to present themselves as caring therapists, with the risk that some people may be exploited or poorly served without awareness.

> *An associate gave me the name of an Internet counseling service to check out. When I clicked on the site, all of the faces were white and a prominent appeal mid-page said: "Quit being a slave to your old habits—find help here." I responded with a message that the all-white faces and the appeal to "quit being a slave" felt insensitive and racist in a rainbow society. A reply came right back that day: "Thank you for your feedback. Here, we don't have to be politically correct."*

CONCLUSION

First impressions matter a lot in human service work, not because they can't be altered through subsequent experience, but because people tend to put a lot of stock in them and can really be thrown off by unwelcoming or unsettling beginnings with workers. What a clinician offers has to feel familiar and helpful enough for clients to want to continue the experience, bearing their vulnerabilities and finding their strengths as they do so. Goodness of fit between what's needed and what's offered becomes an important issue in determining whether and how to proceed together.

The interview encounter has to create a meaningful differential between itself and what clients can already find with friends and loved ones or in community programs. Why else would busy people go to the time, trouble, and expense involved in speaking with a clinician? Part of that differential has to be a refreshing experience of confidentiality, unconditional regard, support of strengths and differences, and readiness to work hard.

Working relationships can develop within a single contact, within a brief treatment of a few sessions, or over months or years of work together. Clients and workers can sometimes become disenchanted with one another right up front in the engagement phase, yet have to—or choose to—continue working together. An important part of true engagement is compromising and bearing disappointments in each other without crashing and burning—that is, giving up on each other and the work.

EXERCISES

1. *Reflection.* In your journal, remember some initial encounters you've had with professionals who engaged you positively, and with some who really put you off and tempted you not to return to see them again. Be as specific as you can about both the positives and the negatives that you remember well. Can these interactions bring to mind things that you want to be careful about in your own demeanor, attitude, welcoming, and initial approach in new relationships with clients and colleagues? Discuss any things you may have already altered about yourself once you started work in practicum or agency.

2. *Large Group Discussion.* Discuss special challenges or problems you're encountering in your engagement of new clients or in meeting and bonding with colleagues. Have you noticed any things about your engagement style that you'd like to improve? Discuss the things you do well in meeting with new clients, and what it is about you that brings clients back for more work with you.

3. *Instructor Activity.* Divide the class into groups of four. Ask them to devise and then role play challenging situations they've encountered in trying to engage new clients. Reconvene the group and have them suggest alternative approaches for reworking problematic scenarios presented. Later, describe to the class some challenges or miscalculations you've experienced in trying to engage clients, and how you resolved them.

4. *Author Sharing for Further Discussion.* A woman on a psychiatric unit was referred to me for psychosocial evaluation before plans were made for her return home. She was said to be psychotic, and I'd never before met alone with someone hallucinating or deluded. I was afraid of what might happen, or what I would say if she shared strange thoughts with me. She came to

the first meeting about twenty minutes late, chain smoking, although a sign on the door said "No Smoking." This alone made me think to myself, "See? Out of control." I invited her to be seated, which she did in a friendly way that reassured me I was going to be okay. I asked if she was nervous about meeting me, since I was new on the unit and we'd never met. She laughed gently and asked: "If *I'm* so nervous, how come *your* palms are sweating? Look at mine—dry as a bone!" I looked at my palms, and they were indeed wet and shiny. I blushed and laughed uncomfortably. She looked at me kindly and asked, "What's the matter, honey, scared I'm going to do something mental?" She then assured me that she wasn't a scary person, and asked me what I needed to know about her in order to help her get home again. Later I thought to myself how tired these folks must be of dealing with one rookie after another.

For Class Discussion. How would you assess this first encounter on an inpatient psychiatric unit? Why would I be so nervous, and the client, so at ease? What similar and different things might we two be feeling as human beings at this moment? What responses might you make to her question about me being afraid of her "doing something mental"? What can a worker and a client learn from an encounter like this?

RECOMMENDED READING

Daniel, J. H. (2000). The courage to hear: African American women's memories of racial trauma. In L. C. Jackson & B. Greene (Eds.), *Psychotherapy with African American women* (pp. 126–144). New York: Guilford.

DeJong, P., & Miller, S. D. (1995). How to interview for client strengths. *Social Work, 40,* 729–736.

Delgado, M. (1999). Engagement of nontraditional settings. In *Social work practice in non-traditional urban settings* (pp. 159–174). New York: Oxford University Press.

Leigh, J. W. (1998). Assessment, negotiated consensus, treatment planning, and culturally relevant interventions and treatment. In *Communicating for cultural competence* (Appendix C, pp. 125–144). Needham Heights, MA: Allyn & Bacon.

Malgady, R. G., & Zayas, L. H. (2001). Cultural and linguistic considerations in psychodiagnosis with Hispanics: The need for an empirically informed process model. *Social Work, 46,* 39–49.

Rooney, R. H. (1992). *Strategies for work with involuntary clients.* New York: Columbia.

Shulman, L. (1999). The preliminary phase of work. In *The skills of helping individuals, families, groups, and communities* (pp. 40–92). Itasca, IL: Peacock.

Weingarten, K. (1992). A consideration of intimate and non-intimate interactions in therapy. *Family Process, 31,* 45–58.

4

Professional Relationships: Steps and Missteps

The Centrality of Relationship in Practice

Relationship suffuses everything we think about and do in clinical work. The worker–client relationship acts as a conduit and cushion for work together, and expresses each participant's capacity to proceed collaboratively utilizing coauthored goals to guide client-centered activities. Our relationships with colleagues, service agencies, and community institutions are developed and maintained as a support matrix that also enhances access to broader services and networks. Even when we work apparently alone on an issue or task, we're actually thinking all the time about the impact of our conclusions, decision making, and action on others, about their reactions to what we're thinking and doing, and about the other people that need to be involved for proposals or activities to come to fruition.

Relationship is also a developmental process and challenge that many clients and communities focus on in consultation, large meetings, and therapy. Relationship is a professional capacity that workers can improve through study, practice, feedback, and personal work. The client–worker relationship itself can become a purposeful and generative focus of the work at times, and can bring about increased relational capacity in both worker and client as a memorable outcome of the work done together.

Although action towards achievement of client goals is the overarching focus of clinical work, relationships are the powerful medium for that action. Where two or more people act together to define and achieve shared goals through a collaborative process, there is usually a heightened capacity to maintain hope, energy, focus, and direction in ways that individuals can't always sustain when frustrated or blocked by others' competing agendas and needs.

> I had been working with Tracy for a long time in her efforts to try to get public housing, and we both were excited that she was now almost approved for a one-bedroom place. At that very moment, her sister and two kids arrived on her doorstep, as they'd just been kicked out of their apartment due to bad behaviors on the boys' part. Because of their desperate need of a place to stay, Tracy had to take them in, which made her ineligible for the small apartment she was all set to enter. When I had to call her to tell her this, she said that she could tell by my voice that I was "downhearted and on the edge of giving up." I didn't know what to say next, because that was exactly what I was feeling, but I didn't want to discourage her. She said she learned long ago that nothing is ever easy, so I shouldn't give up, because one way or the other, she was going to finally get this housing and complete nurse's aid training. She said she needed me to keep faith, too. I told her she was right, and apologized for sounding so defeated. I thought of this exchange as a role reversal then, but looking back, I can see that Tracy taught me about her own skills, my use of self, and the work process itself.

UNIQUE FEATURES OF THE WORKER–CLIENT RELATIONSHIP

The worker–client relationship often provides a unique level of focused attention and safe intimacy. People often find novel and refreshing the purposeful, client-centered responsiveness of workers who ask for little in return other than investment in agreed-upon work together. The time, emotional commitment, energy, and activity invested in working together also lend a special kind of dignity to the work process.

Another pleasant surprise for many clients is that, while we may be seen as authority figures by virtue of our professions' or agencies' authority and role in the community, we try to use that authority benignly and in the client's behalf, as when instituting services or bringing about connections likely to improve the client's situation or well-being. Our ethical stance can also be novel for clients who are used to seeing people with power use that power for their own gain. Worker ethics may be tested time and again to see if they hold up.

> Curtis saw me smoking not far from a sign that said "No smoking." He asked me if it would be okay if he went up to the neighborhood bar and just had one beer, since he'd been clean of all street drugs for almost five weeks now. I asked him if this request could be connected to my smoking where I wasn't supposed to. He grinned and said that what's good for the goose should be good for the gander. I realized I was living in a fishbowl here where the things I did and said could really matter, so I said that I had a saying to match his: two wrongs don't make a right. He laughed. I said I regretted smoking in the house, and that

even one wrong is wrong. He asked me if I wanted to go shoot some baskets now, and I said I did. On the way, he said solemnly that smoking could be dangerous to my health. I was affected by his worry, realizing that I just hadn't stopped to think through the impact of my behavior on him and our other clients. I honestly hadn't realized either that a resident would actually care that much if I lived or died.

Curtis, a young adult with few sober ties, is really saying to his residence counselor something very hard and new for him: "I like you and I need you to last. I want you to be somebody I can respect and learn from. I also have some things to teach *you*." He and his worker are a good example of relational tending: actively keeping a relationship on track by noting a problem within it, thinking about what the problem represents in the relationship, and addressing the problem together because participants want the relationship to last and grow rather than deteriorate or end due to disconnection and pretending that nothing is wrong.

Miller and Stiver (1997) suggest that such relational tending is at the core of human development and of all effective work with people, whether with individuals, families, groups, or communities. Relational tending—"seeing and telling it like it is"—is one of the hardest things we have to learn to do in life as well as in clinical work, as it requires accurately spotting and verbally taking ownership of our mistakes and hurtful behaviors in relationships with clients and colleagues.

According to Miller and Stiver, mutual tending results in mutual growth in five dimensions that coalesce as mutual empowerment: *zest* or *vitality* ("the energizing effect of emotional joining"); *action* ("in the moment of the immediate exchange" and experiencing one's positive impact on process); *knowledge* (greater understanding, through authentic exchanges, of self, other, and "the way the world goes"); *sense of worth* (from validating attention and recognition); and *greater sense of connection and a desire for more* (motivation to move into a widening circle of growth-fostering connections). Surrey (1991) affirms that the mutual empowerment born of positive relational interchange leads to greater relational responsibility or *"response-ability"*—a fuller appreciation of what relationships mean and require, and an enhanced capacity to develop, tend, and remain faithful to them.

WORKER SELF-DISCLOSURE AS A FORM OF RELATIONAL TENDING

Lum (2000) has found that in cross-cultural counseling, the culturally different client's seeing and "telling it like it is" can be undercut from the outset unless workers share more about their own backgrounds and perspectives than they may be used to sharing. He suggests that appropriate areas of disclosure that can ease clients' reservations about professionals include a brief introduction of self and role, a bit of personal and family background relating to the client's known experience, something about the worker's helping philosophy, and points of interest or concern shared with the client (p. 167).

This kind of disclosure expresses an understanding that many clients have been misunderstood, misrepresented, and oppressed by people and systems connoted as "helping." To counter these alienating experiences, workers try to establish early on an environment of mutual trust and respect through identification of common ground and shared human experience and concern. Pope-Davis and Constantine (1996) believe that most counselors have minimal experience and training in the accurate use of self-disclosure skills, and may be "seriously disadvantaged in their ability to form a helpful relationship with a culturally different client" (p. 119).

EMPATHY: BEING WHERE THE CLIENT IS

Few things are as central to maintaining relationships as empathy—the worker's close cognitive and emotional alignment with the experience, feelings, and perspective of the client. This process of alignment involves "being where the client is," yet paradoxically also involves a mildly dissociative process unfolding in several purposeful steps. First, while remaining attentive to what the client says or does at the moment, we send some of our own feeling and observing capacity over into the client's inner experience. We attempt to experience the client's thoughts, feelings, and intentions as fully as we can, *as though we were the client* in the moment. In doing so, however, *we purposefully retain an observer's capacity* to stand back and evaluate what we are experiencing as the client. Then we have to carefully decide whether to share, or simply store for later use, our experience as the client.

Beginning practitioners often ask how they can possibly execute the multiple functions of empathy all at once, especially when still developing knowledge and awareness of their own inner lives and perspectives. Honing a complex, multifaceted capacity is clearly the work of many years. It involves a knowledge of human behavior and of each particular client's story, feelings, and nuanced style; and of our own story and personal dynamics as they relate to each client's situation, themes, and emerging content.

Empathy requires that the self of the worker be sufficiently secure and "boundaried" to allow the worker to travel to and from the client's position wordlessly, without panicking or losing a sense of stable and organized self (Jordan, 1991). For example, we might say that empathizing with a certain client's story "gives us the creeps." Yet, while shaken, we don't begin to be confused about who or where we are at the moment, or overwhelmed by "the creeps." It's this highly developed ability of excellent clinicians to be able to be fully present while experiencing alternating perspectives and feelings that distinguishes the care they provide. Chapter 1 described how capacity for empathy can be advanced by periodically assuming a metaposition so as to watch yourself in action and check for anything that could interfere with being where the client is.

CONDITIONS CONDUCIVE
TO ACCURATE EMPATHY

A number of conditions make it easier for you and your clients to align and attune in a solid and resilient empathic connection. Although the reality of practice is that very little interviewing takes place under optimal circumstances, an awareness of supportive conditions can spur you to try to effect those changes necessary to support good worker–client attunement and mutual responsiveness.

Worker Calm and Repose

An atmosphere of encircling calm and quiet greatly enhances opportunities for empathic attunement to what is happening, whether it's happening over the course of the work or in one particular session or moment. Observing and responding are easier when there is stillness of mind, body, and spirit, conveyed as a sort of quieting bubble around the work (Murphy & Dillon, 1998). Clearly, that kind of calm is harder if the worker isn't at ease, or the interview environment itself is chaotic, intrusive, or full of distractions.

> *Because I meditate, I have calming things I can do when the demands of the day or the particulars of clients' stories stir me up. Before each client comes, I try to sit quietly where they will, as though to leave a calm aura of care and support there. I make sure the phone ringers are turned off, plenty of tissues are available, and that there are real or paper cups in case a person needs to go for water and come back with it. Then I sit in my chair and picture a valley by a stream where people and animals all rest or drink safely side by side, as in the painting, "The Peaceable Kingdom." Then I inhale and exhale slowly and deeply a few times and ask for patience, guidance, and focus for the meeting to come. Some time back, I used to jiggle or switch around a lot, and I knew this was disconcerting because I could sometimes see different clients looking at my movements. Meditation has really helped, and takes five minutes or less.*

Accurate Discernment of Who Is
Experiencing What, When

Accurately discerning who experiences what in an interaction is a challenge in any relationship. Workers use human behavior knowledge, a growing knowledge of client and self, and well-informed suggestions from supervisors and consultants to begin to sort through the thickets of what's happening within and between self and others at any given time. Because interpersonal process is dynamic and circular, with reciprocal influences rippling between and around participants, often what seems to be happening "in one person" is actually a shared process.

> *When I sent myself into Edna's experience while she looked out the window, I felt angry at all the helpers who had not understood me and had kept me locked up in the state hospital all these years, with very few visits from family. I*

felt so lonely and hopeless—I actually shivered even though it was early summer and hot. I then wondered if this was how the hospital felt to her—lonely and cold—and if she'd ever talk with me, since she was so resolutely shut down— and why not? Suddenly she turned and asked me if I was looking at her "that way" because I thought she was a crazy woman. I asked her what "way" I was looking. She said, "Like at a funeral or something." I said I was appreciating what all these years here must have been like for her. She cackled loudly in a way that didn't feel funny at all, and then said sadly, "Nothing to write home about—if you had a home." This last remark really "hit home," because I was in a period of postdivorce feelings of homelessness at that time. I suddenly realized that some of the sad way I looked was a reaction to my own life as well as to hers; but I'd initially thought of my reaction as only having to do with her story.

Worker thought and feeling, like client thought and feeling, are a rich source of empathic resonance between participants, and can be examined as a way of looking at what happens between people in safe relationship— something with which clients and clinicians may have little experience (Jordan, 1993; Miller & Stiver, 1999).

Lorene worked with a legally blind girl whose parents rarely expressed feeling unless they were annoyed or disappointed at her for having troubles being "mainstreamed" at school when she could barely see to get around or learn. Lorene thus decided to "join" with her by playing appropriate latency-age games with her on the floor, where the nine-year-old could be right next to her and see her better. At a given moment in a game, the girl began to cry, for the first time saying she'd never be like other kids and was so tired of trying to be. This so touched the worker that she began to feel tears welling up, unbeknownst to the girl. Lorene thought it important that this isolated girl experience real emotion from a caring figure, and recognize her impact on another person. She said, "Maybe you can't see this, but your words have touched my heart and I am tearful, too." The girl reached out her hand, touched Lorene, and thanked her for being "so nice."

It's important that you learn to discern the multiple and complex sources of feeling experienced with and about clients, and to review their manifestations in your work with various clients and colleagues.

Empathy The client has a feeling or inner experience and then the worker joins with it and experiences it, too, *as though the client* at the moment. The first part is the client; the second part is the worker vicariously experiencing the client's internal process. Clients can often sense accurately what is happening within the worker, too, and convey noticing and caring. Here, the first part is the worker's experience; the second part is the client's accurate perceptions of it and joining with it.

Miller and Stiver (1997) identify a "central paradox" in human relationships: that people will actually keep parts of themselves (for example, real wishes, feelings, or truths) *out of relation* in order to try to maintain a relationship they fear cannot bear these held-back parts. Clients, for example, may hold back their empathy if they sense that a worker is uncomfortable receiving their accurate observations and feedback. Jordan (1990) describes the courage it takes for both clients and workers to stay in connection when experiencing conflict with each other, and to own their contributions to difficulties when these arise.

> *Aldana said I could dish it out in the group but not take it. This was a really uncomfortable thing for me to hear, even though I could feel myself blush every time she or other members gave me feedback that was other than positive. I always thanked people for the feedback, but then kept reacting to it visibly. I hadn't known much "good criticism" in the foster home I grew up in, and thanks to these women, I came to realize how much corrective feedback felt like criticism from the foster home. My supervisor had already suggested something similar in supervision, so when it came up in the group, too, I got myself a therapist to talk with about my reactions and my history.*

Countertransference   Countertransference may be thought of as an unconscious reenactment of an unresolved part of the worker's relational history with a client who's experienced as a stand-in for a figure in that history. The first part is similarly stuck relational history in worker and client; the second part is an unconscious replay of it in the moment, each believing they are simply reacting to something the other has initiated. Unlike empathy, which takes the worker *towards* the client's experience, the intensely personal worker reactions of countertransference take the worker *away* from the client's here-and-now experience and back into the worker's own unresolved tensions or conflicts.

Projection   In projection, an unconscious, disavowed feeling or belief of the worker is attributed to the client. Where previously there was irritation in the worker, there is now a blank space of unfeeling. "Why are you irritated with me so often?", the worker may ask the client, who isn't actually feeling irritated "so much." But if the worker nags about the subject, the client may in fact get irritated and say so. As long as an unconscious projection is at work, the worker's real feelings can't be evaluated and used for growth in self or client.

Complications from a worker's unknowing blank space arise when empathy cannot form in this feeling vacuum, and when the client is regarded as the initiator of a problem sequence instead of its target. Often projection is most clearly seen in dyads, where one member is felt to be the "good one" and the other member, the "bad one." When either member is absent or the partnership breaks up, frequently each will begin to manifest more of the traits that the other had "carried" for both in the dyad.

Identification   Identification with the client describes the emotional process of finding things in common with the client's experience, feelings, and agenda, and seeing the client as similar to oneself in special ways. A temptation for workers in identification is to focus only on the matching and likeable dimensions of worker and client, filtering out those attributes of the client or worker that differentiate them from each other. Identification while trying to empathize with the client can lead to oversimplification and incompleteness of evaluation and understanding, and can blind the worker about problem areas in both parties that need further attention.

In **overidentification,** the worker is so twinned with the client that a kind of sleepwalking relationship ensues. The worker begins to make assumptions about what the client feels and thinks based on the worker's own feelings and thoughts. Questions and probes are less and less used to elicit differentiating details of the story. The worker begins to speak *for* the client: "That must have hit you pretty hard," or "As a fellow adoptive mom, I can guess what you're thinking." Overidentification can induce a false or distorted perspective—one good reason why workers are asked to maintain some intellectual detachment from those they serve so as to retain a psychological center and perspective distinct from the client's. Book (1988) encourages a balanced therapist oscillation between the role of participant and that of observer (the metaposition), but notes that clinicians too often get stuck in the participant stance through overidentification with the client's issues or feelings. Only when sufficiently differentiated within a relationship can each participant bring fresh perspectives and potentials to problem resolution when the work process gets stuck.

Interest and Nonintrusive Curiosity

Having and showing curiosity about the client is a sustaining relational technique, and leaves most clients feeling that we are genuinely invested in them and eager to learn the details of their experience. The worker's curiosity usually encourages more sharing by the client, just as the client's interest in what the worker has to say often elicits more talk by the worker. In rare instances, however, certain clients may become suspicious of worker curiosity because of past exploitation by others, but this fear can usually be softened through a gentle style of exploration while maintaining very respectful boundaries, attitudes, and behaviors.

The goal in all exploration is not simply to collect data, but to help unfold client experience supportively and safely so as not to overwhelm the client's established adaptive strategies. The more we find out about clients and their stories, the more there is to join with through empathic alignment, and the more that alignment may cushion further disclosure by the client as trust is built.

Openness to Many Kinds of Narratives

Empathy flourishes when a worker communicates an accepting openness to whatever the client has to say, no matter how alien the content is to a worker's experience or understanding. Experience from *within* a variety of communities and perspectives immeasurably enhances a worker's ability to immerse in others' experience. As we come to know communities better through direct participation in them, we also begin to appreciate why many people prefer family, neighborhood, and faith-based organizational assistance to that offered by human service agencies and workers, who can seem so detached from "street realities" (Briar-Lawson, 1998; Taylor, Ellison, Chatters, Levin, & Lincoln, 2000).

When Timothy, a black teacher, was found to be HIV-positive, he dropped out of a psychology PhD program to help found a Multicultural AIDS Center in the black community of his city. Through his practicum, he had seen that most of the big money was going to the long-established AIDS Action program in the mostly white downtown area. In spite of that center's outreach by a few predominantly African American staff, clients of color were not really coming to that center because it was accurately perceived by them to be white dominant and nowhere near the social and spiritual power centers of communities of color. Timothy and leaders from various other minority communities ended up creating a roving health bus outreach program, a street ministry, a leafleting campaign, a needle exchange program, and two HIV clinics related to neighborhood health centers that served newcomer groups. Articulate ex-addicts from several language groups turned out to be some of the most effective education and outreach staff because they were indigenous to the areas targeted and had also "walked the walk."

Another aspect of openness is our openness to our own family and personal stories and our willingness to get in touch with our own privilege, cultural blinders, and biases. McIntosh (1989) provides a compelling framework for examining unacknowledged dimensions of white privilege and blind spots that permit white people to think and behave offensively in the presence of nonwhite clients and colleagues with little or no awareness of having done so.

Close Following of the Client's Story

Enhancement of empathy occurs whenever workers are able to follow the client's story very closely and stay focused on it, since learning more about the client can facilitate a quicker, more accurate alignment with him or her. One of the best ways to follow the story closely is simply to stay out of the client's way whenever she or he is on already on track with well-focused material or feelings—an example of the "don't just do something, sit there" approach.

Supervision and Mentoring
in the Development of Empathy

Many workers have had positive life experience in a variety of relationships, entering clinical educational programs or roles with a good capacity for closely following conversations and demonstrating caring and concern for others. What good supervision can add to these relational capacities is a theoretical understanding of their differential use with different people. As noted in Chapter 1, you'll be helped to recognize and work with mutual influence and reciprocity in interactions and appreciate the parallel process that can ripple through the client–worker relationship, the supervisory relationship, the relationships of worker and supervisor within agency hierarchies, and the relationships of the client, worker, supervisor, and agency with outside forces and institutions (Ganzer & Ornstein, 1999).

Effective relationships between you and your instructors afford opportunities to experience *in vivo* many of the constructive attitudes and insightful approaches useful in work with clients. Good supervisory relationships possess clarity of expectations and roles, open knowledge exchange, a strengths approach to learning and work, and authenticity in interaction (Gardner, 1995). The instructor's empathy with your excitement and anxiety can be a great support for learning, as well as a demonstration of how empathy sounds and feels.

Relationship modeling and skill building, while clearly embedded in the experiential aspects of the relationship, are predominantly work-focused and client-centered, much as client interviews are. At times a supervisor, modeling relational tending, will attend to problems or issues that might arise between you, or to expectable anxieties and needs as these may affect attending and working well with clients. Instructors may also provide readings, suggest conferences to attend, and share examples from their own or colleagues' practice experience in order to advance knowledge and skill.

MISSTEPS IN TRYING TO EMPATHIZE

Workers can mean well and still make mistakes when trying to convert empathic responsiveness into statements and behaviors with clients. All too often, in "feeling sorry for" clients, we are mistaking sympathy (a feeling *towards* or *about* the other) for empathy (a feeling *with* or *as* the other). Inexperienced workers can become confused when trying to determine when they are joining the client's experience and when they are misperceiving their own feelings as those of the client. The following are other very common errors that, while enacted with the best intentions, can leave clients feeling inaccurately heard and feeling rather alone, in spite of workers' physical presence.

Boilerplate Empathy

Boilerplate refers to repetitively stamped out and stockpiled materials or communications that can be used for many different purposes. A salesperson might use the boilerplate "Is there anything I can help you with today?", while a lawyer might say, "I'll see you in court." There shouldn't be boilerplate or stockpiled phrases in empathizing with another person, but there are. Statements like "I feel your pain," "Oh, *my!*" and "I see what you're saying" are very overused, perhaps learned as much from TV sitcoms as from instructors and supervisors.

To be meaningful, *empathy has to feel and sound to the client like what he or she experiences.* Until it does, workers will often receive redirection from them in statements such as "That's not what I meant," or "Huh?" These responses may tempt the worker to make another mistake by saying, "Let me explain what I was thinking when I said that," which focuses on the worker instead of asking

"What's happening for you right now?" At the very least, a concerted effort to avoid the overuse of boilerplate is crucial in creating an atmosphere that feels respectful and genuine.

Piling It On

Workers "pile it on" by making empathic comments and sounds that are too numerous, too exaggerated, too childlike in tone, or so repetitious that they feel inauthentic and lacking in specialness. The nicest responses can lose their power and meaning if they become repetitious or are inappropriate to age or culture.

Example of Piling It On

Client: My cousin's house is flooded, they're staying with us.

Worker: Wow, awful . . . what happened?

Client: That river near St Louis that crested?—that got them.

Worker: Wow . . . terrible . . .

Client: They lost everything. We're trying to help.

Worker: How generous . . . but then, you guys always are.

Client: Actually, we tried to get my brother in Michigan to take them because of the new baby and all . . .

Worker: Makes sense . . . goodness, what a lot of stuff. Hard. Wow. How are they faring?

Client: First, what about how WE are faring?

Here the worker focuses empathy off of the client and onto her relatives, and in that moment, captures the client's full attention as someone who is not "where she is" at the moment. She then attempts to re-engage and redirect the worker with the heartfelt plea, "What about how are *we* faring?"—letting him know that he is off track at a difficult time for her. It's at this point that many workers make the mistake of getting defensive instead of just apologizing and asking how the client *is* faring, since the client has just generously suggested where the work should be refocused.

Another common worker mistake is to empathize with the wrong one of several experiences the client has just described. When this happens, clients will often simply say something like, "No, that's not it," and redirect the worker with a sigh, or nonverbal signals like a frown, a change in eye contact, or a glance at a watch or clock.

Roz had been telling me for a long time about an abusive drinking buddy of hers who was constantly verbally abusing her. When I asked why she stayed with this friend, she consistently said this was her one best friend, and took the friend's side, explaining that she'd been abused like that in her own family of origin and had developed the same habits of putting people down. The last few weeks, this abuse had taken on a more violent character. Both women, longtime mill workers together, were trying to change their lives by taking training or classes and getting involved with new friends a little bit more. This was definitely rocking the friendship that both had counted on for ages. Roz came in one evening with a black eye and bruise on her nose, with broken glasses, caused when her friend hit her in the face while mad about a change in schedule. She cried about how mad she was at Bea, and how she'd like to kill her. I said that she'd often helped me get beneath Bea's anger, to remember that Bea acted the way she did due to her history of abuse, and that this had helped me feel more empathy for Bea. I wondered if that could help Roz now. She was outraged with this idea and, raising her voice, said, "Hey, I don't pay you to feel sorry for Bea, I pay you to feel sorry for me! You'd better remember where your bread is buttered."

Here the worker moves swiftly away from Roz's feelings, perhaps out of discomfort with so much rage. Instead of giving Roz special concern and empathy, she asks Roz to feel some compassion for her abusive friend. This misstep leaves the client feeling very deserted, experiencing the worker as siding emotionally with the enemy instead of with her, and just when she is feeling estranged from Bea, her only real friend. With an uncharacteristic grandiosity prompted by outrage and desperation, Roz then orders the worker to remember "who she is" (a disguised plea for recognition, dignity, accurate empathy, and emotional support).

Another similar mistake interns and workers make is to get the facts wrong just when they're trying to empathize in order to consolidate a feeling of relationship. The worker will look at a client and say caringly, "This is the anniversary of your brother's suicide . . . an important day," and the client will say, "My *sister's* suicide," appearing let down. Often the client will then protect the worker by saying, "I wouldn't expect you to remember details like that with all the people you see," a statement to be explored for meaning.

TRIVIALIZING VIA EXCESSIVE UNIVERSALIZING

In universalizing, workers attempt to locate client experience in a large cohort of people who've been through similar things, in order to normalize client behaviors and reduce shame or embarrassment felt about them. For example, when a man says he felt ashamed after running from snakes on a hike with his date, the worker might at some later point say, "Who wouldn't run from a group of snakes?", or "That's such a normal reaction—why would you feel ashamed of that?"

This reframe can help people feel understood, but if offered too quickly or too frequently, it can make the recipient feel that his or her situation, still being experienced powerfully as uniquely painful, is being trivialized as "just one of" a hundred similar instances. Exploring the man's shame further may yield deeper meanings embedded in it. Since this may not be the first time he feels—or others have judged him to be—lacking, this would be a very important subplot of the story to explore for its deeper meaning and feeling.

Excessive Personal Sharing in Efforts to Empathize

Clients don't expect their doctors, nurses, lawyers, or ministers to be just like them, or to derive their professional authority from having gone down exactly the same life pathways as they have. They usually don't expect their workers to be exactly like them either, expecting instead that we be cordial, accepting, knowledgeable, and helpful in a deliberate and focused way. While clients may want to know a little about who you are as a person, they usually don't expect to hear a great deal of detail, and may actually feel displaced if the worker shares too many personal experiences, problems, and dilemmas.

Sometimes, inexperienced workers can mistake self-disclosure for authenticity, which is more about being genuinely oneself in responsiveness than it is about sharing personal material in order to demonstrate similarities with the client.

Needing to Demonstrate Competency

Some workers mistakenly believe that unless they share meaningful insights and interpretations with clients, they are not doing a competent job as a clinician. As a result, instead of exploring client experience or feeling their way intuitively into it, they think about what they want to say next when the client finishes. Clients who experience a worker's repeated need to demonstrate knowledge may be impressed initially, but may tire over time of the worker's inability to hear them out or explore in more depth.

Distractions

Distractions come up for workers all the time. If the worker is covering a small agency alone at night, he or she may listen to the client with one ear, but have the other ear geared to register any sound that might indicate someone entering the building or waiting room, or of phones ringing with no one else to answer them. Workers with worries on their minds may find themselves following the client only spottily, just as tired workers may listen less well as the day or evening goes on. Outside distractions like loud conversation, helicopters flying over low, skateboarders practicing on the building steps, or fire engines passing can also disturb both worker and client attention. Sudden events can also draw the worker's attention away.

> I saw Kumi just after the staff had been watching the Challenger disaster on the agency's TV set. She looked expectant, and I thought that meant she, too, had seen it, so I said, "Can you believe what happened to those poor astronauts?" She looked perturbed and flew into the office, saying, "If you think that's bad, wait until you hear what's just happened to me." That reaction told me that I was focusing on my own reactions, leaving her feeling pushed aside, so I got back on track by showing extra concern that she tell me more about what had happened to her.

Rapidly Shifting Between Cognition and Feelings

Miller and Stiver (1997) describe thoughts and feelings as so intertwined as to be practically inseparable. They describe this amalgam as "thought-feelings," and ask their clients often about their thought-feelings, opening the way for them to choose where to begin and what to include, in what order. Workers who cannot so easily synthesize thought and feeling sometimes move too quickly from the one to the other with clients when trying to capture the client's moment, as observed in the following example of an effort to empathize.

> When Luann triumphantly told her worker Jeremy that she'd not only made an A in her nursing course, but was also going to graduate with honors from the Associate Degree program, he was as elated as she was and tried to show her that he was by exclaiming "Yes!" and making a gesture of triumph. She had just started beaming when he asked her how she would make it now on the low starting pay for her specialty.

Here the worker clearly makes himself the driver of the conversation, taking the wind out of the client's sails by moving abruptly off of her celebration and onto thinking about living expenses as compared with starting pay—a glum subject indeed. It would be strengthening for her to spend some time celebrating her achievement and the happy feelings surrounding it, a novel experience for her.

Mind Reading

Mind reading when intending to empathize with client experience is a frequent mistake of inexperienced workers. For example, "That must have been hard for you" is a student response that often appears in process recordings, videotapes, and role plays as an attempt at empathy. The suggestion of what the client feels—"that must have been hard for you"—gets in the way of the client's reaching more deeply for personal reactions, which are often far more complex than one single feeling like "good" or "bad." Sometimes clients cry when they're mad, look angry when they're about to burst into tears, and feel relief instead of sadness about particular losses or changes. With experience, workers develop a more open stance in which they explore for, rather than suggest, client thoughts and feelings.

No Worker Response at All,
When One Is Sorely Needed

A worker who's not following closely may miss important moments where attunement and responsiveness are vital to a client's sense of being safely anchored by the attentive presence of a caring other. The absence of a response at a crucial moment can be experienced as a lack of interest or as the worker's having his or her mind on "more important" things. The worker's mind may in fact be elsewhere, propelled there by external events, inner turmoil, or the client's material or feelings. In addition, some workers may not care about some clients enough to pay close and consistent attention to their stories or respond in a heartfelt manner.

When a worker is unresponsive, a client may keep talking as though nothing has happened, and yet feel let down. Psychologically vulnerable clients may begin to feel disorganized or confused about how to continue without the worker's active participation and responsiveness. Others—like the client above displaced by the *Challenger* crisis—may get mad or curious about why the worker isn't reacting to important material. Workers who miss opportune moments in the client's story can apologize and rejoin with the material they missed by asking the client to restate it. You may worry that apologizing will call attention to your lapses in attention, but clients often spot breaks in attention right as they happen. More often, it's our own embarrassment about drifting that prevents more authentic discussion of lapses in attention.

Veering Away from Distressing Topics

Ironically, it has sometimes proved easier for workers to focus on two things at once (the client's story and the worker's reactions) than to focus on the thing that most leaves clients feeling heard, understood, and appreciated—*being fully with the client in the moment.* We often veer off or detour around topics that distress us. Clients can interpret these moves as something they caused by introducing certain topics or feelings. The temptation then arises for them to protect the worker by not raising such matters again, even though they are a significant part of the story that needs unfolding.

Other Impediments to Empathy

Hepworth, Rooney, and Larsen (1997) review client behaviors that make it difficult for workers to sustain empathy and positive regard. These include unyielding client protests of helplessness when asked to participate actively in problem solving, leaving workers feeling frustrated and hopeless themselves. Stubborn or sullen silences and aggressive behaviors can trigger overtalking in workers trying hard to jumpstart conversation instead of exploring what may lie beneath these manifest behaviors. Exploitative or untruthful behavior can leave workers feeling used or tricked, while nonadherence with working agreements can leave workers disappointed and annoyed (p. 62).

RESTORING EMPATHIC ALIGNMENT

Several steps help to restore empathic alignment when dealing with provocation or disappointment. The first is to remember times in our own lives when we or people close to us have behaved as the client is behaving—to recall foibles and relate them to conditions that may have contributed to them. Next, instead of keeping difficult moments in clinical relationships a secret due to embarrassment or fear, turn to a supervisor or consultant who can suggest new understanding and fresh approaches to the problem at hand. Work towards conceptualizing difficult client behavior as information about that's person's life experience and functioning, rather than personalizing it as a direct attack on you. Try to recall any strengths or positives about the client that may have faded from memory with the onset of problem behaviors, and keep these positives in mind in contemplating reparative action.

With the help of a supervisor, explore the meaning of the behavior directly with the client in a compassionate way—relational tending in action. Don't try a reparative conversation if you are still angry or are being compelled by someone else to try to work a relationship out when you are in no frame of mind to do so. Don't expect miracles, since empathic breaks can hurt feelings and require time and persistence to repair. In all of this process, reexamine your own feelings and behaviors regarding this particular client to make sure you have not unwittingly triggered or reinforced unproductive client behaviors.

Client Concerns About Clinical Relationships

Clients often know far better than we do that not all human service workers are client-centered and eager to work hard in their behalf. They may have had their personal information shared with others without their permission, or had children removed by a harshly judgmental "protective" worker, or had a family member deported without due process. They may have seen workers treat other people poorly or unjustly, favoring some and withholding service from others. All of these things can and do happen in the human services, so clients may approach workers with caution or with grave doubts as to the wisdom of trusting an outsider who may or may not prove safe and reliable.

> *Liz told me shortly after we met that her male welfare worker had fathered the last two of her five children, but that she was afraid that if she reported him, he would find a way to hurt her. She knew three other women that this same worker had had affairs with and gotten pregnant, and all were scared to say anything. She said that this man took advantage of lonely single mothers. Then she looked at me tiredly and said, "I've been waiting to see when you people would want something from me. There's no such thing as something for nothing."*

Clients can also worry that their relationship with a worker is going to make others in their present relational system upset, perhaps by making them feel jealous of the client's admiration for the worker, suspicious that the work may harm them in some way, inadequate compared with how the worker seems to understand and handle things, envious of the time spent with the worker, or angry about the time going to the relationship with the worker, instead of to friends and family.

Other clients may fear the intensity of their feelings for the worker, or want more from a relationship than a worker is willing to provide. These concerns may cause clients to break off contacts, space meetings out to dilute risk or intensity, refuse to be authentic in what they share with the worker, or not say much to family and friends about the importance of the clinical alliance to them. Workers can approach many of these concerns and ease them by asking clients periodically how they are experiencing the relationship and the work, and how other people feel about the work and its wider effects.

WORKER CONCERNS
ABOUT RELATING WITH CLIENTS

We, too, can bring anxieties with us in trying to relate in a purposeful and other-centered way. If shy, you may wonder if you will be able to relate to numbers of new people comfortably and helpfully. If young or brand new to counseling roles, you may feel that everyone will see that you're a rookie, and will think you won't be of much use to them. If you're from a background different from that of clients and other workers at an agency, you may wonder if you'll get acceptance and respect from others around you.

Some workers may have a hard time respecting clients who've mistreated or deserted others depending on them. These colleagues may pretend to be caring and nonjudgmental when they aren't feeling that way, and eventually this will show in the process. In addition, taking on the problems and needs of many clients at once can trigger feelings of being the overburdened "good one," even though other workers are burdened, too.

At times, workers worry that personal problems or stresses will make it hard to concentrate on others' needs, so that clients or colleagues will find them distracted or unhelpful. We can feel internal pressure to see that every case goes perfectly so that others admire us. We might also worry about potential client violence, lawsuits, or terminations that could show us in a bad light. It's interesting to note how parallel the worries of workers and clients can be because of shared humanness, and in some cases, some shared human experience. Worries can dovetail around themes such as:

Will things go okay with this person?

Can I appreciate this person for what she is, instead of what she isn't?

Will this relationship affect other ones negatively and prove to be more trouble than it's worth?

Will I be able to report accurately and honestly to others what goes on in this relationship, or will I hold some things back?

Am I capable of the trust and cooperation this venture requires?

Do I have to stay with this person if we don't get along?

Will I find respect and a sense of belonging in this group of people?

If I blunder, will I still be liked and respected?

SHARED CONCERNS ABOUT RELATING
WITH OTHER AGENCIES AND HELPERS

Workers and clients sometimes hesitate to involve other staff and services, even when they see that these colleagues can bring information or services to bear that might greatly improve the client's situation. Multiple providers must all set aside extra time for coordination and monitoring of service delivery and appointment scheduling. Outsiders may have opinions or ways of operating that conflict with those the worker—client pair have established. They may have tight schedules to which you and your client have to adapt if you want particular services from particular agencies or staff, a situation that can inspire resentment.

Powerful specialists may want to come in and change your current plans and goals—sometimes collaboratively, sometimes arbitrarily—leaving people on edge. We sometimes worry that clients working with other providers will prefer their care to ours. If tightly scheduled, clients may actually have to choose to attend other crucial health or mental health appointments instead of meetings with the worker, leaving the latter feeling devalued. Any of these concerns can trigger mistakes in relationships or work.

COMMON MISTAKES
IN RELATING WITH CLIENTS

You've likely come to clinical education pretty aware of your relational gifts and rough edges from past social and work experience. You may or may not have realized that the rough edges can contribute to many of the following frequently observed mistakes in relating with clients.

Thinking That Poor Relationship Skills Don't Matter

Some workers and students are uncomfortable around others and show this through nervousness, shyness, awkwardness of style or manner, or trouble engaging with clients and colleagues. They can't remain still in their seats, jiggling their legs or playing with pens while conversing with clients. They may not be able to maintain good eye contact, extend a warm handshake, or make statements and ask questions confidently. They may appear overly serious, intellectualized, distant—even cold or officious, believing that these things don't matter so long as problem-solving work gets done.

Nothing could be further from the truth. In human service work, much as in complementary medicine and people-centered politics or ministry, the medium (the personhood of the worker) is an enormously important part of the message conveyed to clients about what they may expect from a particular agency or individual staff member. Rogers (1967) was among the first practitioners to identify "necessary and sufficient conditions" (p. 95) for effective work with clients, identifying the important qualities of openness, positive regard for clients, genuineness, and congruence between worker beliefs and actions. Following her own extensive review of research studies on positive helper characteristics, Okun (1992) finds that "an increasing amount of evidence supports the idea that helpers are only as effective as they are self-aware and able to use themselves as vehicles of change" (p. 30).

Sometimes workers forget that counseling is a mutually observing fishbowl experience for all participants. Clients often leave counseling sessions and talk with friends or loved ones about their worker's demeanor, beliefs, behaviors, and idiosyncrasies. Since they miss very little of who we are and what we communicate, we have to be especially careful to maintain professionalism in all that we say and do on the job, and to use good judgment in our private lives as well, since we never know when we may encounter clients or others expecting—and relying on—high standards of conduct from people in fiduciary positions such as those workers hold.

> Dora, a counselor in private practice, tried to help some poor clients who came to a support group by having them work for her in her home. One shopped for her, noticing how much money Dora spent on lavish entertainment. Another cleaned, often finding clothes strewn all over and the kitchen a mess from lots of dinner parties. Some served at the parties and saw friends get tipsy and silly. All of the women were initially grateful for the help, but their work for this therapist introduced them to a side of her that caused them to lose respect for her. They dropped out of the group and stopped working for her, too.

The Setting Speaks Volumes

Interview settings have a language all their own, and communicate something about the dignity and worth of both workers and clients. Some settings seem pleasant, calm, and welcoming, while others seem dilapidated, overcrowded, and bleak. Clients and staff often judge each other by the looks of the setting in which they meet, whether this be home or office, so attention to the setting is an important sign of caring about the comfort and feelings of others who enter that space. An interview space that's dirty or in disarray communicates indifference to others' comfort.

> In my work as a mental health treatment consultant, I've met with staff from a lot of state hospitals. Most of these institutions have fixed windows to prevent suicide, insufficient air conditioning, locked doors to prevent running away, and a TV going in the day room—whether people watch or not. In spite of all of the upgrading of facilities and staff in these hospitals, many still feel old, decrepit, and thick with cigarette smoke, something that's not permitted in regular hospitals these days. With all the TV that patients watch, I'm sure that some know by now that even secondhand smoke can cause cancer or heart disease. Being in these hospitals over time must feel like being condemned, and I always come away down in my spirit, as though I've been in a story out of Dickens, where those left behind can't exit like I can.

Seeming Not to Care

Busy workers and interns can race through assessment protocols with clients, look at their watches while families cry about the loss of a son to an overdose, ask intimate questions while walking towards an office, or leave clients sitting in waiting rooms for long periods of time without any information provided as to when they will be seen. Workers have been known to fall asleep in individual sessions; leave settings early, forgetting client appointments until hours later; repeatedly call clients by incorrect names; and not show up for appointments at all.

If clients behaved the way some staff do, some might quickly assess them as "acting out." Too often, when workers behave in exactly the same ways, they are described as "stressed out"—obviously a more forgiving connotation. Such behaviors undermine the establishment of respectful relationships, and they communicate that the worker has more important things to do. Elaborate justifications of uncaring behaviors just magnify the problem.

> *A social worker on my team went to see a clinician at a private clinic across town. She felt she was boring as a person, and that people who asked her out rarely called a second time. In the fifth or sixth time with the counselor, he fell asleep while my friend was ticking off the names of various men who had come and gone in her dating history. For a few minutes she did nothing. Then, mad, she went over and tapped the therapist's shoulder to wake him up. She asked him how he could fall asleep when her very problem is that men don't stay with her. He told her huffily that she just kept repeating the same things over again, and that when she had meaningful things to say, he would stay awake and respond to them. Shocked, she left and never went back.*

Lack of Unconditional Positive Regard

Unconditional acceptance is a value and state of mind, and not just an ethical prescription. One form of messaging a client judgmentally is the impatient lecture: "Myron, you haven't tried harder like you said you would . . . do we need to talk about this again?" Another is using comparisons in which we come out superior: "In my day, we had it a lot worse than this and were not allowed to complain like you kids do here at the center." Still another is the putdown exhortation: "Ellis, you've just got to go back to school if you ever want to have anything for your family . . . do this for your boys' sake if you don't want to do it for yourself."

Judgmentalism is also expressed in the wide-eyed exclamations "You *what?*", and "Oh no, not again." These devices often trigger resentment or withdrawal in those on the receiving end, as the tone feels disrespectful and puts clients on the defensive, as in the following example.

> *When Lucky told me she was going off to a weekend conference with a married boss she had a crush on, I spontaneously exclaimed, "What?" She looked at me with surprise and said, "I count on you to be the person I turn to who tries to understand my thoughts rather than make me feel bad for having them, like my mom did."*

Trying to Impress

Sometimes workers make it hard to relate with them by trying too hard to impress. Clients don't need boasts from a worker that he or she has successfully treated dozens of people with similar problems with tremendous success, although they may like a simple statement about the worker's training and experience, without ruffles and flourishes. Though we don't usually think of ourselves as having either the disposition or the wherewithal to initiate self-serving behaviors, some colleagues can and do, often without much sense of the effect they're having on others. Usually a supervisor or senior colleague is asked to discuss with that individual the complaints from others regarding self-promoting behaviors. Clients may not complain, but instead, may "vote with their feet" by not returning for further meetings.

Infantilizing Clients

From a strengths perspective, relationships between workers and clients are thought of as collaborations between people who each have life experience, some knowledge of coping strategies, and other strengths and potentials that will interact synergistically to produce more understanding, ideas for work, and goal-related activity than any of the participants could marshal alone.

Infantilizing is the opposite process, in which workers treat some clients like children who need parental guidance. They regard these clients as too naïve, limited in skills, or damaged to find workable solutions to problems without a great deal of leadership and control by the worker. Infantilizing can take place at many levels, with workers treated like bad or ineffectual children by their employers. A patronizing attitude trickles down from top management, and workers then pass on that attitude to each other and clients. Workers who find themselves relating more parentally to clients will find supervision a useful place to discuss more balanced and respectful ways of approaching relationships.

Maintaining Good Interagency and Community Relationships

Workers who relate well with clients and colleagues also appreciate the importance of maintaining excellent interagency ties that build a matrix of committed service allies who can at times join forces to create or lobby for services that clients need but can't find in their area or language. When starting out in an agency or geographic area, workers try to learn who key providers are in related systems, and then meet with these providers to introduce themselves and initiate bonds around shared work and interests.

This network of allies can also diminish the isolation experienced by many workers who spend a good deal of time alone writing in client records, entering data on computers, traveling between sites, or interviewing solo. Sometimes agencies develop continuing education consortia for their staff, which makes getting to know each other much easier. At other times workers simply reach out to each other in a geographic area or widespread system of care and alliances build that way.

CONCLUSION

Effective relating is at the heart of all good clinical work, because people are relationship-oriented by nature and usually function best when affiliated with committed allies. Relationships with clients cannot be forced, for unless mandated and under court supervision, clients can leave at any time, or not be home when workers reach out to them there. This "voting power" acts as a counterbalance to the potentially daunting power and authority of large service agencies and their staffs.

Workers, instructors, and scholars have begun to appreciate the mutual benefits inherent in working alliances (Coleman, 2000). Just as the client receives support, validation, new information for problem solving, and a feeling of meaning and connectedness, so do we. A singular difference is that we remain responsible for keeping working relationships client-centered, purposefully focused on mutually defined goals, safe, and productively on track.

EXERCISES

1. *Reflection.* In your journal, recall two of the most memorable relationships you've had in your private life, and two in your educational or work life. Picture each person and the qualities each brought to the relationship that made it very special for you. How did each of the relationships empower you? What qualities did each of these "good relaters" build or bring out in you? Which of those good relating qualities can you now find in yourself? Which do you hope to develop or refine?

2. *Small Group Discussion.* Break up into groups of four or five and take 15 minutes to discuss common mistakes you have made in relating with clients. What were the effects of your mistakes? If you attempted to repair them, what did you say or do, and how well did the repair work? List the mistakes you found you had in common, and *prepare to share your observations with the larger group when it reconvenes.*

3. *Instructor Activity.* Use role play to practice empathic responsiveness to client experience. Give each other feedback about the genuineness or naturalness of responses, suggesting variations in "response-ability" as these occur to you and other participants.

4. *Class Activity.* Have the class discuss what interferes with their empathy with certain clients and not others. Discuss what we can do as professionals when we find people hard to like or to listen to over time, especially when there are no other care providers available to see these clients.

5. *Author Sharing for Further Discussion.* A client of mine in several years of therapy for childhood trauma moved to a distant state after her dad died. She wanted to be nearer her mother to provide more support. Working on various leads together, we found her a good therapist in her new city. She called me every few weeks or so to update me on her work and on her mostly positive feelings about her new worker. She acknowledged missing me, and I said I missed working with her, too, but was very glad to see her

working so well with someone who sounded easy to sit with and good at listening and understanding. Gradually the phone calls tapered off, but after some time, I began to get telephone call-like letters detailing her therapeutic work and daily life successes and challenges. I never answered these because she never asked for a reply.

In the second year of her relocation, she suddenly called to say she was coming to see friends in this area and needed to speak to me, so we set up an appointment. She was very mad with me that I hadn't answered her letters, feeling that I had been so close and helpful, and then suddenly was so silent. She wanted an explanation of my unresponsiveness. The only explanation I could offer was that I hadn't realized she needed a response from me to the letters. She'd evidently regarded the letters as a continuing relationship with me, and now became tearful while still mad. I said I'd thought she was all set with the new therapist and didn't need me any more. The look on her face told me this wasn't helping to soothe feelings of rejection, so I extended a heartfelt apology for not understanding her need for me to respond. I never heard from her again after that.

For Class Discussion. What factors in worker and client could contribute to a miscalculation and rupture such as this one? Why were explanations of little use in the last encounter? If the client had ended work with me, why was I still so powerfully in her thoughts? What might I have done differently to help ease her transition? What relational strengths does the client exhibit in this vignette? Find and discuss evidence of relational tending in the relationship.

RECOMMENDED READING

Coleman, D. (2000). The therapeutic alliance in multicultural practice. *Psychoanalytic Social Work, 7,* 65–90.

Jordan, J. (1991). Empathy and self boundaries. In J. V. Jordan, A. G. Kaplan, J. B. Miller, I. P. Stiver, & J. L. Surrey (Eds.), *Women's growth in connection: Writings from the Stone Center* (pp. 67–80). New York: Guilford.

Miller, J. B., & Stiver, I. P. (1997). *The healing connection: How women make relationships in therapy and in life.* Boston: Beacon.

Nicholson, B., & Kay, D. M. (1999). Group treatment of traumatized Cambodian women: A culture-specific approach. *Social Work, 44,* 470–480.

Rogers, C. (1967). The necessary and sufficient conditions of therapeutic personality change. *Journal of Consulting Psychology, 21,* 95–103.

5

Assessment
and Contracting

Skills and Pitfalls

ASSESSMENT

Assessment involves techniques of exploration and support that encourage and gently assist in the unfolding of the client's narrative or story. It's more than just a product or outcome of initial exploration of what brings clients in to see someone. It's also *an ongoing process,* one of gathering and evaluating information and direct experience with clients, and of tracking subtle shifts in understanding, feelings, and behavior as workers and clients explore together. Compton and Galaway (1994) emphasize that an ongoing assessment of problems, strengths, objectives, and methods employed towards change provides continuous feedback loops that reduce linearity in the process, allowing it to take on a dynamic, systemic, constantly changing quality (p. 550).

For example, in initial meetings, the client may say, "I'm getting upset as I think of that," while tears start to fill her eyes. The worker may assume that "upset" equals "tears" equals "sad," and respond: "Thinking of that makes you sad," attempting to join with the client. Many visits later, the client has begun to relax more in the meetings and finally lets the worker know that when tears come to her eyes in relation to certain topics, she's actually feeling mad, not sad, but finds it hard to express anger. This clarification enriches the worker's assessment understanding and allows for further exploration of how the client's expression of genuine feeling got turned into something else—an important addition to the narrative. In this sense, evaluation begins with the first verbal or written contact ("Hmmm . . . her tone suddenly changed just then . . . I wonder what that might mean . . . I think I'll ask"), and continues throughout the work together, whatever its nature and length.

OBSERVATION CHANGES THE OBSERVER AND THE OBSERVED

Systems tend to draw in observers, turning them into active participants. We can see this in the way we are drawn rapidly into caring about new clients, often beginning to support and encourage them like good travel hosts, even before we know them very well. After all, empathic attunement and alignment with the client is not a stance of great scientific detachment and neutrality, but one of active mutual engagement.

Once we've joined with the experience and perspective of the other, it's hard to think about that person as simply an object of detached study, or of ourselves as simply good data processors. We do proceed to stand back intellectually, in order to formulate impressions and hunches regarding the client. However, we also become emotionally attuned and attached as a function of purposeful relating with clients and of providing a holding environment for anxiety-producing work (Meyer, 1993).

In so doing, we can become enrolled subtly as a limit setter or referee in the family, or as a rescuer, a coach, or a connecter of the family with the outside world of opportunities and expectations. As continuous evaluators whose impressions and findings can greatly influence the kind and extent of services clients receive, it's important that we remember how our joining with a system can activate and sustain its potentials while simultaneously affecting our judgment, decision making, and capacity to think and plan from a metaposition.

The client system itself may also change under observation, perking up due to professional interest and caring, feeling more accepted and worthwhile because of the worker's respect and involvement, and consequently producing special efforts in behalf of its members. On the other hand, an observed system can also deteriorate if the demands put upon it are too great or unfamiliar, creating more stress and tension. Secret-keeping systems may also quit pretending all is well once under professional care. For example, once referred by his school principal for evaluation of apparent depression, a sad, constricted teen delegated by substance-abusing parents to be the primary caretaker of siblings and household may finally disclose the level of dysfunction in his parents and ask that the school "make" them get help—or else.

ELEMENTS OF GOOD ASSESSMENT

The primary task of a good working assessment and formulation is to develop understanding of clients' assets and needs in the context of their previous and current life experience. The worker-client exchange in pulling together information and impressions can lead to a working agreement, to a referral elsewhere for more appropriate services, or to an ending of the help-seeking process for now, with no agreement to continue work with anyone at this time.

All participants need to realize that the worker's or the team's ideas are simply their own best working formulations at a given point in time, clearly subject to alteration as new experiences and ideas develop. Because initial evaluations are collaborations between relative strangers, it's likely that many assessments only begin to scratch the surface of potential understanding. First impressions are but one version of the client's story.

> *Eugene, a college counselor, thought a pregnant student might be exaggerating her relationship with a professor in describing the well-known scholar as the father of her baby. Later, when asked to evaluate a depressed spouse of a faculty member, he suddenly realized during evaluation that this might be the wife of that very same professor. She said her husband spent many evenings in "research" with a graduate student who sounded to Eugene like the pregnant student he was seeing in counseling. The wife had no idea that the student was pregnant by her husband. She simply knew something was terribly wrong.*

Embedding Exploration in Support

A second goal of assessment is to help the client feel supported as the evaluation proceeds. The evaluation process should leave the client feeling safe with the worker, the content, the pace and focus of the conversation, and the agency environment and requirements. In every way, the evaluator must communicate the idea that it's okay to tell one's story outside of the usual supports and constraints of family, friends, and familiar cultural or spiritual institutions. We have to remember, though, that such a concept can seem disrespectful and distressing within cultures where family privacy is a dominant value. Okun, Fried, and Okun (1999) note that "North Americans . . . have a reputation for wanting to achieve 'instant' intimacy" and ". . . frequently are considered insincere and intrusive by members of other cultures" (p. 203).

The assessment phase is one in which clients will need you to provide a lot of support, mutual feeling, and appreciation of the courage it takes to reveal oneself to another person who is often an outsider to one's own culture, primary language, and folkways. Sometimes assessment interviews evoke a lot of sudden and deep feeling in people. If prepared for this possibility, you'll be aware of the way these moments illuminate the degree to which clients have stored up many unexpressed human reactions to powerful life events.

Including Important Others

One of the most important determinants of positive coping and resilience is the extent of family, friendship, or community network supports (Devore & Schlesinger, 1996; Poindexter, Valentine, & Conway, 1999). It's very important to help clients and significant others comment on who they think should and should not be present during assessment meetings to outline strengths and service needs of clients. In Asian families, for example, elders usually speak for the extended family group (Chao, 1992). In some families in which elders may have limited fluency in the dominant language of the agency or the worker, younger English-speaking members may be asked by them to represent what is needed by the family, even though the worker guesses that youthful members may have less perspective and evaluative experience than older family members. Lesbian and gay families and kinship foster care providers may bring a number of cohelpers to the meeting to assist in describing the needs of various members of a wide circle of people relating as family.

In some family constellations, pets and next-door neighbors may be introduced, further filling in the picture of significant relationships and coping resources, while in others, a rabbi, imam, or other spiritual leader who has been helping the family may be asked to be present to speak for the family and keep a watchful eye on the fairness of the proceedings with a professional. Nowhere is inclusiveness more crucial than in life-threatening health crises, where important loved ones like longtime roommates, fellow members of religious orders, tribal group members, and gay partners have been forbidden lengthy visits in emergency rooms because they are not recognized by the facility or the family as "legal" family, yet would be defined by the patient as beloved family. Client-centered care involves making every effort to find times and spaces that accommodate the needs and comfort of clients rather than just those of staff.

> *A Roma family of fifteen, previously referred to in the area as "gypsies," came to sit in the hospital lounges in order to be near the King of their group, recovering from surgery. Several times they were asked to quiet down as they talked nervously between themselves to pass the time, and several times they were asked to wait outside because their numbers were bothering the nurses. The patient was remarkably cheered by their presence, and so they stayed. The social worker met with their King first, who filled in details of his medical history. He then invited the worker to meet with his whole group in one of the big lounges. During the meeting they identified two children and four women who were also showing signs of illness. The worker arranged for them to be seen at the nearby neighborhood health clinic that offered care to those who had no insurance, and they were seen promptly for diagnosis and treatment.*

Responding to Absences or Exclusions

Sometimes both staff members and family members ask that people be excluded from participation in assessment because they don't like the way they speak or behave in meetings or while in the setting. These are not good reasons to exclude someone, unless that person is violent, disorganized, or so disruptive that necessary conversation can't proceed. Even when certain staff and clients may not be able to work together easily, every effort should be made to negotiate cooperation before exclusion decisions are made. Both staff and family judgments can be personally and culturally biased and arbitrary. Exclusions can hurt feelings and leave out important informants. Murphy and Dillon (2003) note that those excluded sometimes hold important information or clues to painful events or dynamics in families. Undisclosed information or themes residing in a missing family member might be about undocumented residency, sweatshop labor, family violence, unlawful activities, surrendered parental rights, or secret affairs or intentions.

Using a Comprehensive Assessment Framework

Assessment frameworks suggest important basic questions that can help identify immediate and past stressors and strengths in sufficiently focused detail to allow the worker to think and plan ahead wisely. Most interns and workers familiarize themselves with important questions from agency intake frameworks, and develop a style of exploration tailored for the client at hand, the time and resources available, and the nature and extent of problems to be resolved. Several good comprehensive frameworks for assessment exist to guide intern and worker exploration in initial assessments with clients (Brems, 2000; Cormier & Cormier, 1998; Garvin & Seabury, 1997; Hepworth, Rooney, & Larsen, 2002; Lum, 2000).

It's all too easy to develop a routine of starting evaluations with demographic questions: "Your address, please? A way we can reach you? Who should we notify in case of an emergency? What's your employment or source of income?" In addition to contextualizing the client's presenting story in everyday realities, these questions can be used to help you and clients ease gradually into inquiry of a more intimate nature (relationships, sexual activities, violence in the home, substance use, dreams realized or shattered, etc.).

A disadvantage to such an approach is that it tends to present the interviewer more as a functionary than a fellow human being intent on finding out where the client is at the outset of the meeting. While very personal and potentially emotion-laden content may feel harder to explore initially, demographic questions may actually be harder for some clients because initial probes by a stranger of one's family, financial, and health circumstances can feel very exposing in some cultures, and very inappropriate to ask about in others.

Asking Meaningful, Appropriate Questions

Good questions deepen participants' understanding of the breadth and depth of the narrative relevant to the client's request for help and the agency's capacity to provide needed services expeditiously. Fishing expeditions—forays into personal areas not clearly related to the client's needs—are discouraged. Experience within and across cultures helps workers become aware of those questions and topics that may be taboo or offensive within particular cultures and those that may ease the way, especially when there are significant differences between workers and clients (Delgado, 1999; Gutierrez, Parsons, & Cox, 2000). Delgado provides many useful illustrations of ways in which community workers have tailored their use of self, language, dress, and outreach methodology to the unique needs and strengths of the diverse urban populations they hope to engage in work with. Laird (1999) encourages us to take an ethnographer's stance:

> . . . the ethnographer is not without knowledge, experience, theory. She uses her long period of professional study and life experience not to predict answers or to surface some pattern, structure, or organization of experience she is sure exists, but to ask the best questions possible, the questions that will surface her cultural informant's narrative (p. 75).

Techniques of Information Gathering

Clearly, *asking direct questions* such as "What are you thinking right now?" and "What happened next?" is a primary technique of assessment. Most people applying to speak with someone about problems understand that workers will need to ask them lots of questions about their situation before providing services, and are usually patient about being questioned, as long as the questions are pertinent and sensitively framed within relevant cultural norms. With very sensitive clients unused to sharing personal questions, sometimes *indirect questions and prompts* like those that follow are easier to bear while still giving workers a sense of how the client thinks and feels about things. Indirect questions allow clients who wish to, to address an issue or theme, one step removed, as though describing someone else's life.

Examples of Indirect Questions
To an elderly gay man living alone: I wonder what it's like for gay seniors living in this area, knowing that younger men have been assaulted close by.

To a new immigrant: Someday I would love to be able to sit down with a person from your country and just hear him or her talk about what it has taken to get here and make it here.

Prompts are utterances, gestures, brief statements, questions, or cues from the worker that encourage the client to continue or to say more. They bring some variety to exploration, so that the client does not feel like the object of an inquisition. Prompts routinely include head nodding, "mmhmm," "Really . . . ", and "Oh?" Using the same prompt too much can cause clients to notice and focus on the word or technique rather than continue recounting their stories. The following prompts are commonly used by workers to expand or deepen the inquiry.

Could you say more about that?

Yes . . . I see.

Please continue, or, Please go ahead.

And after that? . . . And then?

You were about to say . . . ?

Let's see . . . we were talking about . . . ?

I'd like to hear more about this if you feel like saying more.

Did you want to add anything more before we move on?

Reflections involve several possibilities in technique, and are mirrors of what the client has said or done. *Postural reflection* involves unobtrusively assuming the client's body posture or gestures. *Verbal reflection* involves picking up the client's statement and repeating it back as an embodiment of empathy or join-ing, as when the client says "It's real cold outside today, but warm in here," and the worker nods and replies, "It sure is cold outside, but nice and warm in here." Workers can also employ a *dot-dot-dot technique* in which they take the last few words of the client's last sentence and repeat them back to prompt con-tinued talking when the client has trailed off midthought: "So then you stopped him and said . . ."

Nonverbals can also be prompts and probes. Speakers usually watch for cues from listeners to indicate whether it's okay to proceed or not. Widening the eyes or raising an eyebrow can represent a silent question hoping for a reply. Smiling, nodding, a puzzled look, and signaling with hands can encourage more verbal-ization. A sympathetic look can express appreciation for the teller and the story. Frowns and judgmental or fearful expressions can shut down or dramatically alter the narrative. In our pluralistic society, it's very important that we get to know our own nonverbals as well as those of a wide variety of cultures, so that we don't unwittingly employ gestures or facial expressions offensive to others.

Children, teens, and some adults express themselves more fully through action than in talking and reflecting. They are often evaluated through games, art, writing, music, and play therapy that reflect patterns and dynamics of relat-ing and of self-expression (Webb, 1999). Adults can use artwork, journal and diary entries, descriptions of video and fictional plots and characters, and music or poetry to express their stories and feelings. Clients have even brought in home videos at times to show the worker people, pets, and circumstances important in their stories.

FREQUENT MISTAKES IN ASSESSMENT

The following are very common missteps that can muddle focus and under-standing, lessening the client's confidence in both the worker and the process.

Questioning Without Clear Purpose

The purpose of the assessment guides the selection of questions to ask. When workers don't yet appreciate this, they can ask whatever comes to mind with-out realizing that while they are eliciting some facts, they may not be eliciting the core information necessary for making decisions about what will happen next regarding client needs and requests.

Two easy interviewing devices help check the goodness of fit between the exploration we're doing at the moment and the established purpose of the meeting. One device is to imagine an unspoken title or rubric for the session, for example: "Explore Friendships/Other Supports," or "Explore Work History/Future Career Goals." These silent headings are good benchmarks to ensure that the ensuing client-worker process follows the stated purpose of the meeting. Your aim is then to keep the main work of the session within the established heading, unless the client introduces compelling new material to explore.

A second tracking device is to check in with yourself periodically during sessions, hovering over the dialogue and asking:

- What was our primary reason for meeting?
- Where are we right now, related to that primary reason?
- Given the amount of time we have, is this focus wise?
- Should we be refocusing in some other direction?
- If a trusted advisor were here right now, what might he or she suggest?

As a rule of thumb in assessment, the client is responsible for presenting the story, codeveloping realistic goals and plans related to stated problems and resources, and deciding whether to continue work or not. The worker retains the responsibility for maintaining the purpose and focus of the work, developing the kind of information and formulation needed for planning and action, tending the relationship as needed, and keeping goals, time, and resources in mind at important choice points in the work.

Excessive Focus on Some Things and Not on Others

Sometimes interns and workers get interested in some aspect of the client's story that they find more engaging, and focus on that area too much instead of carrying out a balanced evaluation. This kind of skewed focusing can leave out or minimize aspects of the client life and strengths that might lead to more balanced and informed planning.

Lack of Attention to Time as Structure

It helps to think of the beginning and ending of the time available for initial assessment as bookends between which we have to wedge everything we need to get done in a particular session. We also have to leave time in assessment work for surprises—unexpected behaviors or information that spontaneously crop up importantly and bump other foci. If you pay attention to the phasing of work—settling in, exploring for information and feelings, tapering down, planning ahead, and ending for now—you can think ahead about how much time will likely be spent in the various phases with each particular client and situation. If you hope to spend at least thirty to forty minutes on exploration of pressing concerns, that leaves only about fifteen minutes for everything else mentioned above. The skills of partializing and prioritizing are crucial in assessment, so that clients have a comfortable as well as a meaningful experience, and aren't left feeling rushed, jerked around, or overwhelmed at point of exit.

It's important that you understand and utilize *time as structure that organizes* the workday and client sessions so that numerous people can rely on each other at set times and can plan and interact purposefully, rather than randomly within a complex matrix of responsibilities and relationships. Inexperienced workers need to be helped to feel more comfortable in *unobtrusively tracking time and developing a sense of time* related to the many tasks that have to be accomplished in a given session. It's hard to think of other professions whose members work with such guilt and awkwardness in tracking time, marking it out loud in sessions, and accommodating work to its passing. These three aspects of time management are very important to master early on in professional development, since they model good reality testing and respectful collaboration with clients and colleagues.

Poor Questioning

Multiple questions in the same breath leave the client confused about which one the worker wants answered first ("Should we stop here, or should we go on for a bit, or should we just hold this for next time?"). "Why?" questions ("Why do you think you did that?") are usually unproductive dead ends, as people often turn to counselors precisely because they don't understand why things are happening or how to make them better. "Why?" often elicits the reply, "I don't know," with accompanying feelings of deflation, and is therefore avoided. Kadushin and Kadushin (1997) have found that, in response to "why?" questions, clients may try, impromptu, to reason out their past behaviors in order to please the interviewer or to feel less embarrassed by past actions, even though they don't really know why they behaved as they did (p. 257).

Good focused questions elicit both more information *and* more client observations and feelings about that information. Stick with themes most closely related to the client's initial concerns and feelings and gently ask one question at a time about a particular theme. Don't leave that theme until there is increased understanding of the meaning, importance, and feeling the client attaches to it.

Preempting the Client

Telling clients who they are, why they came, and what they're thinking and feeling as the assessment moves along is a big mistake that workers can make as a time-saving shortcut in the evaluative process. Such a worker might begin, "I see from the intake form that you came about your little boy's problems in class—what's going on with him?" This worker may quickly learn, though, that while a note from a teacher about the boy's poor performance did prompt this mother to call about seeing a counselor, the son's problem turns out to be just the tip of the iceberg, there being much larger marital and financial problems of concern to the mother.

By preempting the client's selection of an opening theme, the worker makes assumptions and closes off other openings that the client may have preferred. Another mistake here is that the worker focuses on the boy rather than on the mother, before the latter has scarcely settled in. That can suggest to the client that the worker is to be the leader of the conversation, and that the client should wait to be "led by the expert," a misunderstanding that many people have when consulting with a professional.

Examples of Preempting Assessment Statements

The questions I'll be asking may seem unfeeling, but they're not.

You'll likely be getting chemo for that tumor, right?

You probably just forgot to fill in this space where it asked about significant others.

I'm sorry to cut you short, but there are some important things I need to get to with you before our time is up today.

Not Pausing for Reactions to "Fact Giving"

While data gathering is central in evaluation, the point of assessment is not the size of the mass of information gathered, but rather *how meaningful* the particular information we gather is for purposes of understanding and planning. Sometimes when asked their thoughts or feelings about something, clients will immediately say, "I don't have any thoughts," or "I don't feel anything," expecting to go no further than that. If you simply accept that premise and move too quickly to communicate your own ideas, the client isn't helped to reach within for more. Clients often do turn out to have more to say if encouraged, as in: "Take a moment and let's see what comes to mind."

Too Much, Too Soon or Too Little, Too Late

Sometimes out of anxiety, a worker cuts abruptly to the chase of a story before the client knows or trusts him or her. For example, in beginning a bedside meeting with a hospital patient, a worker might blurt out, "The nurse asked me to come by to see how you are doing since the doctor told you this morning that you had MS." The opposite happens as well, if a worker, dreading the conversation about MS and hearing beforehand that the patient doesn't like talking with staff, goes in to see the patient and chats about everything *but* MS. As a result, the patient is discharged without the team learning much about her adjustment to the diagnosis or her possible needs for counseling or a support group once home.

When clients initially *can't stop* talking about an overwhelming topic once they're asked, you can move gently to curtail the conversation to protect the client from being overwhelmed by themes or feelings. You can prepare the way by sharing concern for the client's well-being: "You are looking really upset by this right now . . . take a moment to catch your breath." You and the client can then agree to move on for now to other topics, or you can end the session with some calming review of the work so far and plans for any future meetings or activity. It can help to explain: "People can feel shaken by getting too deeply into upsetting things all at once. How about we move to other subjects for now, but plan more time to talk about this again very soon?"

Pressuring Clients After They've Balked

Balking is a form of pulling up short and indicating strongly that one doesn't want to "go there" in conversation. This can happen when we unknowingly wander onto forbidden ground while innocently exploring a part of the client's story—for example, asking about a gap of twelve years between children, then watching as the client becomes flustered or defensive. Continuing to push and probe once a client has firmly signaled opposition shows disregard for the client's feelings and sensitivities. In assessment work, clients get a foretaste of what a particular worker will be like to work with over time, so respect for client tolerance levels is at a premium if we hope to continue with the client.

Not Searching Out Strengths
if Clients Don't Mention Them

Clients beset by problems sometimes feel so down and stuck that they fail to note positives and achievements. If they've been in service systems before, they may have experienced some professionals whose focus was on diagnosing and treating psychopathology, or exploring what was "dysfunctional" in the client or family. Clients may also assume that everyone has resilience and capabilities, so that their own are not worthy of special mention. Sometimes people under stress also *appear* so stuck, disheveled, and momentarily disorganized that workers mistakenly forget to pursue, and highlight, the strengths in their story, since the focus is on crises and gaps in functioning or resources. In addition, agencies and workers steeped in a deficit model of assessment or reimbursed for treating "the disabled" or "the ill" may still employ practice frameworks that focus on "diagnosing and treating pathology" in order to secure reimbursement or collegial admiration (Holmes, 1997).

Every individual and family has strengths, no matter how troubled a situation appears. Many clients show impressive resilience in spite of enormous problems and daunting social barriers to achievement. Asking about what is working in a group or family, or what has worked in the past, gives the client a window of opportunity to review successes and take from these a taste of capability that can lift spirits, restore some pride in resourcefulness, honor treasured connections, and motivate efforts to resolve current crises (Bricker-Jenkins, 1997; McMillen, 1999; Rose, 2000).

Not Being or Appearing to Be Moved
by the Client's Narrative

A mistake made by many inexperienced workers is that of not showing reactions and human feelings when these are sorely needed by the client as validation of common humanness. A client may begin to cry about a series of losses and disappointments, and the worker shows little reaction, worried whether a supervisor would approve. A woman may be exultant about a winning lottery ticket that allows her to bring her siblings in Central America to join her in this country, but the worker, not believing in lotteries, looks unreceptive.

Miller and Stiver (1997) emphasize the way in which seeing that one can move or impact another person *visibly* contributes to a client's feelings of esteem, validation, and capacity to act, in therapy as in life. In the situations previously presented, the responsiveness needed to stimulate growth is not occurring because professionals' belief systems and agendas block emotional alignment with the client in the moment. Some workers' theoretical perspectives, professional mentors, or their own personal development lead them to hold back human reactions (Shulman, 1991). Others may have trouble experiencing or showing feelings even if they want to, and may continue taking notes in an earnest way while the client emotes; or may just stare at the client, nodding silently. Sadly, this kind of unresponsiveness often happens with the very clients whose histories of relational deprivation leave them the hungriest for experiences of human reaction and kinship.

Not Utilizing Multiple Forms of Information Gathering

If people haven't been strengthened and encouraged in verbal communication, keep struggling with a second language, or have been silenced by others from expressing personal truths, it isn't accurate to label such clients as "nonverbal," since in their private lives they may be very forthcoming with the right people and under supportive circumstances.

As noted earlier, adults and young people may be more expressive through activities than words, or when meeting in their own communities instead of in a formal office setting. Depending on the safety of their homes, they may even feel better at times talking elsewhere, particularly if they know in advance that the likelihood of interruption or threat is great. Talking while walking in nature or sitting over coffee may help some people open up more, but may close other people down if they feel too exposed or fear bumping into a friend while with a worker.

Not Recording Information as the Evaluation Proceeds

Workers who simply think of record documentation as drudgery or a waste of time fail to appreciate the importance of a material record in keeping work on track with subjects covered and subjects yet to be explored (Brems, 2000). In teamwork, the need for documentation is even greater, since members count on each other's assessments and experience with clients to help shape their own ensuing work with them. They are left flying blind if some colleagues haven't recorded important interactions, events, or findings that might alter overall treatment significantly. Health and mental health reviewers also require that notes on contacts be kept and updated so that judgments can be made about quality of care and reimbursement of procedures.

A nurse on an alcohol treatment unit decided on her own to ask one of the "pets" on the unit (a man frequently detoxed there and helpful to staff) to be in charge of about $200 collected for a party on the unit that was to celebrate fellowship. The fellow with the money was sent out alone to buy decorations, since the nurse hadn't charted his recent conversation with her about feeling like drinking again. She thought her vote of confidence might sustain him under pressure. Instead, he spent the money on a bender, disappearing for two weeks and cutting his wrists because he felt so guilty for what he'd done. He later told the staff that handling the money made him feel people were expecting too much of him too early in his recovery, and that he needed to show people how he "really" was.

In the event of a lawsuit, the record is one of the important documents subpoenaed as evidence, so appropriate and timely content and accuracy are crucial in defense of good work by individuals or teams. Clients also have the right to ask for copies of their records at any time in the work—another reason for keeping notes current and free of jargon.

In a famous medical malpractice case, parents of a disabled child sued hospital staff when they got a copy of their child's record and saw that he had been diagnosed as having "FLK Syndrome." When asked what this meant, a doctor explained that the initials stood for "funny looking kid" syndrome. He said that experienced staff had seen many children with a chronic blank look about them that indicated a neurological anomaly of unknown origin. It was by this look that they were diagnosed and assigned treatment. The parents were appalled and moved their child's care elsewhere, subsequently winning their lawsuit.

Misattributing Causation

Workers may wrongly attribute client behaviors and situations to personal psychological problems, overlooking biological causes. For example, bipolar disorder can be masked beneath overfunctioning in a high-pressure system that values and encourages overwork. Workers can also focus on "the disorder in the patient" and overlook family or larger systems influences (Kleinman, 1988). For example, apparent attention deficit hyperactivity disorder (ADHD) in children can at times reveal itself to be anxiety in reaction to current, undisclosed sexual or physical violence at home, the neighborhood, or school. Teams can label individuals as being lazy, procrastinating, or cranky when these traits can turn out to be clustered features of an undiagnosed clinical depression missed by evaluators unfamiliar with the symptoms of depression.

Noting his many symptoms that fit the bill, I diagnosed Les as having agitated and possibly suicidal depression, described this to my busy backup physician by phone, and with his approval, sent the man by ambulance to the state hospital for further evaluation and protection. The receiving doctor there phoned me, livid. He yelled, "Didn't you notice that his pupils were as big as saucers?

The guy's coming off drugs . . . he could have had a seizure in the ambulance and died. What kind of place are you running there?!" I felt ashamed and dumb, because the man had denied drug use and I took his word, not knowing to look for pupil dilation. After this incident, every intake client with any bodily signs or symptoms had to be seen face-to-face by the psychiatric backups. I felt very relieved by that.

Up-to-date physical exams, psychological testing, reports from a variety of observers, and home and classroom visits can all assist in clarifying the contributions of biology, psychology, and the environment to client functioning. Workers and teams may have to advocate intensively to get important evaluation activities approved, covered by insurers, and carried out by skilled professionals, especially when clients lack a strong voice or political lobby of their own.

Playing Doctor

When working on or around medical personnel, or in an agency where people with illnesses or disabilities are commonly treated, it's very easy for people new to clinical work to pick up both "Medical Students' Disease" (the worry that one might have every condition treated) and medical lingo and jargon. Workers can even develop a feeling of being able to diagnose symptoms and understand their ramifications and treatments. This is an extremely commonplace development starting out, perhaps because it makes anxious people feel wiser or more worthy of respect in multidisciplinary hierarchies.

Assiduously avoid telling clients what doctors and nurses say about their condition, diagnosis, or prognosis, and equally avoid discussing medication use or dosages or withdrawal from drugs or protocols unless you are legally empowered to do so in your state. Also avoid telling clients about your own favorite treatments, herbal remedies, and the like. What we *do* need to ask clients about is how they're faring with their medical providers, treatments, and medications, and whether they are following medical advice given. Such discussion often discloses that people can't afford their medications, don't like their side effects, or don't really understand their benefit, so have stopped taking them. In response to such concerns, we can help by encouraging or arranging no or low-cost medical consultations for clients. The strength of the worker-client relationship can be used to support follow-through with needed check-ups and medication consultations.

Randy had been paying over $400 per month for his heart medications and other crucial drugs when I saw him following his latest heart attack. I checked with the VA and discovered that as a Korean War era veteran, he was eligible to get his prescriptions for less than $5.00 each at a nearby VA pharmacy. Randy hadn't actually gone to Korea, but his work as an officer at a national traning base throughout that war still qualified him for the benefits. He never dreamed he would be eligible. The drug savings could now be applied to paying for participation in a heart exercise program at a local gym.

Not Following Up if Clients Drop Out

Good practice usually dictates that we reach out to clients who suddenly drop out during the assessment process. We explore the client's reasons for ending so soon, and invite him or her to return for at least one session to discuss what may have happened, in hopes of working things out productively. Sometimes, though, client sessions may have been contentious around assessment probing, so that workers may secretly feel relieved if clients don't complete the assessment, glad never to see them or their upsetting themes and reactions again. To say the least, this relief signals the opposite of unconditional positive regard. Such feelings need to be worked through in supervision in order to prevent their undermining a professional commitment to work with all people in an informed and patient way.

When we know we've blundered with a client, we try to own the behavior with him or her and apologize, essentially requesting a second chance to resolve problems and move ahead with the assessment. Clients do the very same thing at times, calling the worker after a "meltdown" and asking to meet again to sort things out better.

Overgeneralizing

In assessments, we are often seeing clients at times of great stress, when coping resources are stretched thin. A mother may push her child in the hallway; a dad may get angry quickly and slam out of the room. People may forget their appointments with workers or think these appointments aren't important when compared with crucial visits to a loved one undergoing breast surgery. Workers store these experiences for further observation and inquiry rather than rushing to judgment or overgeneralizing observations into grand conclusions about client functioning.

It's important to establish whether current behaviors are established patterns or current stress responses. To answer these questions, we can ask clients direct questions about their behaviors, amass further experience with clients to see for ourselves, and seek out the observations of others involved with the situation. If we could see people at their best, at less crisis–ridden moments or in situations with more resources, we might see them functioning much more skillfully.

> *Sanjay, 12, was a bright, successful child in school, when his dad suddenly left the family and moved across the state with another woman. Ashamed, Sanjay's mother only told her two boys that dad had left to "find himself." Sanjay blamed his mom for his dad's leaving. A year later, his adored older brother suddenly died of a rare disease, again leaving Sanjay devastated. Unable to tell his teachers of his losses, the boy began to make trouble in classes, get in fights with former friends, and truant school. Teachers chalked Sanjay's behavior up to "adolescence," and suspended him for several days "to set limits." During that time he was able to call a suicide hotline he'd seen listed on TV and cry with the male worker about the loss of his dad and brother. He then followed up faithfully by attending counseling sessions at a health center near his school, something no one would have predicted.*

The Working Agreement or Contract

The worker should use assessment findings and suggestions (along with client reactions and preferences) to guide the development of a plan for work together. This may also be known as the service plan, intervention plan, or treatment plan, depending on the setting. Within this plan, specific goals and objectives are developed, partialized, and prioritized, emphasizing the most critical or urgent foci for work.

The plan then outlines prioritized items for work in a verbal or written working agreement that usually describes:

- agreed upon goals and objectives for focused work (in order of urgency)
- methods to be used towards reaching desired ends (modalities, strategies, techniques, evaluative protocols)
- locus for the work (home, church, office, bedside in health setting)
- roles of participants (listening/responding, time keeping, room access, control of interruptions and noise)
- division of labor in managing identified tasks (making applications, completing homework and evaluative inventories, attending team meetings)
- resources to be linked with or developed (benefits, transportation, training, health care)
- other people to be involved (family, collateral systems, colleagues, friends and advocates)
- things that *won't* be focused on at present (situation-dependent topics such as drinking exploits while in sobriety counseling; talk of another pregnancy while in deep mourning over a first infant's death)
- estimated length of time of the course of work and of each meeting (the "bookends" of work)
- other (confidentiality; any protocols to be used; emergency help between visits)

The Function of Working Agreements

Like a good travel guide or map, a good working agreement provides clear guidelines for the journey ahead. Clear objectives and plans provide a focus for activities and conversation to follow, and help both worker and client recognize when work is and isn't on track. Clearly specified objectives also allow us to track and measure progress formally and informally in order to determine which approaches best help with particular problems and which are less effective.

Garvin and Seabury (1997) believe that to be effective, a contract must be clear and understandable, framed in the client's own language whenever possible. It should be mutually agreed upon and acceptable to all parties, as well as dynamic and flexible, leaving room for change and creativity. It should also be realistic and pragmatic, not full of ambitions and ideals that will likely never be realized (pp. 157–159). For them, "a contract based on false hope or intimidating demands may be more harmful than no contract at all" (p. 161).

Form and Flexibility of Agreements

Sometimes a service plan or agreement is written and signed to emphasize seriousness of purpose or to minimize ambiguity or gray areas. Agencies may present workers with printed service plan and contract forms to be filled in and reviewed by quality assessment managers at regular intervals. At other times, participants use less businesslike verbal clarifications and agreements.

Clients and workers realize that as more understanding is gained through experience, flexibility will allow for plans and methods to change as necessary. Surprises can and do happen to alter prospects, so the worker and client discuss the possibility of the unanticipated, agreeing to work together around surprises as they occur. Job changes, serious illnesses, prison sentences, and deportations can suddenly take people away. Family crises can affect the frequency and focus of sessions. Some initial plans and ideas may prove to be too grandiose or poorly conceived, so conversation must confront unknown aspects of the work, to help minimize unrealistic worker and client fantasies of what counseling can accomplish.

Contracting time is also a good time to discuss expectations of each other and the work: session length and scheduling, expectations of starting and ending on time, plans for notifying each other and rescheduling if someone can't make it, trying to minimize intrusions on the work, and so on. The worker encourages participants to put feelings and preferences on the table for clarification or negotiation. Is smoking allowed? Can the client bring coffee to the meeting, and does the worker want some, too? If the client's wife wants to come and meet with you too, is that okay? Who will track the time in the meeting? Can an officer wear her uniform and weapon to the meeting if she has to report for duty as soon as they finish? No one can think of everything up front, and such matters will continue to arise and be dealt with as flexibly as possible.

This exchange is much more important symbolically than the content of each separate question would indicate at first glance. Such a far-reaching conversation hints at how level the playing field will be between the participants, and can reveal awkwardness, rigidities, and uncompromising tendencies in the worker and the client. Participants are expected to be as genuine as they possibly can instead of pretending to agree on things when they don't, or that things are fine when in fact they aren't. Discussions give us a feel for each other's values, work style, and degree of ease with collaboration and speaking our minds.

Priorities Can't Always Be Determined by the Client

A teen may have to remain in residential treatment because of violent tantrums, though his most urgent personal priority is to return home. Even though his mother is newly ill and could use his help at home right away, he previously hurt her twice while out of control, so must now demonstrate more consistent self-calming and controls before he can return home. A policeman may want a periodically hallucinating woman off the streets because she upsets passers-by, but the priorities of the day treatment staff and the client are to maintain her in the community and to help her learn to use medication and discussion groups at the center to contain her hallucinations and advance appropriate expression of her needs and feelings.

Some of the hardest tasks we face are those of explaining steps that have to happen before other objectives can be tackled: parenting skills training before getting a child out of protective foster care, more job training before getting a promotion, or completion of a high school equivalency before becoming a nurse's aide. This may be the first opportunity some clients have had to experience the steps of achieving a goal through the development of the patience, new knowledge, confidence, and skills that can lead to meaningful mastery and growth.

Pressure from Clients

Occasionally, clients put pressure on workers to cut corners for them or move them ahead in line as they await assessment for services. Much patience and skill is needed to maintain firm and fair procedures when services are limited and many people need and want them urgently. Our job is not to punish people who become angry and demanding, but to hold firm in explaining any limits on time, commodities, or services, as well as explaining the appeal process if they think they are being unfairly treated. In busy agencies, it's important to remember that an apparently "entitled" client pressuring to be moved ahead of others waiting for service may actually have a dire emergency that can't wait. It would then be a mistake to value "limit setting" more than needed emergency responsiveness in such situations, which is why agencies often use triage, a process of quickly assessing severity of all applicants' needs in order to determine priority of service provision.

Shulman's "Three Decisions"

Shulman (1999) writes of three important decisions a client must make in regard to the commitment to see a worker and uphold a working agreement at the beginning, middle, and end phases of the work (p. 200). The first decision is that of making up one's mind to actually go and see a worker and then commit to the work suggested—a courageous and difficult step for many people. A second decision arises once clients have begun counseling work and know what the process requires and is like. Now clients must decide if they wish to continue, and if so, with this particular worker, in this modality, style, and pace.

Shulman's third decision arises when, after a period of productive work together in a meaningful relationship, the client has to decide to finish up with the worker for now and bear the work and feelings attendant to saying good-bye. Clients and workers sensitive to loss and separations may want to continue rather than stop, and may keep finding things to talk about; in fact, they may even unwittingly generate crises as a basis for continuing. Or, they can zoom through the ending conversation, minimizing its emotional focus and impact while celebrating gains.

Understanding these decision points helps workers keep an eye out for reluctances or ambivalences that could undermine the early work of engagement, assessment, and contracting if not discussed and resolved. For example, when tapering down a session, the worker might say, "Sometimes people worry that they won't like counseling once they've started down the trail, but will be afraid to say so, and they'll get stuck in something that doesn't feel good. What about yourself?" If no comments are forthcoming, at least the client knows that the worker is open to discussing worries of this kind.

IMPLICATIONS FOR CONTRACTING
WITH INVOLUNTARY CLIENTS

Kadushin and Kadushin (1997) and Shulman (1999) suggest empathic attunement with the involuntary client's feelings of anger or outrage at being "made" to see a counselor "or else," putting into words what anyone might feel if forced to speak with a professional against their will. Kadushin and Kadushin refer to this joining with the client's perspective as "rolling with the resistance"(p. 367), noting that empathy, positive regard, and expressed interest in helping this situation work for the client often diminishes anger and piques interest in hearing more about what the worker might have to offer. Rooney (1992) speaks of helping clients move from "involuntary" to "semivoluntary" status by locating issues that the client might never have sought help for, but might actually choose to work on now that he or she is obliged to attend.

We're usually not very comfortable having to "make" someone participate, so it's easy to come across as more businesslike, distant, and formal when feeling ill at ease as an agent of authority. Garvin and Seabury discuss workers' historic concerns about being agents of control, about participating in legal mandates that *de facto* void client rights to silence and to self-determination, and about having to cast about for issues the client may want to talk about when we're more used to clients coming in with specific requests for help.

There could be times when workers might actually want to empower clients by helping them *become or remain involuntary* by the standards of the agency that has power over them and has insisted that they have counseling. Rooney (1992) reviews assistance given by workers to war resisters and people jailed for civil and human rights advocacy, or during public protests aimed at extending benefits and social participation. These clients might be referred against their will to counselors who could then actually extend them support around their resistance. It's good to remember that our professional *codes of ethics affirm that our primary service obligation is to the client, and that this service obligation takes precedence over all other considerations except those of safety.* This obligation protects and supports us in situations in which a government or institution might pressure us to treat clients in ways that we believe are counter to the client's best interest; for example, involving clients in research projects without their fully informed consent, or reporting gays in the military identified through other clients' disclosures while in therapy with a military counselor.

MISTAKES IN CONTRACTING

It's easy to make mistakes while discussing and negotiating working agreements, because there is often time pressure to complete initial assessment and contracting and move on into problem-solving work without delay. People can also go back and forth about what they think they can or ought to do about problems. Workers can be responsible for several intakes at once, and rush through them because of their level of stress at the moment. People can also get excited by prospects and get ahead of themselves in planning, not taking into sufficient consideration the huge number of system factors that may limit opportunity and discourage change. The following mistakes often flow from numerous factors such as these.

Promising More Than Can Be Delivered

In *false reassurance*, you may innocently try to cheer clients on by reassuring them that work together will resolve complicated matters, or bring new happiness in relationships. Interns often ask why reassurance is a problem if the worker's hope, optimism, and confidence are identified as important factors in client continuance. The nature and extent of worker statements is crucial here. Saying "I've seen this work help people make some important changes, I think it might help you with some things, too," is different from saying "The kids who come here change—we don't see them back here because what we do works." The first statement offers hope born of experience, while the second offers a cure that hasn't yet been identified. The more realistic the bargains struck about the work to come, the less the disappointment of both worker and client when problems take time, resources aren't as forthcoming or generous as expected, imagined allies undermine efforts, or service needs prove greater than the worker or agency can handle.

Confusing Clients by Using Contract Jargon

As previously noted, jargon disempowers consumers and makes interns and workers appear more allied with the professional team than with the client. For example, with the client at her side in a care planning meeting, the worker might look at the psychiatrist and ask, "After we '460' her (the number designating a legal paper used in hospitalizing someone), will she have WPH (weekend privileges home) if she doesn't go AWAL (away without administrative leave) again?"

The last thing clients in crisis need is to have service plans, procedures, and take-home materials that they can't understand. Sometimes family members can't read, or are poor readers in the language of the agency, and they may misunderstand agreements and instructions, particularly if these employ jargon. If jargon slips into conversations, you should translate it right away into plain language before clients have to ask what it means. The same principle holds true in translating obscure diagnostic terms into plain language and implications clients can understand and act on.

The agency has been trying to move to a system where we sit side-by-side with clients to review all of our recorded formulations and treatment plans and goals with them so there are no surprises or mysteries about diagnoses or plans. I give every client a copy of their initial and ongoing file notes if they want them (and a lot don't), for them to reflect on at home if they want to, and bring in questions or comments. Not all of the workers do this, and some expressly do not want their clients to see what they formulate or note about them, because they are still using diagnoses that pathologize clients, focusing on their extreme behaviors rather than on their capabilities. Actually, the state is helping us now by requiring that all clients read their assessments and treatment plans and sign off on them. I think the state is doing this because of a growing list of complaints and lawsuits from irate mental health consumers who feel poorly understood and treated.

Proceeding Without Real Agreement

Sometimes workers try to talk clients into a treatment they provide or espouse instead of dealing first with ambivalences they hear in the client's misgivings, or see in the client's hesitations or newly tensed up body language. You may lean on a wife to come to the center's evening NarcAnon meeting, when she has already expressed fear about being seen there so close to her bank job. You may try pressuring a divorcee to come to a Parents Without Partners dance in order to socialize more, when she's said she needs to get her confidence back before meeting more people.

These examples evidence worker problems of failing to start and remain where the client is. Sometimes this failure is due to overestimating the client's wish or capacity to change or choosing *for* the client a goal that means more to the worker than it does to the client. At other times, the nature of the task (for example, dating, or revealing one's relationship with an addict) may be daunting and needs further discussion prior to action. It's important that we not look or sound disappointed when clients don't share or agree with some of our hopes and goals. *Disappointment is a subtle form of judgmentalism* regarding client priorities and capacities. It exposes clients to double messages about who's in charge of the client's narrative, goals, and work.

Agreements with Built-In Problems

Garvin and Seabury (1997) note three problems workers frequently get into around contracting. *Hidden agendas* (pp 164–165) are secret aims of the worker, unexpressed to the client. The worker feels these aims will greatly improve the client's situation or functioning, but fears that the client will balk at them, and hopes that the power of relationship will later make the goals possible to pursue openly. The authors warn that a hidden agenda often dooms work to failure later, as "it is close to impossible . . . to change people against their will, especially when they recognize that they have been deceived" (p. 165).

Corrupt contracts (p. 165) occur when multiple service providers, working separately, make different agreements with clients, or clients with them, without all of the parties realizing that different goals or methods have been agreed upon. A client may tell a probation officer that she is attending a weekly support group for former sex workers, while telling that group's leader that mandated attendance at an AIDS support meeting prevents her attending the sex workers group more than once every other week. The worker and probation officer are not communicating; the treatment plans established with the client are inauthentic for all practical purposes, and the client will attend no meetings whatsoever as a result.

Sabotage (p. 165–166) can occur when an angry worker encourages a client to act out against the treatment team because the worker doesn't believe in the goals and plans the team has established. The worker, feeling sorry for a client with whose wish for more freedom he identifies, might help her secretly go off of the unit for the day while supposedly working in the laundry, because the worker feels the limits imposed on the particular client are unjust or inappropriate.

Splits in teams or between agencies often mirror emotional or psychological splits within the team members themselves (Nason, 1990). Staff can feel both a respect for limits *and* an ambivalence about limits, for example. They can believe in community treatment of mental illness *and* have fears of people with mental illness living in their own neighborhood. Families can also sabotage treatment plans by threatening members with negative consequences if they reveal concealed or sensitive family information or behaviors.

Potential problems in contracts can often be resolved by getting all participants together up front. All participants need to make their hopes and conflicts explicit and try to hash out differences. Only then can realistic compromises be reached that allow workers and clients to proceed above board and responsibly in league in the work.

Intentionally Vague Agreements

Vague working agreements usually characterize the work of someone who is either afraid to speak frankly about why the client needs to be seen, or hasn't been well trained to carry out an assessment and working agreement. Another reason for vagueness in interns and new workers is that they can fear losing the client if they are frank about problems they suspect are present, but unmentioned by the client. The following is a vague agreement that fails to clarify what the client's own goals or interest might be in seeing the worker, or how objectives will be realized through clear component objectives in order of urgency.

> *How would it be if we talked every week about whatever your concerns might be? We could meet for an hour, we could see how the week was going for you, how the family is taking your surgery and walking with a cane now. We could talk about whatever comes up for you. How's that sound?*

Vagueness can be observed rather frequently in the supervision of work with people thought to need help but who are not directly asking for help: lonely seniors or newcomer populations reluctant to identify problems, distressed teens leery of discussing personal business with an adult worker, young moms in protective services who resent being referred, and incarcerated or chronically hospitalized individuals for whom service is folded into a routine plan of care for those admitted.

While it's true that supportive alliances can sometimes lead to clients' gradually sharing personal concerns that can be worked on at "deeper" levels, people are still more likely to work toward change if they are in overt agreement about the need for and design of the work towards change, and can articulate a vision or sense of what that change would look like in their daily lives.

Agreements That Empower Workers More Than Clients

Sometimes workers proceed with clients in ways that are clearly going to disempower them. When rushed or impatient, it's all too easy to do *for* rather than *with* clients, believing that this changes lives and circumstances more rapidly than waiting for clients to deliberate and act. We can do many subtly self-centered things early on that we'll later remember with dismay. For example, without discussion with the client, you might arrange a weekend pass for her, thinking she needs a break from the treatment unit. The written pass is handed to the client triumphantly, only to have her burst into tears because she wants to go bowling and shopping on Saturday with her friends on the unit, yet feels conflicted because also grateful for your effort.

> *Ada was a chronically mute and depressed woman of 52 living on the long term unit of a psych hospital. The social worker and nursing staff decided for her that weekends home with her only surviving relative, her older brother, would "help her regain some sense of normalcy in her life." Ada complied, going home with her brother every Saturday and returning dutifully on Sunday nights, everyone telling her how glad they were to see her having such a nice time outside. Then a new worker introduced a behavioral modification program that, over a two year period, finally helped Ada talk. She was able to disclose to the worker that on all of those weekends home, her brother had been forcing sexual relations on her, threatening never to take her home again unless she complied.*

Keeping Secrets from Supervisors
and Other Authorities

Sometimes inexperienced workers plan with clients to carry out activities forbidden by agency policy or supervisors. For example, a residential worker with a motorcycle may think that a secret ride on his bike may increase bonding with a shy teen. A supervisor may ask workers in a high-risk neighborhood not to work alone in the building after dark. While saying they won't, they actually do regularly stay late and fib about it in order to finish case notes or meet with working clients who can't get off in the daytime. This ostensibly generous work sets unprotected workers, clients, and the agency itself up for unnecessary risk and possible injury.

Work rules and taboos are often created because of painful past experience, such as a staff member being mugged or a worker having an automobile accident that injured a client. Equally importantly, workers are not only bound by ethical considerations; they're also liable for the messes they create. If the agency is sued or attracts negative media attention, the worker and client are targeted, too. Finally, supervisors and agencies rapidly lose faith in workers whose behaviors put self, clients, supervisors, and the agency at risk.

The Impact of Assessment
and Contracting on People and Systems

Workers have to attend to the impact that the planning and agreement processes may have on clients and others, and be ready to check in about reactions to the process of talking with a stranger about very private matters and feelings, now that more such work is planned. People often come for therapy, advice, or concrete services without ever having experienced any of these processes, met or known a clinician, or been inside a social agency.

You also need to check with clients about the responses of significant others to planned work together. Some of them may fear that if the client changes because of the meetings with a counselor, relationships may be irrevocably altered or lost, without their even having a vote. People can also have uncomfortable feelings about a loved one's sharing a version of a narrative without other participants in it being present to add their own views. Initially encouraging, they may now ask, "Why do you need to talk with somebody besides us? I thought we were your best friends. Can't you tell us and let us help you without going to see some stranger who doesn't know anything about how we do things?"

Exploratory questions such as the following can be used to check in with clients and important others.

How will Lynette's meetings with me likely affect you and your family?

What are your partner's thoughts about your coming to see me without her?

Will our meetings create any new problems for you?

Are you getting any feedback from anyone about our plan for work on your fears?

Angry people who feel diminished or insulted by the assessment process or planning recommendations can also suddenly threaten the worker who is doing the evaluation, particularly when they feel they have something important to hide (e.g., drugs, weapons, or violence) or lose (e.g., partner, children, or home). An immediate consultation with a supervisor is indicated if any threats have been made against the worker during or following an assessment.

Recently an experienced worker in a nearby state was killed by an angry father in a family whose children were at risk of being removed due to the father's violence in the home. The worker had gone to the home to evaluate anew the possibilities and conditions of the kids remaining at home, but was attacked on the street by the father before he could enter the home. The father thought the worker was coming to take the kids away that day.

Today many agencies see the whole client system for the entire process of evaluation, planning, contracting, and work; with individual or dyadic meetings only scheduled by special request.

When the oncology worker did a psychosocial assessment with a new patient on the unit in his final weeks of life, his urgent request was that he be allowed to have both his wife and family and his beloved mistress of many years to visit him, but at separate times so as not to hurt his wife and children. This was like a dying wish, and we didn't think it was our place to interfere with what had worked for the patient and his networks for so long. We thus arranged that his wife and kids would visit every day, any time, until about eight at night, and then leave. In an unusual exception to visiting hours, his mistress would arrive about nine and stay until the patient drifted off around eleven or midnight. We remained afraid that something would blow up about this but it never did. Eventually the man died peacefully, having said all of his goodbyes and received support from all who loved him. Some staff objected to these arrangements on religious or moral grounds, and were not obligated to be involved in the care plan if they didn't want to be.

Workers can be surprised by how much evaluations and treatment planning affect them. It feels very gratifying to elicit and honor client, family, and neighborhood strengths, but it can be very stressful to carry out numerous assessments during a day or week in which the worker must also elicit details and feelings about family violence and neglect, or the unabated destructive effects of homelessness, substance abuse, or incapacitating mental and physical illnesses. Sometimes clients who don't know anything about the worker's social life tell the worker things the latter would prefer not to know about behaviors of colleagues or friends. Workers can also hear disillusioning things about their own neighborhood's or town's practices that discriminate against clients. Sitting repeatedly with frankly expressed despair, outrage, suspicion of others' intentions, and stories of betrayal can also cause occasional worker despair about the human condition and widespread oppression that never seems to end.

Pearlman and Saakvitne (1995) have described the vicarious trauma experienced by caregivers who repeatedly attend to and empathize with client trauma narratives, as they sometimes develop symptoms similar to those of their affected clients. Workers can also experience their own issues or histories being tapped into by the emerging narratives of clients. This evocation of unresolved dilemmas or conflicts can occur within or after interviews, or after evaluating a series of clients whose issues closely conform with stressful current preoccupations of the worker.

In effect, we have to make Shulman's three commitment decisions ourselves if we're to stay emotionally involved with clients who touch us deeply by virtue of their heroic resilience against great odds, and despite frequent injustice and abuse. We have to commit initially to carrying out considerate and thoroughgoing assessments during which we may have to spend many extra hours responding to emergency needs and calls, legal and protective service inquiries, upset and overwhelmed family members and neighbors, and lack of adequate local services. If work with the client continues beyond assessment, we have to commit to remaining emotionally engaged, patiently available, and promptly responsive during the frequent crises that arise for many poor, oppressed, and highly stressed families today. Eventually, we also have to let go when it's time.

The Positive Impact of Assessments on Assessors

A great positive impact of numerous assessments on workers is the vast amount of knowledge, skills, and community contacts we accumulate through facing new situations and people repeatedly, and receiving excellent supervisory advice about how to focus in on the most relevant aspects of narratives without needing to find out every detail. We continue to learn how to help clients be more comfortable in revealing intimate details and feelings without feeling too overwhelmed, exposed, or disloyal to systems of which we've long been a part.

Experienced evaluators gradually develop facility in shaping conversation, becoming more adept at judging when to refocus conversation, do nothing, or bring a theme to conclusion, while at the same time respectfully witnessing or hearing people out when they need to linger longer on experience or feelings. We also get more comfortable asking the really hard questions because we've learned that it can be a great relief to people to unburden themselves confidentially in a way that doesn't overwhelm them or hurt others unnecessarily.

Client assessments affect everyone on the unit or in the agency or department in a number of ways. Discovering through multiple assessments that a number of clients need interpreters, wheelchair accessibility, home visits, or on-site childcare can change dramatically what the agency offers, and can reshape its budgets to meet appropriate special needs. When an outpatient mental health clinic wins a contract to evaluate people for admission to a state hospital, or to evaluate persons before the nearby court, clients may come in with police or medical escorts, and may require immediate medications that have to be given on site by new staff hired for emergency consultation for these purposes.

At the same time, workers may become part of emergency teams who act together in evaluating clients in-house or in homes or shelters. In-service training and supervision will highlight new knowledge and skills needed for emergency psychiatric evaluations, and roles will be divided up between the biomedical and the psychosocial aspects of evaluation. Teams may begin to identify service gaps or a lack of coordination between agencies involved with the client, and may advocate for changes in how things are organized. Case-finding—outreach into neighborhoods to identify populations at risk—and political work often become very important parts of a team or worker's work responsibilities.

In the space of four months, our hospital's emergency room staff noted that three workers in a nearby factory came in with finger or hand injuries described as occurring in the same unit of the factory. The doctor on call called the factory manager, who wasn't responsive, blaming many "foreign-born workers" for not paying good attention on the job. When the fifth and sixth men came in with hand injuries, the social worker got in touch with the federal agency OSHA (Occupational Health and Safety Administration), and a speedy inspection turned up a malfunctioning machine responsible for the injuries. An attorney organized the workers into a class action suit against their employer and won coverage of their medical treatment and hand rehabilitation. They were also awarded damages for their wrongful injuries, and the company was punished for trying to cover up the injuries and intimidate the injured workers.

LARGER SYSTEMS ISSUES

The setting and the surroundings can importantly influence the depth and breadth of assessment and planning activities. Some staff and families may not like it that the court refers alleged batterers or stalkers for evaluation at a family agency licensed as a mental health clinic, and may shun these and other people in the waiting areas and ask not to be assigned them. Curiously, mothers openly nursing babies, large, chatty family groups, and clients who are hallucinating or have mental retardation are also sometimes made to feel less welcome in some settings, and may not get as thorough and respectful an assessment or offer of ongoing treatment. Staff can also feel uneasy when the police sit in on the evaluation with a client for safety purposes, or may gather inappropriately to have a look at the "unusual" client.

Clients who feel poorly received may or may not register this with the worker or other authorities. Feeling stigmatized or shortchanged, they may participate in assessment reluctantly or angrily, without the worker realizing that his or her judgmental or hostile reception is causing the client's reactions. (Medical professionals use the term *iatrogenic* to connote problems or illnesses *caused by* professional settings or practices, as when an otherwise healthy person enters a hospital to have a broken leg set, only to catch an institutional airborne virus while there.) Settings can also group or categorize people and devise uniform referrals and services for them instead of tailoring responses to the unique needs of individuals and families. For example, a town may send all newly pregnant teens to be evaluated at a specially designated community agency; all teens entering there, pregnant or not, worry that observers will think (or know) that they are pregnant.

Financial matters obviously influence evaluation process and outcome. Federally or locally subsidized health care and other funding programs often begin to tap their fund sources at the beginning of the fiscal year, and indigent or uninsured clients may be delayed for evaluation in order that services be covered at that particular start time. Clients may be seen in brief treatment thought to be more economical, where evaluation and treatment proceed together rapidly from point of first meeting. People may begin an assessment, realize they have very serious problems, and leave before help is received because they don't want or can't afford the follow up care offered. They may resent workers who cannot offer free care or reduced fees because the workers or agencies themselves are struggling financially.

CONCLUSION

Assessment and contracting processes are rich sources of data and experience for both clients and workers. An emphasis on client assets and potentials moves assessment from an exploration and labeling of pathology, to a journey of discovery with people whose problems and prospects may be best understood when viewed within their own natural helping systems and sociocultural contexts. Assessment is not considered to be a neutral or easy process for workers or clients, as it requires an intensely focused review between relative strangers regarding material, feelings, and events that are in most cultures kept private within individuals and family groups. The assessment process will therefore require of you:

- a high degree of comfort with self and with many other people
- good collaborative skills used to develop and share understanding
- an ever-refining knowledge of human behavior within and across cultures
- well-developed exploration and support skills
- attunement to changing moods, themes, and shifts in the evolving narrative
- knowing when to proceed and when enough is enough
- the ability to communicate hunches and information in plain and easily understood language that informs, guides, and is open to feedback

EXERCISES

1. *Reflection.* In your journal, remember a time when you underwent some type of assessment, and picture it as fully as possible. What techniques did the other person use to inquire into aspects of your life or functioning (e.g., direct questions, invitation for you to reveal needed detail, forms to fill out, pressure on you to talk)? What worked well to engage you in talking, and what was less effective? Which aspects of the inquiry were comfortable and which were not? Recall things you might have held back, and why you decided to do what you did. Looking back, can anything from that experience contribute to your own assessment understandings and skills?

2. *Small Group Discussion.* Discuss situations in which you have found it difficult to contract with clients, and review factors within your own, the agency's, or the clients' situation that compounded the difficulties.

3. *Class Discussion.* Using this chapter as a reference point, discuss mistakes you all have made in assessment work with clients, and what you might do

differently now. Share any constructive feedback you've received from clients that has helped you alter your assessment style or ways of thinking about getting to know people.

4. *Instructor Activity.* Discuss with the class some mistakes you have made in assessment work or in constructing a working agreement. If you've unwittingly disempowered a client while having every good intention of empowering him or her, give examples so that the group can see what that looks like. Share with them any feedback you got from clients about your assessment or contracting work that still guides your practice today.

5. *Author Sharing for Further Discussion.* Once when I was a student reporting out an intake phone call to my supervisor, I said with assurance that I could tell the man was drunk due to the way he talked. She asked me what his manner of talking was, and I described slurred speech. She reminded me that slurred speech could be caused by many other conditions, such as stroke, other brain injury, speech impairment, effects of medication, and dental problems. She didn't inquire further, but later, on my own, it occurred to me that this man sounded a lot like a person I knew who spoke like this when drunk. Realizing this helped me understand why I had begun to feel irritated by the man on the phone when he threatened to harm himself but refused to come in to see me in person in order to get some help.

For Class Discussion. What happened to me during my phone contact with this client is an example of the frequently observed phenomenon of countertransference distortion. Discuss the manner in which a good supervisor got me to a point of greater self-awareness without "therapizing" me. Discuss together incidents in which you have experienced or observed how assessment and contracting can become distorted by bias, cultural or family taboos, or other personal experiences.

RECOMMENDED READING

Amodeo, M., & Jones, L. K. (1998). Using the AOD cultural framework to view alcohol and drug issues through various cultural lenses. *Journal of Social Work Education, 34,* 387–399.

Cowger, C. (1997). Assessing client strengths: Assessing for client empowerment. In D. Saleebey (Ed.), *The strengths perspective in social work practice* (pp. 59–73). White Plains, NY: Longman.

Garvin, C., & Seabury, B. (1997). Contracting. In *Interpersonal practice in social work: Promoting competence and social justice* (pp. 153–171). Boston: Allyn & Bacon.

Lum, D. (2000). Assessment. In *Social work practice and people of color: A process-stage approach* (pp. 210–253). Pacific Grove, CA: Brooks/Cole.

Pinderhughes, E. (1998). Black genealogy revisited: Restorying an African American family. In M. McGoldrick (Ed.), *Re-visioning family therapy: Race, culture, and gender in clinical practice* (pp. 179–199). New York: Guilford.

Webb, N. B. (1999). *Play therapy with children in crisis.* New York: Guilford.

6

The Middle Phase of Work

Prospects and Problems

The client and worker move into the middle phase of work on goal-directed changes because of identification of those goals and contracting. This is also known as the implementation, developmental, or intervention phase of practice. Now, the worker and client intentionally focus on conversation and activities designed to support and achieve identified goals. Unexpected positive changes in participants and related systems can be gratifying side benefits of this work, as when distant friends or relatives move closer to where the client lives, providing new support and connection.

COMMON FOCI FOR WORK

Whatever the theoretical model we use in helping clients improve their lives and prospects, we often focus on problems or dissatisfactions in the following domains of experience: relationships; troubling thoughts, feelings, or behaviors; motivations to change; sociopolitical barriers to success; and resources to enhance daily living. The professional usually moves work on these domains towards supporting existing client strengths and connections with others, as well as towards enhancement of knowledge, self-awareness, skills, and resources related to developing more positive experiences within these domains.

Motivation for Change

Initial conversations with a helping professional begin to clarify for a client just what the desired change may entail in terms of personal, family, or systems commitments to collaborate forthrightly, as well as energy, time, and space commitments for meeting and working together. The notion of "getting help" now takes on real form and implications, especially as workers emphasize client strengths, decision making, and working as a collaborative team—no mean feat for very busy or troubled people in crisis. People begin to realize that "help" and "change" are not prepackaged procedures or supplies they will "get from a helper." Instead, these are supportive but exacting participatory and dynamic processes that worker and client must coproduce from shared vision, capacity for change, determination, and support from service networks.

Some clients drop out of the work early on, realizing that more is required than they are interested in or can commit to giving at the present time. Others realize that at some point they are going to have to make fundamental changes in their familiar ways of thinking, relating, and behaving within their complex role responsibilities. They may proceed to work with a counselor, but with some ambivalence, self-doubt, or trepidation about risks and benefits as they contemplate change. In order to continue—that is, to "experience motivation"—people need to be able to find the trust, time, resources, and compelling purpose and focus necessary to sustain the sometimes stressful work of change.

The research of Prochaska, Norcross, and DiClemente (1994) reveals that people attempting change are more likely to change if they feel they have some choice in the matter, and several change strategies to choose from. The authors identify *six stages of change* occurring uniformly across a wide variety of people and problems. They describe change as involving a spiraling, rather than a directly linear, process, with people "recycling" between stages a number of times in the course of making sustainable changes.

In the first stage of change, *Pre-Contemplation,* individuals may be in denial about the presence or importance of a problem, even though people around them see it and urge change. The authors observe that in this stage, "people often blame their problems or habits on family influences, genetic makeup, societal models and pressures, or destiny, and as such, that their problems are out of their control" (p. 41).

We usually don't see "precontemplators" in counseling unless someone else has forced them to come. If they do come in, advice-giving, moralizing, and the force-feeding of dire predictions of negative consequences do not work, although empathy and enlistment of the client's ideas about how best to use mandated meetings may soften reluctance to participate. From their work with addictive behaviors, Miller and Rollnick (1997) suggest that at this stage, providing encouraging feedback and information to help build self-awareness can sometimes be useful.

> *Several members of a local family tried to get their cousin to attend Gamblers Anonymous because of the destructive effects wagering was having on family life. At first he pooh-poohed their suggestions that he had a problem, and*

would clip out articles in the paper about how gambling had helped bring in billions of dollars to enrich the lives of Native Americans on the East Coast. But his wife and son left him when their home was threatened by his use of the mortgage money to pay off debts from gambling, and he was left alone and depressed. At this point, he was open to at least trying a program for gamblers in a nearby town. He'd seen it advertised on TV, and while he didn't stick after the first meeting, at least by choosing that program he indicated that he was beginning to grasp his situation.

The second stage of change, *Contemplation,* involves a dawning awareness of something that needs changing. People can spend a long time thinking about pros and cons of possible change and examining various alternative suggestions and programs available to help with that change. Miller and Rollnick describe contemplators as "see-sawing between reasons to change and reasons to stay the same . . . reasons for concern and reasons for unconcern" (p. 16). It's often at this stage that people seek out advice and support from a wise friend or counselor, and ensuing empathic discussions can help gradually to "tip the seesaw" towards constructive action. Neither pushing nor arguing speeds what has to become an inner process of reconciliation with disavowed aspects of oneself.

This ambivalence—feeling two ways at once about something—is common to all human change efforts and is not unique to people trying to change self-destructive habits. We usually like our familiar ways of doing things and can develop elaborate rationales for these behaviors over time. According to Miller and Rollnick, any attempts to support only one side of a client's thinking, such as giving something up, are likely to trigger a defense of or clinging more closely to that thing, whether out of habit, attachment, or use of it as a major coping strategy for which there's no adequate substitution yet.

Orlie, an older woman with many losses, wanted to discuss her mother's aging and loss of memory with a social worker, but went from worker to worker looking for someone who would validate that her mother belonged in a nursing home for her own safety, and could not be looked after safely in Orlie's home. On the other hand, she wanted someone to understand that going to a nursing home might kill her mother because her mother would have to give up the family home nearby. Her solution was to see one worker who advocated nursing home admission, and then see a physician who believed long-term care should be given in the home. As a result, no action was taken until her mother fell down a few steps and broke her arm and hip, thereby necessitating placement. At that point, Orlie lashed out at the hospital staff for being so heartless as to insist on both the placement of her mother and the sale of her home. Clearly her behavior was a visible manifestation of an intense inner struggle.

Empathy with the client's struggle, validation of the need to take one's time and make one's own decisions, and encouragement to examine the pros and cons of changing and staying the same, can all help the move towards more clarity and self-awareness. Expressing appreciation of roadblocks, acknowledging temptations as a human given, and working on development of insight can also help clients feel respected and understood while still struggling and feeling confused.

The third stage, *Preparation* (Prochaska, Norcross, & DiClemente, 1994), or *Determination* (Miller & Rollnick, 1997), is characterized by small steps towards behavior-based change. Worker and client set a start date for a change program and agree on first steps, and review careful examples of the client's ability to make a change. When trying to change, it's normal to slip backwards into denial or contemplation or leap forward impulsively into action. It's important for the worker to normalize these phenomena as they occur, and support the client's taking leave as taking the time needed to get a footing in new thinking, activities, and relationships. Workers commend clients for accomplishments in order to counter any feelings of embarrassment or discouragement that may arise. Both client and worker can strategize around different ways to make and sustain small changes, with role play of optional behaviors often useful in anticipating steps and challenges ahead.

In the ensuing *Action* and *Behavior Maintenance* stages, worker and client keep goals small, and reinforce positive steps through review, praise, and examination of any benefits of new behaviors. The worker also expresses appreciation for normal feelings of anxiety and temptation at this time, and encourages the client to stick with the new program, in spite of occasional missteps. In the change phase, clients are also helped by attending meetings or programs where they can exchange ideas and feelings with others who share their hopes and goals, and hear testimony from people who have made and sustained similar changes. Having a sponsor to whom one can turn for support and advice can also foster feelings of hope, acceptance, encouragement, and a sense of belonging.

> *Michael had been sober for a year, working part time as an assistant at a greenhouse after a high-stress career as an insurance salesman. He loved his outdoor work and flexible hours, allowing him to spend a lot of time in his sobriety program and in supporting others in recovery, but he thought he should be making more money and working more steadily if he was ever going to have a home of his own. His worker helped him slow down and keep his dreams and steps small, perhaps taking on a few more hours at the greenhouse. She emphasized that the important thing now was to reduce stress and build positive people skills. He revealed that he was embarrassed by living in a trailer near the greenhouse, the only place he could afford. It was something he never thought he would "sink to." This disclosure gave the worker a chance to help Michael share more of the shame he felt for problem drinking, and to validate the strength he was showing in working his way back slowly. She then wondered about a career as a greenhouse man for himself, since he'd taken to the work but never seemed to think of it as valid employment. She mentioned her own love of gardening and some courses she'd enjoyed taking at her local greenhouse.*

Miller and Rollnick disagree strongly with longstanding worker definitions of motivation as something *the client* has or feels inside. Instead, they define motivation as *worker and program activities* that increase the probability of a client's behavioral change, and they suggest techniques for motivational interviewing, instead of focusing on the presence or absence of motivation in clients (see the discussion in the next section on changing behaviors). They point out that clients who *appear* unmotivated at a given time or with a given worker or program may go on to change behaviors with the help other workers or programs. Some clients might even be able to change on their own, given the proper moment, circumstances, advice, and support.

A central focus of motivational work is to discern and amplify even the smallest part of a client that recognizes a problem and a need for behavior change, in order to provide what Shulman (1999) calls "a handle for work" (p. 101). This discussion often begins with an exploration of what is and isn't working in the client's life. Client statements about what isn't working may provide a focus for behavioral change work.

Working on Relationships

Clients often note problems in relationships, or the problem of having few relationships to count on, as part of their agenda for work. Poverty, for example, often brings extended families together for mutual assistance with child and elder care and transportation to school or work, but its grinding effects often leave people too tired, depressed, or discouraged to enjoy life's renewing pleasures together for very long at any one time (Organista, Dwyer, & Azocar, 1993). Family members may be absent for long stretches of time while working more than one job, in order to pay for basics and to provide additional support for loved ones living abroad, education of children, or expensive medications for ill members. Members often pass in the night, with mosque, church, or temple participation as their chief social outlet and support. For these reasons, family relationships sometimes bear the brunt of built-up tensions, especially if some members use violence or substances to express or mask resentments and despair.

Even when they want help with relationships at home, school, or on the job, it's understandable that some highly stressed and isolated families may feel incredulous that workers expect them to leave their overwhelming responsibilities to have a relationship with a stranger through a distant, unfamiliar counseling process when they barely have time to sustain relationships with the people they are closest to and count on most for help. Other families may simply lack the funds to pay for bus or subway fare, or be so embarrassed about their perceived lack of resources and achievement that they don't want to go to professional settings and expose themselves to expected judgment and misunderstanding from people often very unlike themselves. In instances of family disorganization due to mental or emotional illness, substance use, or domestic violence, no member may be organized enough to reach out for, schedule, or attend assessment meetings in order to identify needs and potential services.

In all of these instances, any relationship with a "noncommunity" worker often needs to be arranged by intermediate providers located nearer to clients in home visiting programs, neighborhood health centers, faith-based service centers, Visiting Nurse Associations, or school-based programs. Referrals often come from religious, health, mental health, legal, or educational colleagues who identify issues for further assessment and work as they carry out their own roles with families. Once invited in, worker outreach to identified clients has to be cordial, respectful, vigorous, persistent, and down to earth. Initial contacts with clients are often characterized by widely supported client suspicions that the worker has come to judge, lecture, or take something or someone away. While some families may come to treat their worker like a helpful relative, others may need to think of him or her as a revered wise person, and may be horrified to see the worker volunteer to perform a menial service like letting the cat out or helping move the chairs for a meeting while visiting them as an honored advisor.

Our strengths perspective must be demonstrated early and often by honoring with clients any obvious skills and knowledge they've developed in dealing with adversity (McMillen, 1999). Clients can be so tired and depressed that they forget that their "street smarts" are very valuable and admirable qualities-not in merely surviving, but in moving ahead and achieving more complex goals than previously imagined.

Work with Religious and Spiritual Relationships

Clients have been far ahead of workers in bringing to public and professional attention the enormous support that they and others find in spiritual and religious relationships with a god, goddess, or guiding spirit of their understanding; with spiritual healers; and with pastors, rabbis, imams, and larger faith communities (Cascio, 1998; Poindexter & Linsk, 1999). For example, Haight (1998) has found that spiritual socialization can be central to African American children's healthy development (p. 213). Research by Poindexter and Linsk reveals that many minority elder caregivers of HIV-affected persons derive unique support from spirituality when so many other resources seem to ignore, stigmatize, or fail them.

At the same time, very few agency assessment forms and protocols contain any reference to or questions about client beliefs about or use of spiritual resources in sustaining and enriching their lives, and workers often receive little or no professional education concerning the integration of spiritual matters into their practice. Meanwhile, community religious leaders, complementary medicine practitioners, and spiritual healers increasingly assume the calming, mediating, inspirational, and advice-giving functions once provided by professionals and elders or wise persons in many cultures.

Taylor, Ellison, Chatters, Levin, and Lincoln (2000) note that in the African American community, ministers are sometimes the first and only professional that individuals encounter, and that they give important support and counsel about wide-ranging matters, including serious illness and health care needs, bereavement, marital and childrearing problems, and distressing personal problems. Longstanding relationships, easy access to consultation, and receipt of free counsel through faith communities are viewed as important benefits of faith-based services (p. 75). At their best, these ministries *provide* relationships, *support* relationships between individuals and their families and communities, and *define and express* relationship through this presence, support, and array of services. The authors suggest a number of helpful linkages that workers can make with churches for purposes of crossfertilizing educational sessions and crossreferrals when the skills of a particular organization or mission makes most sense for a particular client.

Understanding how spirituality does or doesn't support or affect individuals and families must be an important part of intake assessment with clients. Organista, Dwyer, and Azocar (1993) found in their health work with poor Latina women that some women felt that health events were "God's will," some believed that prayer alone was sufficient to change things favorably, and others could resonate with the saying that "God helps those who help themselves" (p. 231). Use of prayer was encouraged in their work, and clients were asked to share contents of their prayers in order to distinguish those who expected God alone to alter their situations, and those who felt they were working as a partner with God to shape their destinies. The latter belief could dovetail nicely with a worker's framing of the clinical relationship as a partnership for work to shape new possibilities and outcomes.

Cascio (cited previously) describes a number of techniques that can enhance interested clients' sense of connection with a god, goddess, or the spiritual. For example, the gestalt technique of *conversing with an empty chair representing a spiritual presence* allows clients to sort through issues aloud with the power they most relate to, and then switch places with that power, assuming the imagined perspective of that power to address issues or questions raised. We can also help clients utilize sustaining metaphors related to Mohammed, Buddha, a god or goddess, angels, powerful spirits, or the like. Cascio recommends that clients develop images of these presences accompanying them at *all* times, not just at times of crisis. If clients wish it, time can be made for quiet or uttered prayer during meetings, and these moments of prayer do not have to be confined to deathbed grieving or hospice bedside work, although those can be excellent venues for joining in spiritual support.

> During my hospitalization for surgery, the woman beside me introduced herself as Haitian American and confided about a scary procedure she was about to undergo. She had called her minister to ask for support, and after supper, she asked a second patient and myself if we minded if her prayer circle came to comfort her and provide a service of support. It was fine with us, and after dinner the small group arrived, circled her bed, and all soothed her with their hands while they sang some hymns in Creole and prayed for her wellness. After she was rolled out for surgery the next morning, the other lady and I laughed about how we wished we had had a circle like that to come and comfort us. It turned out that we had both lain there silently participating in the hymns and prayers. There was a different quality of peacefulness we felt then compared with our feelings during the visits of worried friends and family.

In a study of Native American clients by the Native American scholar Weaver (1999), some respondents reported that they'd found that many non-indigenous workers appeared unhealthy and ungrounded spiritually, and were not positive representatives of the strengths perspective they purported to utilize. It may be the absence of focus on spirituality in clinical practice curricula that leaves workers unprepared and ill at ease in exploring and helping clients to develop richer connections with spiritual resources.

Imposing one's beliefs and practices on others is never appropriate. Students and workers often express a worry that talk of religion or spiritual practice will offend or distance clients, but this seems rarely to be the case. Those who aren't interested will say so, but many are used to people discussing alternative healing and spiritual practice from watching films and television, or from living with someone who practices a faith. It helps to explore with clients at some point whether they can use prayer or religious practice for support or to ward off feelings of isolation. At times of death or loss, it can also be very comforting to clients to have workers appear briefly at wakes or funerals or to come to the home or institutional bedside to say goodbye to client and family prior to an impending death.

A good spiritual assessment may also turn up instances in which clients have been harmed or excluded by faith communities. For example, there have been instances in which newcomer populations, individuals with mental illness, transgendered people, and people affected by HIV have not been welcomed into full membership or provided with the traditional supports and opportunities that others enjoy within faith communities (Canda & Phaobtong, 1992; Poindexter & Linsk, 1999). In other instances, some spiritual leaders have sexually abused members of their faith communities or enticed members into cult-like associations.

Connecting with Others Like Oneself

Relational norms, styles, and behaviors are usefully learned in support and educational groups, and workers can greatly help isolated clients by identifying local mutual aid or activity groups through which clients are likely to get support, information, and feedback regarding ideas and relating style. Whole families may wish to become part of groups such as AMI (The Alliance for the Mentally Ill), P-FLAG (Parents and Families of Lesbians and Gays), or MADD (Mothers Against Drunk Driving). In such groups, they can experience the exhilaration of acceptance and validation of their struggles as well as the warm support of continuous community.

Clients may have to search a little in order to find the right group for them; they may also wish to begin a group with a specialized focus if nothing is available, and may need the worker's help with publicity, ideas for screening members, understanding about possible group dynamics, and potential issues in group formation and maintenance. Sometimes clients initially form groups themselves, later seeking out a worker to facilitate some or all of their meetings.

Their auditioning of workers around goodness of fit is a healthy sign of self-regard and efficacy.

Working on Unproductive Thought Patterns

Derubeis and Beck (1988) suggest that faulty or distorted thinking is often at the root of unhappy feeling and unproductive behaviors, and that distorted or unsubstantiated thinking often occurs in three domains: *view of self, view of the world, and view of expectations or prospects for the future.* They refer to these three domains as a "cognitive triad" necessary to assess in understanding unhappy or unproductive thoughts and feelings. For example, the view of oneself as a "loser" can rapidly lead to depressed feelings. In turn, these feelings can fuel social withdrawal and a hesitation to seek out new people and opportunities. Resignation and social withdrawal can be easily misinterpreted by others as a sign that withdrawn people actually don't want contact, so that people quit reaching out to them. An absence of invitations to socialize can then be misinterpreted by withdrawn people as "evidence of being a loser, just like I thought." This thought can trigger a descent into further negative thoughts and feelings, perpetuated by personal misinterpretations and a lack of balancing experience or feedback. To break up this spiraling process, we have to counter one kind of logic with another. Reassurances ("You're not a loser, you've very nice to be with") usually bounce right off core negative beliefs, and are of little real use in reducing distortions.

At some point in work together, clients from many different backgrounds are likely mention one or more of the following ideas or experiences troubling their thinking:

- disrespect from other people who matter to them
- fear of rejection in social situations
- feeling like a fraud or pretender who will be discovered as deficient beneath an apparently competent exterior
- feeling unattractive or undesirable via one or more personal characteristics
- fear of failing or looking foolish in front of others
- thinking they have nothing to say or add, no valid opinions of their own
- feeling odd, different, or negatively unique in ways no one else could understand
- suspecting that everyone else is calmer, happier, "more normal," out there having fun while the individual suffers uniquely
- feeling hopelessly broken, stuck, or incapable of change

Work on such deflating ideas is based on the premise that, since ideas are socially learned and reinforced, they can be socially unlearned through corrective experiences that provide support, fresh feedback and information, validation of self and efforts, and gentle challenges to fixed negative beliefs (Beck, 1995). When clients frequently describe unhappy moods, low self-esteem, and negative self-talk, workers can try to get behind these "givens" to identify the deeply ingrained core schemata that engender these assumptions. Misinformation, distortion in thinking, and misinterpretation frequently dishearten and undermine people of all ages and backgrounds, so that work on irrational or distorted guiding ideas need not be confined to the formal practice of cognitive and behavioral therapies, but can be integrated into a variety of approaches.

Importance of the Worker's Ideas and Images

The worker's hopefulness about change often positively kindles and reinforces the client's willingness to persist in identifying and tackling ideas that are undermining comfort, confidence, and the capacity to act (Miller & Rollnick, 1997; Saleebey, 1997). Because worker optimism is crucial in change work, it's important that we examine the ideas and images *we* bring to our work with each unique client system. When agency and worker stress levels are high, negativism about clients and difficult work can be contagious, and can cause us to distance ourselves when working with people or situations that seem to promise great difficulty and complex service networking.

You may find that you share the mistaken notion that work focused on an individual's thinking is superficial or intellectualized, leaving his or her personality unchanged unless "deeper" or "longer" psychodynamic work is done. However, numerous theorists representing different developmental perspectives believe that personality and adaptive resources are grounded in and constantly influenced by core images and interpretations of the self in relation to others, as well as to prospects in the outside world (Beck & Freeman, 1990; Surrey, 1991; White & Epston, 1990).

According to White and Epston, "persons give meaning to their lives and relationships by storying their experience . . . in interacting with others in the performance of these stories, they are active in the shaping of their lives and relationships" (p. 13). We can regularly observe the phenomena our narrative constructions shaping feelings and activities. When people experience small successes—such as converting a negative thought pattern into a more positive, accepting, and guiding one—this change in the way they "story" themselves can lift mood and free energy for use in more creative and productive behavior within their daily lives.

TECHNIQUES FOR UPDATING
UNHELPFUL THOUGHTS

The old principle that "nothing succeeds like success" is key to working with ideas that disempower, for the more people experience their own strengths, effectiveness, and increased esteem in relationships and activities with others, the more likely they are to tackle new challenges with increased zest and confidence. Each small success has the potential to lift mood and increase hope for the future, as well as to heighten positive thinking about self and world.

Taking an Ideas History

When taking an initial history and reviewing the client's current situation for its strengths, connections, and problem areas, workers focus interest on the formative history of the distorted ideas themselves through such questions as:

- When did distorted or negative thinking begin to take hold?
- Who—or what events—may have reinforced them?
- What subsequent experiences seemed to "prove" these beliefs?
- What, if any, exceptions to them may the client have experienced?
- How aware is the client of the powerful negative influence of these ideas, and that others may not share his or her views?
- How ready is the client to struggle with stuck ideas, as opposed to trying to convince the worker of their special worth and validity?

We are careful to *store identified exceptions to negative certainties,* using these along the way to challenge unreasonable beliefs by reminding the client of acknowledged successes—even minor ones—that counter their "logic."

Apart from family of origin influences and personal developmental problems, many sociopolitical factors can contribute to negative or distorted thinking (Berlin, 1983). These include *lack of information or incorrect information* (for example, about the rights and benefits of newcomer populations), *social isolation due to migration from a safe base elsewhere* (fleeing home for safety but landing in an area where there is no one like oneself), and *socially conditioned and reinforced helplessness or passivity* ("In my culture, the man is the strong one and the woman supports him at all costs").

According to Berlin, unhappy thoughts can also stem from *racist or otherwise negative and oppressive constructions of personal or group characteristics or traditions* ("Religious fundamentalists cannot be unbiased counselors"), *negative myths and stereotypes internalized by individuals* ("As a person of color, I'll never be elected to national office due to racism"), and *lack of resources for advancement, especially due to socially imposed barriers to empowerment and achievement* ("Because we're poor, they'll never put a good transit line in here, so we can't get to good jobs on the other side of the city").

Factors like poverty, lack of information, and social barriers to achievement call for wider social action by workers in the larger systems, because clients's lives are imbedded in these systems (Gutierrez, DeLois, & GlenMaye, 1995; Swenson, 1998). Thousands of counseling clients also need advocacy, legal services, and skills training in order to position themselves differently in their environments, either in their current locales or in other ones that can welcome them and appreciate their presence in the neighborhood. People affected by other conditions—social isolation, internalized disrespect, and stereotyping—respond well to mutual aid and discussion groups in which members with situations or characteristics in common can challenge each other's mistaken beliefs and counter with stories of positive, self-affirming experiences and coping strategies (Nicholson & Kay, 1999; Saleebey, 1997; Shulman, 1999).

Identifying the Powerful Sway of the Negative

A first action step is to simply help clients appreciate the degree to which their lives are hostage to automatic negative thinking and withering self-reproach. Some know this but can't see a way out due to limiting realities. For example, a spouse might be trapped with a battering wage earner, having no other source of income or place to live. Others are surprised when the worker's gentle but repeated noting of patterns brings these vividly into awareness. This new awareness can bring about enough dissatisfaction to motivate further self-examination and efforts to change some negative images and ideas step-by-step.

> *Laurette, a successful artist who kept linking up to production people who were negative or controlling like her deceased mom had been, understood that this was an old scenario for her. Approaching her fiftieth birthday, she was furious with her "inability" to get out of the habit of involving herself in these angry, frustrating collaborations when she "knows" better. In a midlife reexamination of herself, she realized she didn't want to spend the rest of her life in struggles at work. She could see that her home life was peaceful, but her work life was curiously themed with repeated battles for respect from "haughty" people.*

Pausing Periodically to Examine Negative Ideas

After noticing a pattern of negative thinking in a client's story (e.g., "Real men don't cry," or "I can't make it without them"), workers can begin gently to interrupt the conversation occasionally to note a recurring pattern of negatives with clients—always with respect and curiosity, and usually noting only one pattern at a time, for the sake of clarity and depth of exploration. Cognitive theorists (Beck, 1995; Burns, 1989) have described a number of common distortions that appear in people's automatic thinking. These include *catastrophizing* events or possibilities ("The millenium bug will destroy all computer programs and documents, and nothing can prevent this"), *minimizing self positives and magnifying* shortcomings and missteps ("Anybody would have done the same thing, and wouldn't have waited as long as I did to come to the rescue"), *overgeneralizing* from one situation to another ("That poor grade in math means I won't do well in computer courses"), *all-or-nothing thinking* ("I must always play first string or I'll never make a college team"), and *should/ought thinking* ("I should do better than this in school in spite of working two jobs, and I ought to have done better last semester, too"). Clients often quickly begin to spot their own distorting patterns following regular reviews of these problematic schemas. These nonjudgmental reviews can also help decrease some of the embarrassment clients first feel when identifying and discussing automatic habits of mind.

Eliciting and Supporting Positive or Hopeful Ideas

It is easy to mistake clients' frequent negative thinking as the predominant thinking that they do. This isn't always the case, and shouldn't be assumed about people, just as clients shouldn't assume that because a worker discusses a client's diagnosis with her, it means that the worker pathologizes clients or concentrates on pathology. Many clients have been conditioned through use of human services to expect workers to concentrate on the negative or the "dysfunctional" aspects of their thoughts and experiences, in order to identify and apply remedies (a medical model of a sick or broken person fixed by a self-styled wise helper). These clients may not know how to focus on exceptions to perceived failures—those times or contexts in their lives in which they have had positive experiences and thoughts, no matter how briefly (Saleebey, 1997). Workers can help to alter this state of things by focusing instead on strengths and possibilities.

> I pointed out to Laurette that her conversation with me was laden with "shoulds," "oughts," and self-condemnations. She could see this, too, but couldn't stop herself from judging. She further judged herself for not being able to stop talking this way about herself. She could see this, too, and finally said, "Let's don't go there, this could go on forever." I agreed and just asked her to try not to judge herself, but to stick with her wonderful vision of "finding a new day" for herself. She proved able to make that switch because she wanted to so much.

DeJong and Miller (1995) describe specific interview questions developed by de Shazer and colleagues (1988) at the Brief Family Therapy Center in Milwaukee, Wisconsin. These questions look for exceptions to described failures and "stuckness," and can be used to elicit and exercise client strengths and resources instead. *Miracle questions* ask clients to imagine that, while they were sleeping, a miracle happened to solve their problems. Next, they have to describe what will be different when they awaken that will indicate resolution of the problem. How will they themselves behave, or experience life differently, and what differences will their changed experience or behaviors bring about in the people around or closest to them? How will the subsequently changed reactions of these loved ones then affect them in turn? These "how would that look?" questions help clients concretize imagined outcomes of their current efforts, so that these are easier to work towards and recognize as they evolve, step by small step.

Exception questions ask about situations or days in which "the problems" haven't happened: who or what things helped or improved the situation? What was different at that moment? When can those very people or things be brought together again in order to experience that positive difference again? What has been learned in these exceptional moments that might be transferred to similar moments and challenges?

Scaling questions ask clients to rank their confidence, beliefs, activities, or usefulness of their ideas on a scale of zero to ten (ten being the most useful or successful in problem solving). The worker uses any increases in ranking to build towards more work; for example, using an increased belief in self to explore how that increase was achieved and how those strategies could be repeated again.

Coping questions focus clients on how they have gotten where they have today, given the chronic adversity of their circumstances: "How have you

managed (or survived), given all that you're up against?" The client will usually note something that keeps them alive when they think all is finished; for
example, kids, prayer, or a cousin who counts on them. The worker can then
explore these activities or relationships to emphasize their power and meaning in the client's life.

What's Better? questions search for anything that may be improving, but
remains unmentioned as the client describes continuing problems: "What's
changed as we've been working together?" may have to be repeated several
times in the work to get the client used to noticing nuances or small details
that are better, recognition of which can build confidence as well as skills for
further problem solving.

Gentle, Respectful Challenges to Stuck Views

There are many ways a worker can question the client's view of self, world, and
prospects for the future. We can ask simple questions such as "What makes you
think that?", "And your evidence for that is . . . ?", or "Really? You believe that
about yourself?" A hint of mild disbelief in the worker's tone signals that already,
the worker is surprised by the point of view and doesn't automatically agree
with it as the client may have expected. Workers can also challenge the client's
perspective by suggesting early on that ideas expressed are just perspectives or
points of view, not concrete, inarguable facts. As such, they are subject to
review and evolution as we mature and our knowledge and circumstances
change. Clients can be helped to see that their ideas are worth discussing with
others, in case there are other interesting ways of thinking about things.

> *Niecie said it was her fault that she was date raped because she shouldn't have
> stayed so late and drunk so much. Her worker asked her if it was her view,
> then, that a girl is 100% responsible for preventing sexual assaults. Niecie
> replied that she had also worn tights and a miniskirt to the party, which was
> "enticing." The worker asked if she was the only girl at the party dressed like
> that, and she thought back and remembered several girls in outfits like hers. The
> worker asked if all the girls in miniskirts had been raped that night. Niecie said
> that she was the only one. The worker then asked again if anything else was
> leaving her blaming herself so much. The client began to cry and confided that
> two years earlier, she had had an abortion and someone had called her a slut,
> and she still had that on her mind a lot. On further questioning, she remembered
> her mother telling her often, "It's the boy's role to try; it's the girl's role to
> prevent." By drinking, she believed she didn't "do her role right."*

Workers can also ask clients to think about whether anything else could
account for a situation. With Niecie above, the worker might ask: "Could anything else have caused the assault besides your 'asking for it' or 'failing to prevent?'," or "Are there any other ways we could understand this assault?" Often
clients have already heard—or asked themselves—these searching questions, yet
have dismissed them as meaningless because of their own overdeveloped sense
of personal responsibility in every situation. The worker specifically chooses the
word "assault" to emphasize a countering viewpoint that Niecie is the victim of
an unprovoked attack, and not the inciter of an act of adolescent passion.

Assigning Homework

Homework encourages and supports carryover from sessions by engaging clients in further activities related to the increasing of awareness and to the rapid blocking of negative thoughts. They may be asked to fill out logs recording triggers for and consequences of bouts of undermining thinking. They might journal about experiences that left them feeling badly about themselves or their prospects. They might be asked to try to speak with someone who makes them feel diminished, and ask for different responses. These activities are then reviewed with the worker in subsequent meetings, examining patterns and reactions together, and reinforcing any efforts to strengthen positive actions (Beck, 1995; Hepworth, Rooney, & Larsen, 1997).

Providing New Information

Another helpful technique in working with stuck negatives is to counter distorted thoughts with new information. While continuing to work on repercussions from the assault, the worker above could also work with Niecie around an informational pamphlet or age-appropriate video, educating her about the frequency, dimensions, and effects of date rape, and helping her be clear that what happened to her is legally defined and punished as statutory rape. The worker might link her with a support group of rape survivors who are gaining new understanding through mutual sharing of ideas and provision of emotional support and reassurance. It can be powerfully mind changing for clients to realize through group exchange and validation that they are "not the only one" as they'd imagined. Such isolation can be very stigmatizing and lonely (Corey, 2000; Shulman, 1999). Support and understanding might empower her to testify in court much more confidently, and to feel less guilty about breaking the mold of her family's construction of "the girl's role" in sexuality and in gender relations.

Making the Personal Political

Often when less despairing, clients begin to notice clearly how much the systems they operate within contribute to their views of self and prospects as limited or hopeless (GlenMaye, 1998; Sue, Ivey, & Pedersen, 1996). This noticing often awakens people from a kind of sleepwalking acceptance of life as it is and has been, stimulating them to reexamine their beliefs and roles. Often this reexamination moves them to work with others to change the way people and organizations view and treat them.

Weaver (1999) believes that the worker's own ideas and perspectives can be an important source of both help and hindrance in working with indigenous populations such as Native Americans. She urges us to "decolonialize" our mindsets, acknowledging that Native Americans need services, "not as a handout or moral obligation," but because land and rights were taken from them during earlier periods of colonial subjugation that defined them as inferior.

Respondents in her study repeatedly mentioned the need for nonindigenous workers to be healthy, positive people, to accord greater respect to Native American clients' values and skills, and to "contain" themselves through respectful listening, tolerance, patience, and containment of urges to speak and act, understanding that "generations of oppression take time to change" (p. 21). Weaver's work is another reminder that oppression often creates unhappy or troubling thinking that is *not* "distorted" or "irrational," for which the best remedies are the collective struggle for social justice and equitable distribution of opportunities and resources for all people.

Teaching and Modeling Self Empowerment

The worker and Niecie might role play to practice different ways of "saying no" (a very difficult skill for status-conscious teens), and teaching her positive self-talk and self-affirmation strategies to counter negative automatic self-evaluations. They could also use role play to reenact and study the sequence of events the night of the party, in order to clarify the client's useful and less helpful ideas and behaviors as time passed.

As long as clients blame themselves for situations beyond their control (poverty, lack of child care, distance from employment opportunities, silence when subjugated), they may not allow themselves to express appropriate anger about injustices worked upon them by more powerful people and systems. Justified but suppressed outrage and sadness can affect health status, self-respect, future vision, achievement levels, and relationships.

Showing Confusion or Bafflement

Another helpful technique is to react to illogical statements with kind puzzlement: "Could you pass that by me once more, please? I don't understand how you came to that conclusion." Here, the worker makes it clear in reacting that the client's idea doesn't make sense to an otherwise accepting and supportive observer. Even though clients may argue vehemently in support of their own views, these are likely never to ring quite as true inside once a respected other person has shown surprise or confusion upon hearing them.

Pursuing an Idea to Its Illogical Extremes

Sometimes we can help to jar stuck thinking loose by verbally pursuing its illogic to its extremes. For example, the worker might ask Niecie if she dresses at other times the way she dressed for the party at which a man assaulted her. She will likely reply that she does, and when she does so, the worker can calmly ask whether these clothes have caused other men to assault her. Following the likely reply that they haven't, we can contrast this finding with Niecie's expressed idea that the way she was dressed "caused" the assault. We might ask her to check with other women who routinely dress as she was dressed that night, to see if they have been assaulted while dressed that way.

We try to stay as close as possible to the client's own use of language and metaphors, even though we mightn't use language except for the purpose of challenging a demoralizing stuck idea. Although the worker might not use the word "slut" like Niecie did, she can usefully go back to the client's use of it and explore the word's longstanding meaning and power in her thinking and the way it's reappearing now. Worker challenges are only made when in the client's best interest, and are expressed with caring and kindness.

Sharing Alternative Perspectives

It's also possible to loosen stuck and distressing ideas by directly encouraging clients to think about the worker's and other people's different opinions, or "takes," on a situation or set of reactions. Already, the worker has told Niecie that the legal system can define what happened to her as a crime, statutory rape, with the man held entirely responsible, since witnesses have come forward to testify in her behalf. The worker can agree that while inebriation may have put Niecie and others at risk for exploitation, it didn't give others free rein to exploit them.

> *Les told me that one of his teachers had told him that there might not be a place in clinical practice for a person with a learning disability that made him a poor speller, since writing was such an important part of the role of a worker. This left him so discouraged that he was afraid to ask other professors for extensions on papers, fearing to hear the same thing. I told him that I knew from my university liaison work that his university had an extensive program for people with disabilities, and that one of his rights was to receive extra time to complete his assignments. I also said it was inappropriate for a social work instructor to predict his career success based on spelling alone, when his participation at the school so strong. He said he was too afraid to give the instructor negative feedback now, but that he would do so before he graduated, when his grades were all in.*

Reframing

Sometimes a picture looks a lot better in a new frame that brings out or emphasizes a different or previously unappreciated aspect of the work. In the same way, a worker can reframe a client's ideas so that they are interpreted or experienced more positively. For example, the client might say, "I get so nervous here, I feel like the Queen of Wimps . . . I know by now you're not about to harm me." The worker might say (to the client's surprise), "Of course you're nervous here . . . so many people you trusted along the way seemed nice but ended up hurting you. Why wouldn't you be nervous? Give yourself time to see how you experience me . . . it could be that you're really the Queen of Wise Carefulness when in the presence of a stranger."

Reframes often evoke from the client a "Hmmm . . ." response—a reflective moment of taking the worker's ideas under consideration, while not yet agreeing entirely. The seed is planted, though, and the worker can repeat this response any time the client makes only one (negative) interpretation of his or her story.

Substituting New Metaphors for Old Ones

A metaphor is a guiding image that represents or stands in for something else, as in "All the world's *a stage*," or "He's *an accident waiting to happen*." Clients often share metaphors of self, sometimes without realizing the power of language to influence perceptions of the world, their prospects, and their psyche. "I'm a tough nut to crack," and "I'm a pain" are examples of self-sticking metaphors that can undermine confidence. The worker in the previous example shifted the meaning of the "Queen of Wimps" metaphor, so that the client could begin to understand that there are many life situations in which vigilance and holding back are valuable commodities. She plants in the client's mind the idea of "wise carefulness" as a potential revised interpretation of the nervousness the client experiences as they begin to get to know each other.

"Stop" Procedures

Especially in instances in which clients can't get negative ideas out of their minds easily (for example, anxious or self-defeating ruminations on failure or personal defects), workers can teach and model thought blocking strategies (Beck, 1995) for use both within and outside meetings. A mental focus on relaxed breathing, and the pathway and process of the breath, can be taught and practiced with the worker coaching the mental process at first, then calling for the client to focus and verbalize the passage, process, and effects of calmed breathing.

Breathing can then be coupled with immediate visualization of a stop sign, a door shutting, or a TV remote clicking off. The worker then coaches the client to let these images of closure screen out all other thoughts or concerns. At a later time, peaceful images of oneself in a safe and affirming environment can be elaborated in detail out loud, coupled with calm breathing (Borysenko, 1987).

Clients can also be taught to interweave breathing and imaging strategies with an inaudible "Stop!" command, to remind themselves to break the circuit of automatic self-undermining thoughts. Workers can narrate audiocassette tapes of these procedures, including the worker issuing the "Stop now, and go to your breathing" request in a way that is kind but memorable, so that it can be internalized as a future self-skill if the client wishes.

Crediting Self

It's not always easy for people to give themselves credit for progress, successes small and large, or mastery of new strategies that update older, more undermining ones. It's therefore important for workers to give verbal praise and credit for hard and good work done, at the language level each particular client finds appropriate. Teens and young adults may respond well to "high fives" or verbal praise ("Way to go!", or "Yes!"). Younger kids may enjoy putting stars or stickers on a page or chart indicating achievements or task completions. Adults may enjoy being told directly that they are trying hard and are doing a good job. Workers can amiably remind clients where they started and where they've come, and can share genuine admiration in witnessing clients examining and guiding themselves more effectively—therefore feeling more positively about self and world. We can also voice pleasure in seeing clients' relationships and desired skills taking hold in empowering and satisfying ways.

Working with Feelings and Behaviors

Thoughts and the sociopolitical environments in which they are kindled are obviously not the only sources of problem behaviors or troubled emotional reactions and states. Workers must also ask about any special family genetic or biological factors, complications, or injuries that may have affected and shaped the reactions and behaviors of people. Individual temperaments and stimulus thresholds vary, and can be greatly overloaded and compromised through domestic violence, substance abuse, and other traumatic life experiences. A good assessment takes all of these biopsychosocial factors into account when hunching about factors contributing to current thoughts, feelings, behaviors, relationships, and overall capacity to interact beneficially with one's environment (Saleebey, 1992).

As noted previously, work on cognitive distortions can in and of itself greatly free and empower clients to feel and act more positively and to design and carry out small changes that favorably impact their own and others' lives. This work can also be effectively knitted into a working agreement and plan that focuses on the client's significant developmental history and relationships (McQuaide, 1999; Sharf, 2000). While we can't alter the past, we may be able to frame and interpret it in new ways, calling on current client skills that were unavailable or discouraged at earlier life stages.

> Bonnie had been driving on an interstate when a truck veered into her lane and cut her off. She swerved left in order not to be hit. Her small car went off the road, rolled over several times, and landed upside down in a ditch behind some shrubbery, where it was hard for others to see it. The friend riding with her died on impact. Bonnie was unable to move because she was strapped in upside down. Many years later, the main thing she could recall was her subsequent rejection by the members of the college church group she belonged to, who felt her driving must have caused the death of the friend, the group's leader and favorite. Bonnie was instantly persona non grata—a huge loss and stigma for her at a lonely time in her life. We were able to relate the group's rejection of her to her own sense of guilt for talking while driving, leading her to blame herself for her friend's death. As we worked to challenge these fifteen-year-old ideas, the realization evolved that her parents had been very critical of her and left her alone a lot as a child. She grew up self-doubting and shy with peers, usually expecting to be criticized and left alone. These experiences left her primed for self-blame for the highway accident, although on close review, her driving had been attentive and well within speed limits. Once she recalled that she had not been responsible for the accident or her friend's death, work focused on expression of anger towards her overly demanding parents and her harshly critical and rejecting church group.

White and Epston (1990) note that power disparities and interpersonal intimidation cause some personal narratives to be "subjugated" to other versions of one's story and core sense of worth. Bonnie's story illustrates how attitudes and demands of her parents and her primary reference group in college caused this lonely young woman to focus her narrative on unjustified self-blame and to live this blame out by undermining herself in a number of domains so that success (rewards) would never be hers due to her "badness." Work with her involved a real coauthoring of a new "self-text" that included a more honest analysis of her upbringing and its influence on many later incorrect assumptions and despairing feelings.

INTEGRATIVE TECHNIQUES FOR WORKING ON FEELINGS AND BEHAVIORS

The work with Bonnie integrates a number of theoretical perspectives and strategies in a way that frees and empowers the client to see and feel differently, as well as to take new action that is more self-fulfilling and connecting with others again. *Cognitive work* on distorted ideas of self-doubt and blame began in the present, focusing on the client's presenting experiences of unhappy go-rounds with critical fellow employees at a design house. Exploration for the history of self-doubt and criticism revealed the *psychodynamics* of a lonely childhood of many house moves in this and other countries, and the severe criticism of a shy daughter from parents who were opinion leaders in their own fields and expected their child to be a little articulate and gregarious "adult" by preschool age (a *focus on family system role pressures and parental modeling of behaviors expected of girls and women*).

For Bonnie, recalling frightening illnesses and isolation as a child intertwined with revisitation the twin traumas: the dreadful highway accident and the expulsion from the church group, the very support network she would have otherwise turned to for comfort and reassurance following her friend's death (*psychodynamic exploration and ventilation of suppressed traumatic experience and reactions*). Each unfolding of a life event was accompanied by discussion of strengths developed or manifested within that event, and of feelings and interpretations distorted by it that required updating (*a strength-based perspective*). Recalling these strengths—as well as acknowledgement of resilience in the face of great adversity—encouraged her to think she could express to access her anger more directly and use it more constructively with her coworkers and family members (*cognitive rehearsal of anticipated encounters*).

Throughout the work, there would be periods of quiet mourning for people and opportunities lost, and for a childhood interrupted by inappropriate demands to "hurry up and be a grownup" (*grief work*). For her own safety, the client was encouraged to confine her frequent road rage to expressions in the session around the traumatic highway accident; to conversations in her mind with the man who cut her off, and to imagined dialogue with her church group members, insisting on their compassion (*restructuring of behaviors*).

A very loving new husband's acceptance and belief in her provided a "corrective emotional experience" (*lucky coincidence!*) to buoy and soften her. At the same time,the worker encouraged her to believe in herself and take on new challenges with money her husband lent her as start-up funding (*cognitive shift, dynamic change*). Utilizing a *group perspective,* the worker remembered the importance of the client's membership in groups when younger, and she encouraged the client to seek out group experience in the present in spite of her traumatic expulsion from her religious support group following the accident. No single aspect of this work was more helpful than any other. The blending of all of these perspectives produced a synergistic effect.

Several other techniques have proved helpful in helping clients work out problems with feelings and behaviors, some of them illustrated in the work described previously with Niecie and Bonnie.

Ventilation: Encouraging Safe Amounts of Expression

One of the oldest techniques in counseling is the invitation to ventilate or express strong emotion a bit at a time, so that clients aren't overwhelmed by pent-up feelings as they emerge. A corollary of the psychoanalytic "talking cure" has been a belief that identifying developmental traumas and losses, and venting bound up emotions associated with them, can increase internal calm and insight (Mitchell & Black, 1995). Ventilation is also expected to free up energy for healthy current pursuits, energy which, previously, would have been expended to defend against painful memories and feelings. Clients can experience relief through expression of feelings so long as ventilation is safely tracked and modulated, and clients are not retraumatized by emotional flooding or the too sudden reexperiencing of catastrophic events (Herman, 1997; Krupnick, 1997).

To assist with ventilation, we can use familiar techniques of open-ended exploration and reflection on current and historical themes raised or suggested by the client. We provide emotional support during feeling expression utilizing minimal empathic sounds and prompts ("Yes, Just let it come," "Try not to censor," or "Try not to fight your natural feelings"). We can also universalize on the hesitation so many people feel about sharing more deeply with a relative stranger, and honor the client's willingness to try.

Some clients' feelings have been frozen inside for so long that they can't find them easily, or when they do, tears don't flow and the face remains expressionless, even while they describe terrible things that have happened to them. Sometimes parts of their humanness *have* been buried for self-protection, and the dynamics of such a process can be briefly explained and honored as a survival strategy. It helps to explain to clients that expressing feelings can start with just describing what someone in his or her culture might feel about a situation just recounted. Real tears often return when experience and feelings thaw out through very gradual and safe review of events and reactions—*if* the client views tears as culturally and personally appropriate.

I was teaching in an area populated by many Cambodians reestablishing themselves here after the Vietnam war. A twenty-eight-year-old Cambodian man who'd been through the Cambodian holocaust under Pol Pot asked to speak to me after class one night. He said that our reading about trauma had caused him to have his first feelings since leaving his country, and he wanted to talk with a Cambodian counselor, but was afraid that he would "go crazy" if he ever began revealing what he'd witnessed and endured. He said that he'd seen a friend of his here start to remember, and he ended up in a mental hospital. The student feared this could happen to him, too. But he was starting to cry while driving and was having some nightmares, so he agreed to see a male Cambodian counselor we knew locally, to talk some things out very slowly.

Discussion to Identify, Differentiate, and Manage Feelings

It's important, though, to remember that they way we register and express reactions may be light years away from the way clients do within cultures other than our own. It helps to ask clients what members of their culture would encourage as reactions if they were present for this discussion. For some, no feeling response at all may in fact be the most culturally aligned response, and workers must respect that and move on.

Sometimes it helps to look at pictures of people expressing a range of emotions, using these to discuss emotions clients have felt from time to time. Children often respond well to a viewing a page that has many faces drawn on it, each expressing a different emotion such as "mad," "happy," "excited," or "worried." The child can point to the face that represents something he or she is feeling at the moment, and then can use paints, pencils, finger puppets, toy figures, or clay to further express inner experience (Webb, 1999).

Practicing Containment and Soothing of Feeling

Some clients express their feelings excessively or without appreciation for context. They might start to sob on the street or in the middle of a department store or bus station, speaking out their story to random passersby. They might feel angry at a perceived workplace slight and begin to make anonymous threatening phone calls or gestures towards the supervisor who offended them.

It's important early on to offer them calming and redirecting strategies for those times when strong feelings overwhelm a client's capacities to contain them. Once an atmosphere and bond of respect and trust have been established, clients can be surprisingly willing to learn containment and also to practice its forms with the worker. Often they describe having grown up in overly stimulating environments full of excessive behaviors, in which the only limits imposed were brutal or shaming, and with no calming and soothing offered.

Containment strategies can include immediate attention to relaxed breathing and counting to ten while concentrating on the look and sound of each counted number. Clients can imagine provocative situations, evoke "in the moment" reactions to them through rehearsal, and practice breathing to calm reactions. Over time, these positive behaviors should become more automatic.

Quick and successful use of helpful strategies is reinforced by worker commendation and noting of improvement in skill use.

Clients are also given encouragement to avoid or disengage quickly from emotionally triggering situations whenever feasible, in order to stay cool or cool down while strategizing alternatives in their heads, calling the worker, calling a friend or sponsor, and the like. They can be invited to journal provocative experiences for later review, talk about them into a cassette recorder or journal, or e-mail the worker about distressing situations, noting how successfully blocking and countering strategies were applied.

Educating About Triggers, Feelings, Behavior Chains, and Consequences

Clients may not be aware that upset feelings or thoughts precede their troubling behaviors. They may believe instead that they "just have" their behaviors and reactions and get caught up in them or lost in them. Some will say, "I got so upset that I just couldn't think, and I hit her, and I felt terrible about it, but it was too late by then." Others have grown up in environments in which key figures behaved impulsively, irrationally, or in out-of-control ways, modeling a random, disorganized, or unpredictable style that clients have assimilated as their own, and carry out without thinking about possible consequences. If clients once belonged to gangs or posses as teens and young adults, they may have normalized impulsivity as a survival skill. If group members validated their reckless behaviors as being "successful," these inclinations can become even further ingrained (Molidor, 1996).

A focus on goals and client strengths provides the perfect lead-in to a discussion of any recent behaviors that the client feels may have put his or her goals at risk: a fight with a partner or boss, excessive drinking that used up money for school loans, or a threat to use a weapon on a neighbor. The worker elicits the client's account of that episode and his or her feelings about it *now* ("I feel terrible, I swore I would never hit her again"), appreciating the authentic pain and remorse that many clients feel about rash actions that undermined potentials. The client is then asked to try to remember the trigger event, the thoughts and feelings arising automatically from that event, the resulting action taken, and its consequences. Worker and client then study antecedent feelings and thoughts in detail, eliciting clarity as much as possible. Statements such as "She's dissing me," "I'll look weak unless I show her who's boss," or "Enough of this!" are common. Time spent on searching out triggering events, thoughts, and feelings is invaluable, because people often remain trapped in their actions until they can liberate themselves through recognition and constructive management of precursors.

Role-play simulations and rehearsals of optional things to say and do when triggered also help the client to gain confidence and skills through trial and error learning. The work on triggers and reflective responding is very akin to the teaching and modeling that goes on in AA and other mutual aid group programs, in which members share tips and alternative coping strategies, illustrated by examples from everyday life (Shulman, 1999).

Medication to Assist with Feeling Management

Early in assessment, people experiencing severe anxiety, depression, stress, and other destabilizing behavioral disorders should be evaluated medically for possible use of medication in addition to counseling.

Numerous well-controlled comparison studies since the 1980s have demonstrated that a combination of medication and counseling focused on enhancing self-efficacy and coping resources is highly effective in reducing depressive symptoms (Feldman & Feldman, 1997). As we work on management of relational or situational stressors, we stay in close contact with the medical staff overseeing use of medications, so that we all are aware of reactions, side effects, and any long range implications of continuous use of medications.

Listening for Problems with Substance Use or Abuse

Workers remember that substance use and abuse can be an important hidden contributor to the inability of some clients to rein in or modulate moods and behaviors that negatively impact other people. Initial and continuing assessment should include direct inquiry about the frequency and amount of drinking and other drug use, including use of so-called designer drugs and marijuana dependency that may have gone unmentioned by the client because of dependence, denial, embarrassment, or a wish to continue to use substances in spite of their effects on daily life functioning.

Client discomfort or irritation around the subject of substance use may be a clue that such use is an issue in the client's life. The earlier suggestions of Miller and Rollnick can be useful in assessing where the client is in the recognition and ownership process that must precede any real change process. Our motivation to respectfully persist in such discussion and assessment is an important factor in helping many clients recognize the effects of substance use on self, world, and prospects for the future. Amodeo and Jones (1997) suggest strategies for engaging in such conversations with persons from diverse cultural backgrounds.

Worker Self-Disclosure

We can at times help clients by briefly describing a behavior we ourselves worked on but found hard to change. Lum (2000) notes that self-disclosure has several levels, and can move from a minor revelation in engagement, to more intimate sharing as the work develops (p. 170). These disclosures show identification with client experience, and reveal a lived understanding of the client's struggles.

For example, brief sharing of anecdotes that illustrate survivorship and contain potential coping tips can be very helpful in work with lesbians who, for various reasons, cannot yet talk over important lifecycle decisions with their families of origin. They may be encouraged by the experiences and perspectives of a worker who's "been there/done that" (Dillon, 1999). Laird (1999) emphasizes the importance of the transparency of the therapist in this work so that her ideas are recognized as coming from her own knowledge and experience base and are therefore not more privileged in the work than the ideas of clients and others.

The important thing about self disclosure is that *it is for the client's sake, not the worker's*. Selective disclosure can have the positive effect, as Laird notes, of keeping the therapist and the therapy "close to the ground" of real world experience and normal human exchange.

Important Relationships Revisited

Patterns of feeling, thought, and behavior are generated in relationships along the life path, and then further refined and reinforced by experiences in here-and-now contexts. Through a dynamic process called "repetition compulsion," people may unconsciously reenact past traumatic relational scenarios with others in the present. In doing so, they are usually unaware that they are living out old themes and dynamics with people unwittingly selected because of their similarities with others who previously harmed or exploited them (Chu, 1991).

For example, a woman may become a sex worker with no awareness that her often abusive sexual encounters reenact sexual molestation by her mother's boyfriends over a period of several years. A man may choose a series of alcoholic partners with no awareness that scenes arising from his partner's drug dependence reenact aspects of his upbringing as the child of an alcoholic.

CONNECTING THE PAST, THE PRESENT, AND HOPES FOR THE FUTURE

On taking a relational history, the worker may see connections and patterns that can be explored together as the work unfolds around the drama of a client's current living situation and feelings of futility about ever changing things. The work can then move between present and past as it did in the work with Bonnie earlier in the chapter, helping clients ventilate feelings about their upbringing so that these are not all dumped into current relationships and mistaken for reactions to the here and now of the client's life.

Confining work entirely to the present can sometimes result in missing important stuck places that need airing with a concerned and empathic listener who can serve as a potential reinterpreter of events as well as of meanings attached to them. Without this work, people are liable to saddle their current relationships with many unresolved images and feelings left over from past events and disappointments.

> *Malik began to appreciate that all the anger he felt towards Tiffany was not just about her criticism of him. Once the grandmother who raised him died, he began to remember how critical she was of him, always putting him down because she thought he was turning out like Malik's dad, a man doing a life sentence for murder. She made fun of Malik in front of others, especially about his wanting to be a jazz horn player. He had known Tiffany was critical of*

the time he spent on the road with musicians, too, but he thought that would change as she got to know him. But he now thought of her as the spitting image of his grandmother, and would either fume, withdraw, or threaten to divorce her all the time. Once we began couple work, he could see that a lot of the anger he let loose on Tiffany was anger he had stifled all those years with his grandmother.

Another benefit to exploration of past relationships is that it often reveals long-forgotten helpers and heroes in the client's life—people who made a difference, and who helped the client feel good about himself and less lonely or hopeless. This could be a nun, imam, coach, neighbor, storekeeper, or playmate whose special approval and encouragement causes the client to beam in simple recollection of moments and times shared. These good feelings and fond memories can act as fuel for self-esteem and further efforts to change aspects of one's life that are unjust or unsatisfying. Angelou (1986) has written a beautiful autobiographical account capturing one such set of childhood memories of a woman—*Mrs. Flowers*—whose neighborly love and ministrations helped her emerge triumphant from trauma-induced mutism and despair.

GOING HOME AGAIN

It's not unusual for people to want to connect with their roots during this work. Adoptees often want to find their birth parents; immigrants and mobile city dwellers often desire to return to their countries of origin, previous homes, or old neighborhoods and to describe richly the enjoyment and sorrows experienced there. Clients can visit their birthplaces, graveyards, school playing fields, and the hangouts of earlier times in order to remember and reconstruct aspects of their stories using their "new eyes" and understandings.

For many years, Artie had held the death of an old boyfriend in his heart without being able to move on emotionally. His psychologist asked him to return to the town where the boyfriend was buried, go to the grave, and have several very plainspoken conversations about the way the boyfriend's risky behaviors led to his death at a very early age. Artie did this, and found himself shouting out angrily at the graveside about the way Gene ruined a lot of people's lives. Then he sat by the marker and had a huge cry for himself. A cemetery groundskeeper came over to ask him if he were okay, and he thanked him, saying that he both was and wasn't okay, but was all right. He went back a couple of times to repeat this process, and felt "really cleaned out" when he came back to town. He had held his anger in for twenty years, and it had often left him with a tight feeling in his chest that was now greatly relieved.

Pinderhughes (1998) movingly recounts her own painstaking retracing of her African American family roots, a search that answered questions about family secrets and cutoffs, and at the same time disclosed great family valor and resilience in responding to cruelly misshaping events and consequences of

THE MIDDLE PHASE OF WORK

slavery and racism. She frames this kind of revisiting as a healing correction of family myths and misrepresentations, and as an opportunity to experience one's own agency in restorying personal and family identity and meaning.

CONCLUSION

Effective work with clients involves provision of relational support and confirmation; activation of concrete services; and coauthoring a hopeful new client narrative through work on thinking, feelings, relationships, behaviors, and situational challenges.

A common mistake in working together is that of *selecting the wrong methods because we like or want to try them* regardless *of their appropriateness* with a particular client or situation. Sometimes we get too far behind or too far ahead of where the client is in resources, readiness, and determination to participate in change. We also unwittingly disempower people by saying or doing too much with or for them, and by emphasizing our knowledge at the expense of theirs. We may at times show impatience, lack of hope, and preference for certain changes over others, putting countertherapeutic pressures on clients without appreciating the way our actions exacerbate their problems.

The current literature on work with clients is replete with appeals for *us* to "get help"—to make an attitude adjustment that brings us spiritually and practically into more appreciative and knowledgeable alignment with clients. "Being where the client is" involves complexity and flexibility today, as clients are more diverse than ever, and a "one size fits all" mentality won't work. Akamatsu (1998; see the Recommended Readings of this chapter) argues compellingly that white workers must shed their fantasies that there already exists a "level playing field" shared by themselves and clients of color. She believes that clients and colleagues of color still suffer from marginalization and discrimination, and that we will continue to live and work as "two nations" divided by unequal privilege, burden, and risk unless we own and alter our parts in that marginalization.

EXERCISES

1. *Reflection.* In your journal, reflect on a change or two that you are trying to make in your own patterns or behaviors. Using Miller and Rollnick's change schema, assess the change stage you are in, as well as the factors in your environment that do or don't increase the possibility that you will make and maintain desired changes. Now think of a client who is ambivalent about change, and assess the change stage he or she seems to be in. Do you have any things in common in your efforts to change? In what ways can your observations about your own change efforts improve your work with clients? In your own successful change efforts, what factors have helped you maintain

changes rather than recycling in and out of them? Does your client have the advantage of these same or other motivating factors?

2. ***Small Group Discussion.*** In groups of three, develop some role-play scenarios in which distorted thinking or incorrect assumptions are causing a client to be excessively depressed or anxious when presenting for counseling. For example, a colonel sexually harasses a female army officer, who then seeks counseling. She believes that if she reports him she will be finished in the "old boy establishment," since fellow officers are likely to blame her or to not want to risk her discovering and reporting something in their own conduct. Choose your scenario, and then plan a five-minute client-worker role play using techniques discussed in this chapter to try to positively influence changes in the client's thinking, feeling, relationships, or behaviors. Two in the group can alternate interviewing the client when scenarios are enacted before the whole class.

3. ***Class Discussion.*** Discuss those aspects of the middle phase of work with clients that are coming more easily to you now, as well as those aspects that are still hard. As a large group, discuss the kinds of evidence that can help a client and worker tell whether the work is working or not in the manner or directions originally intended. If not, what can be done to alter course?

4. ***Instructor Activity.*** Assign reading about, and then facilitate a class discussion of, spirituality and its place in the community, in families, in educational programs, and in caregiving institutions. Consider together various reasons why so many people around the world today are using complementary therapies and spiritual practice to ease health and mental health problems, and why, by comparison, we often seem far behind the public in understanding, utilizing, and supporting these beliefs and practices. If you or other members of the class do not believe in integrating faith or spiritual practices into your work with clients, share your thoughts without silencing those who do, and discuss standards that would need to guide integration of these practices into one's work with clients.

5. ***Author Sharing for Further Discussion.*** A client of mine in her fifties had lost her father, husband, and nephew in short order, all people she adored. She had failed in a serious suicide attempt from which her cat saved her by mewing loudly at the door until someone came and found her. When she subsequently came for counseling, she was almost inconsolable with grief, and often I simply witnessed and supported her crying and her remembering all that she loved about these missing family members. She said at one point that she would never marry again because, while lonely, she would never get over her husband's death, and felt mad at God for taking all these people in this way. After a while I asked if she ever talked with her husband in heaven. She looked surprised and said that none of her friends or work friends had ever asked her that. She said she talks to him all the time, and that he comforts her, but that she gets so sad that she has to shut off the conversation. I said I was glad that she could talk with him, and that I believed in angels and their capacity to comfort and guide us. Maybe he was doing this for her now. She said she'd thought that her own beliefs like that were crazy, so she hadn't revealed her conversations with anyone. She went on to reveal some of the things they said to each other, much of it about love and loss.

I said that, picturing how much he'd loved her, I couldn't imagine him wanting her to be lonely and miserable for years to come. She was a little thrown by this, since she couldn't picture that, either. His particular generosity just made her remember him all the more as irreplaceable. I encouraged her to keep listening in the conversation to what he advised her. I couldn't believe he wanted her dead and with him now—something she sometimes wanted for herself. Eight or ten weeks later, she began to say that she didn't think her husband would want her to die either, because she still had her elderly mom and her cat to take care of, and the husband believed in taking care of loved ones. I said that a little further along in time, I wouldn't be surprised if her husband encouraged her to get out socially again and try to meet some men and women to lift her spirits.

Perhaps two months or three months later she started to play again in a small bell choir at church and really enjoyed that, having abandoned it previously due to her sadness. Her minister then introduced her to a widower whom she felt her husband would approve of if he could meet him. I wondered with a smile whether her husband had already met him, which helped her to laugh for the first time in a long time. When her old cat died, on her own she went out and bought two baby kittens "to keep me company"—a good sign of reinvesting in life, I thought. A year later she married the friend from church, a move she now felt her husband approved of when she visited his gravesite. She made sure always to compare her second husband somewhat unfavorably with her first one, so that Number One would always know that he would never be replaced and that she couldn't wait to see him again someday.

For Class Discussion. What various thoughts do you have about my work with this woman? What were my goals, and how did I go about them? What helped her to choose life instead of death? My disclosing my belief in angel guides was genuine, but some colleagues would say this was perhaps a self-indulgence rather than a client-centered move. What do you say? If you didn't wish to work the way I did, by what strategies might you help this client get to a similar place in her reasoning? How could you help this client work on her "anger at God for taking my husband too early"?

RECOMMENDED READING

Akamatsu, N. N. (1998). The talking oppression blues: Including the experience of power/powerlessness in the teaching of "cultural sensitivity." In M. McGoldrick (Ed.), *Re-visioning family therapy: Race, culture, and gender in clinical practice* (pp. 129–143). New York: Guilford.

Beck, J. (1995). *Cognitive therapy: Basics and beyond.* New York: Guilford.

Berzoff, J., Flanagan, L. M., & Hertz, P. (1996). *Inside out and outside in: Psychodynamic clinical theory and practice in contemporary multicultural contexts.* Northvale, NJ: Jason Aronson.

Canda, E. R., & Phaobtong, T. (1992). Buddhism as a support system for Southeast Asian refugees. *Social Work, 37,* 61–67.

Coady, N., & Wolgien, C. (1996). Good therapists' views of how they are helpful. *Clinical Social Work Journal, 24,* 311–322.

Corsini, R. J., et al. (Eds.) (1991). *Five therapists and one client.* Itasca, IL: Peacock.

Gluhoski, V. (1994). Misconceptions of cognitive therapy. *Psychotherapy, 4,* 594–600.

Haight, W. (1998). "Gathering the Spirit" at First Baptist Church: Spirituality as a protective factor in the lives of African American children. *Social Work, 43,* 213–221.

Johanson, G., & Kurtz, R. (1991). *Grace unfolding: Psychotherapy in the spirit of the Tao-Te-Ching.* New York: Bell Tower/Crown.

Madsen, W. C. (1999). *Collaborative therapy with multi-stressed families: From old problems to new futures.* New York: Guilford.

McQuaide, S. (1999). Using psychodynamic, cognitive-behavioral, and solution-focused questioning to co-construct a new narrative. *Clinical Social Work Journal, 27,* 339–353.

Miller, W. R., & Rollnick, S. (1997). *Motivational interviewing: Preparing people to change addictive behaviors.* New York: Guilford.

7

When the Work Doesn't Work

An irony in clinical work is that the more comfortable participants get in working together, the easier it is to make mistakes. With relaxation and bonding, it becomes easy to slip out of role without thinking, and say or do things we mightn't have earlier when carefully establishing a relationship and agenda for work. While relaxing does provide a positive atmosphere of ease and warmth, it can also bring out in us our old preprofessional habits of mind and speech that aren't always the most helpful for clients. We can identify these moments when we commiserate later with ourselves or colleagues ("I can't believe I actually said that," or "I can't believe I'm still doing that"). The following mistakes are representative of what can happen, especially when working with complicated situations, problems, feelings, and issues.

NOT RESOLVING IMPORTANT CONFLICTS
OVER PLAN OR METHODOLOGY

Sometimes during the contracting phase it's clear that the client and worker have some major differences about what should occur in the ensuing work. A client may apply to a neighborhood health clinic for meetings with a pastoral counselor. Finding none available near home, she decides to accept an "ordinary" clinician. Yet during assessment, she asks the worker repeatedly about spiritual matters, even though the worker shows discomfort or unfamiliarity with the spiritual.

This work will likely end in disappointment for both parties, since the worker has taken on a request for help that he's not really comfortable with or prepared for, and the client has wrongly assumed that any port in a storm is better than no port at all. The participants would do well to stop, reassess the goodness of fit between them, and try to find a way to link the client with a spiritual advisor from a local faith community, if no trained pastoral counselor can be found within a reasonable distance or timeframe.

NOT HELPING CLIENTS OBTAIN NEEDED RESOURCES

In their cognitive and behavioral group work with poor female African American hospital patients, Hatch and Paradis (1993) note that limited resources and social isolation frequently contribute to members' panic attacks. They wouldn't be able to attend psycho-educational group sessions if transportation, child care, financial coverage for the sessions, and attention to other pressing medical concerns weren't provided by the agency throughout the work. These findings are a reminder that mobilization of concrete resources can make all the difference in client selection and use of ongoing services.

GETTING TOO FAR AHEAD OF THE CLIENT

Getting too far ahead of the client in no way implies that the clinician is wiser or quicker. Rather, it refers to a clinician's suggesting interpretations or possibilities while the client is in precontemplation of these, isn't thinking of them at all, or finds them meaningless or untrue. There will be times when we want to put ideas and suggestions on the table to stimulate client reflection on alternative possibilities, but we always watch for the client's reaction with an eye to staying aligned with his or her perspective and timing.

OVERESTIMATING THE EASE OF CHANGE

Sometimes we can assume that because something comes easily for us and our friends and colleagues, it will come easily for most clients, with a little support and coaxing. When it doesn't, we can begin to think of clients as "resistant," and even try to stop working with them instead of trying to understand or work with them differently.

A student reported working with a ninety-year-old woman with mild dementia living alone in elderly housing. Until last year, she was a leader in activities there and spent most of the day socializing or enjoying herself with a neighbor downstairs. Then she fell and had to be hospitalized due to a small stroke. At that time her doctor asked her to stay in bed for ten days then resume normal routines. Ten days later, she remembers the prescription to stay in bed, but has forgotten the request to return to normal activities. First the student tried to coax and cajole the client back into going downstairs with her; then, to go with the nurse or the neighbor. Frustrated after ten weeks of trying, the student asked to stop visiting the client, who didn't seem to want to change. We took down the DSM and reviewed the salient feature of memory loss in dementia. The student was trying each week to enrich the client's thinking about activity, and the client could not remember either the lessons or the doctor's instructions a year ago. I suggested that the student try to get the same doctor to come with her to see the client and to give her a new prescription, verbal and written, that expected daily activity with others down in the programs room—the more the better.

This student's supervisor had gone over DSM with her in relation to brain impairments that often accompany dementia, and yet the student had proceeded on her own folk ideas that anyone will respond quickly and favorably to support, interest, practical advice, and modeling. Her behavior illustrates a stage of learning in which the knower's demonstration of expertise is more important to her than the client's unique situation and special needs (Reynolds, 1942; Saari, 1989). This student had been learning cognitive techniques in class and applying ideas about cognitive restructuring to a client who can't remember what's practiced. She needs to learn more about organic illness, and about the way change takes time, especially when a client has suffered cognitive damage.

SKIPPING THE MIDDLE PART

When workers have incomplete understanding of complex problems or are pressed for time, the mistake of "rushing to fix it" can repeat itself right through the entire developmental phase of work. This mistake involves our giving quick, simplistic advice before thoroughly exploring for more information, feelings, and implications when a client raises a question or issue.

Romeo said that now that he and Sandy are back together again, he doesn't know how to explain to her kids where he was all this time. I asked had he thought of just telling them the truth, that he had been seeing somebody else for awhile, but missed them all and decided to return. He said the teens shouldn't have a father figure who runs around, and he was thinking of saying he had had to take a second job and didn't have time for a family any more. I said the teens might not think that was such a hot reason for leaving them, either, and went back to encouraging him to tell the truth. He finally said he wasn't going to tell them anything: "Let Sandy do it, they're her kids."

Here the worker misses the opportunity to explore several important themes, including how it is for both Romeo and Sandy to be together again, and how the children are reacting both to him and to the idea of a reconciliation. What is bringing up the idea of talking to them about why he left? Have the children expressed feelings or raised questions already? Has Sandy? Have he and Sandy had a chance to think together about how to discuss this together with the kids? What does Sandy suggest? What are the origins of his feeling that kids should not have a father figure who "runs around"? Has he ever been on the receiving end of any such behavior, and if so, how was that for him?

Rushing to fix it is an easy mistake to make until we truly understand the complexity of the counseling process and the centrality of exploration within it. Once we have explored the story more fully, we can begin to understand its subtler aspects. Deeper understanding helps us appreciate why quick fixes suggested by friends, family, or neighbors haven't worked or even been tried out. Examination of interview process flow with a skilled instructor and watching seasoned clinicians interview are good ways to learn how to help clients unfold meaningful detail. These experiences also help clinicians avoid doling out simplistic advice that rarely helps and can make the clinician appear naïve.

STEERING AROUND TOPICS OR FEELINGS

Until you become comfortable with the full range of human experience, impulses, potentials, and frailties, as well as the full range of your own patterns and strengths, you'll likely find yourself detouring around some themes or feelings at times because of discomfort, perhaps due to family, cultural, or religious taboos. You may have been able to tolerate certain topics or feelings initially, thinking that anxiety about these would rapidly dissipate with work, only to find that it doesn't. On the contrary, both subject matter and anxieties may come up again and again in a jarring way.

The following is an example of a detour in the middle phase of work:

Client: I had a scary image of someone watching me from the next building.

Worker: Have you had any other upsetting images this week? They can be jolting.

Client: Yes, one of my priest screaming at me, "You make me sick!"

Worker: And what do you usually do when these images come up for you?

Questions can be mistaken for meaningful exploration when they're really just questions in a row. The worker above fails to explore the client's understanding of or reactions to these distressing images. Helpful clarifying questions might include: "Would it be okay if I asked you more about the image you had of being watched?" "Who seemed to be watching?" "For what reasons?" or "What about you did the priest say made him sick?" Clients may not know how to proceed with images or themes unless workers help them experience the beneficial effects of gentle, patient exploration.

NOT CHALLENGING OR CONFRONTING
THE CLIENT WHEN PROCESS IS STUCK

Egan (1998) notes the importance of challenging the client in order to "help clients develop the kinds of alternative perspectives, internal behavior, and external actions needed to get on with the stages and steps of the helping process" (p. 189). Shulman (1999) describes this technique as making a "demand for work": "the worker's confrontation of the client to work effectively on her or his tasks and to invest that work with energy and affect" (p. 44). This kind of confrontation should not be done when feeling angry or judgmental.

Sometimes workers avoid challenges or confrontations because they fear the client's anger or denial. Some people who don't like conflict avoid it at any price, becoming passive or silent in their work with clients, rather than treading on uncomfortable or uncertain ground. Yet some clients won't be able to realize their hopes and goals until they are helped to own and work on behaviors that cause problems for themselves or others. Such work is often stimulated by the worker's challenges to consider alternative perspectives that might lead to some behavior change. While workers try to remain nonjudgmental and accepting, Heard and Linehan (1994) reaffirm that acceptance should not be confused with agreement with or approval of behaviors that negatively affect others. Acceptance should instead be "understood as validation that acts have happened for reasons that can be understood, owned, and learned from, at the same time as change in behavior may be needed, as evidenced by negative consequences of the acts" (p. 62).

Egan asserts that respectful challenging utilizes a skill that we, too, need to internalize gradually as we practice it with others—the capacity to confront and challenge *ourselves* when things in us aren't moving along as they should (p. 189). Failure to challenge clients is therefore a disservice to them and to us, and highlights an aspect of our understanding and skill building that needs further development or refinement.

GIVING UP TOO SOON

Trial and error learning of new behaviors and coping strategies takes time, repetition, reinforcement, and tinkering with behaviors until they fit comfortably with the client's sense of style and self. Sometimes workers give up on a client just short of her succeeding finally in making an important change. At some point, clients may simply mention without fanfare that they finally accomplished the desired goal—for example, speaking in class though embarrassed by a speech impediment—long after the worker moved on to something else, feeling that the goal of speaking in class was too ambitious for now. It may be that taking the pressure and focus off of a goal for a time allows clients to pursue it with less fear of disappointing themselves, the clinician, or others.

PUSHING THE CLIENT

When all else fails, we sometimes think that if they just give a little nudge here and there, the client will move ahead from contemplation to speedy change. "Want me to go with you to the first Alanon meeting?" could sound to some people as though the worker lacks confidence in the capacity to follow through. Change can't be rushed, and it's very important that clients make decisions about action in their own manner and time. We may not see the results of discussions and strategizing during the time we ourselves have with clients, yet they may be able to make changes in the future based on ideas that began to hatch in our present work together.

USING INAPPROPRIATE
OR MEANINGLESS STRATEGIES

Clinicians can forget that convincing theories and strategies learned in educational programs, supervision, or workshops can't be generalized for use with everyone—especially when the ideas and materials are constructed primarily by and for European Americans, while clients served are from varied backgrounds, eager to learn from people more like themselves. Increasingly diverse client populations may not identify with, subscribe to, feel at ease with, or be engaged by social or psychological frameworks underpinning many of the services and methods developed for work with European American clients (Lum, 2000; Sue, Ivey, & Pedersen, 1996).

For example, the lifecycle theory that proposes the launching of children into school, work, or training at primary school age and adolescence may seem very odd to families who happily spend their whole lives together in the same dwelling and neighborhood, or to families in which children normally run the house while all adults work just to make ends meet. Providing therapy in English to a bilingual client may be better than providing no therapy at all, but we may miss many subtleties and emphases that can only be communicated adequately in the client's primary language. On the other hand, working with a client's spiritual healer or advisor to devise a cleansing or healing ritual to rid the person of a suspected curse might have very beneficial effects if we can be where the client is in a practical sense.

In their aforementioned group work with African American women with panic disorder, Hatch and Paradis further note that in one session, the members commented that very few African Americans appeared in the video clips or self-help material used in the group to learn about panic disorder and its treatments. Members said that it was very important to them to see someone like themselves who had recovered from panic disorder. The group leaders, both white, were able to respond to this complaint by bringing in an African American client who had recovered from panic disorder and was willing to talk with the group about her experiences.

An important notation here, however, is that *these otherwise skilled and helpful group leaders had apparently not anticipated the negative impact on the group of having only white people as facilitators and models.* The white facilitators didn't address racial differences at the outset, either—a focus that might have established a tone of respect and openness to further dialogue on that or other subjects of importance in bonding. The facilitators commented that "racial issues . . . were addressed by group members, who educated us about their unique cultural and sociological experiences"(p. 241). Many of us might make this same mistake ourselves, influenced by North American traditions of expecting nonwhites or newcomers to assimilate within European dominant traditions, rather than expecting ourselves to accommodate to the preferences and styles of richly diverse traditions.

Swigonski (1996) believes that workers have been "too often . . . content to look at culturally diverse groups as representing problems, anomalies, or victims for study and remediation," (p. 150) and that white workers particularly need to recognize the ways in which behaviors from within privileged positions may oppress other groups. In the panic disorder group example, it was oppressive for women of color coming for help with anxiety to have to spend the little free time and group therapy time they had *educating their "facilitators"* on the aspects of the African American inner city experience that can contribute to panic attacks. It was a great sign of strength that these women could voice their needs for more representative models and materials, and could still come to the program and benefit from it rather than dropping out—action that would have been easily justifiable.

SHOWING FAVORITISM

Workers sometimes provide more attention, response time, leadership roles, and opportunities for special contact to group, family, or club members they like better than others. Poindexter, Valentine, and Conway (1999) observe that this problem can arise in the distribution of time and resources in case management activities. They remind us that decisions need to be based on real needs and not on which clients are liked best or are more comfortable to be around.

They also suggest that clients are at times "dumped"—turned away or sent elsewhere without proper staff help in transitioning—because the agency or worker doesn't want to work with them, or they think another agency should instead (p. 156). "Lack of insurance coverage" has been proposed by comedians and political activists alike as an unacknowledged "diagnosis" that prompts financially strapped agencies and institutions to turn some clients away, even though they are urgently in need of services.

TAKING SIDES

A very important role in work with people is that of an "honest broker"—a multiply partial (rather than impartial) advocate who caringly represents all sides in a conflict and tries to work equally well with all towards compromises that include multiple perspectives in arrangements and problem resolutions.

We can fall into the trap of taking the side of a family or group member or agency colleague we identify with, thus seeming to stand *against* others who now perceive unequal power and privilege in action.

Siding can cause important participants in a work process to become angry, drop out of the process, and undermine it publicly. Taking sides is particularly easy to do in instances of domestic abuse evaluations, where labeling one member "the perpetrator" stigmatizes him or her and takes the focus off of other members or allies who may contribute to numerous problems in the system that help to destabilize it. We must ask ourselves how individuals labeled as "perpetrators" or "felons" will ever have any hope of altering their behaviors and prospects if professionals can't move beyond negative labels to extend non-judgmental assessment and treatment services within a caring and empathic relationship.

On the other hand, we realize that individuals who experience a worker as being on their side against a well-identified oppressor can gather much strength from that perceived alliance, and can feel protected enough under an umbrella of services to take first steps towards freeing themselves from oppressive circumstances and relationships. Agencies sometimes help to resolve such conflicts in care by constituting as an intervention team the least biased workers they can identify to carry out tolerant, compassionate assessment and to work with all members of a complex situation, so that all have a chance to benefit.

DEFENDING OUR OWN POINTS OF VIEW

We can be so taken with our own perspective and knowledge that when we offer it—often too liberally—the client's disagreement with it provokes a reexplanation or heated defense of it by the worker. This reaction takes the worker into a focus on self rather than an exploration of the client's reactions and thoughts when disagreeing. It also communicates a tilting of the clinician towards "my way or the highway" thinking.

USING STRATEGIES
THAT EMBARRASS THE CLIENT

When tired or burnt out on the job, workers can begin to say sarcastic things to clients or blurt out parts of their stories to other staff, violating confidentiality as well as embarrassing the client through the type of material shared.

A student recounted this episode about a boy who had to be wrestled to the floor of a residential treatment unit in order to contain his violent throwing of chairs and books at fellow residents and counselors when upset. The boy hurt his hand when he fell, and one of the male counselors smirked and said, "Maybe that'll teach you not to lose it again like this in the future." Another student reported that the week before, in the agency lounge where staff ate lunch, a worker did an imitation of her client's "crocodile tears." It turned out that somebody there knew the client and recognized her through what was said. That woman later told her friend what the worker said about her, which left the client feeling betrayed and disgraced.

Workers taking a group of residential or institutionalized clients out into the community for shopping, recreation, or task mastery (crossing streets safely, taking a bus, doing laundry) have to be particularly sensitive to privacy and tone of communication about learning levels or needs as they go about their public instruction in skills. Avoid sing-songy speech, shouted commands that other people wouldn't make to each other, and other behaviors that might embarrass clients or reveal work with them.

I recently showed a video to a practice class in which the worker in a behavioral program for adolescents with autism was combining verbal reinforcement with a treat as a reward for a teen's accomplishment of a set task. When the fourteen-year-old boy completed his task, the worker exclaimed in a singsongy tone, "Good boy! Nice doing what I say!" When the video ended, we all expressed concern that the words and tone used felt inappropriate with a developing teen, and in the real world, could expose him to ridicule by peers. "Nice doing what I say" could also set him up for exploitation in the community by people who might give the command, "Be good now . . . do as I say."

It's also disrespectful to take clients out with a coworker and then relate mostly with the coworker, talking about personal or staff matters rather than extending companionship and interest to the clients walking behind the staff. Lack of attention can also allow some clients to wander off and be scared or embarrassed later when they have to be found and dealt with by authorities, or through media attention given to their status and situation in order to elicit the public's help in finding them ("Local Mental Patient Lost on Trip to Beach: Have You Seen This Man?")

SKEWING THE WORK

Workers can make the mistake of emphasizing one element of problem solving work while leaving other areas unattended or only superficially touched on. Some colleagues like to focus on historical exploration and ventilation of feeling, while others prefer to focus on problem-solving tasks to be carried out by the client between visits, and still others like to work on helping clients change self-image and mind sets that leave them feeling hopeless and helpless.

It seems wiser to maintain a balanced focus on important areas of client functioning. These might include self-regard and esteem, mood and energy levels, maintenance of important relationships, spiritual practices and support, activities of daily living, parenting skills or concerns, work or educational responsibilities and barriers, bringing in enough money to meet basic needs; and making time for leisure and fun.

Balance in the clinical conversation is facilitated by rereading case notes over a brief period of time, noticing what hasn't been covered for a while. Sometimes clients get out of balance, too, especially during crises that rivet their attention on certain aspects of their lives or on certain needs or goals looming large. Attending to friendships or finding respite may seem impossible to them at those times, yet these may turn out to be the very activities that could renew their energy and spirit under stress. Your awareness of the importance of a balanced focus can play a critical role in helping your clients work with and think through a reasonable number of matters over a given period of time. In discussions regarding individual client strengths and needs, instructors can help you define what "reasonable" may look like in each unique situation.

PROVIDING INADEQUATE SUPPORT AND REINFORCEMENT

It's easy for workers to make the mistake of saying to a client, "Okay, try this, and let me know how it works . . . I'll be interested to see what happens," and then move on to other matters, forgetting to ask the client how a seemingly routine effort worked out. Changing the habits of years involves tackling one hard thing at a time, and receiving meaningful, age-appropriate reinforcement. Attention itself is a reinforcement; as is asking the client to report back in next session on efforts made and results obtained, making that kind of review an integral part of the planned agenda. When people know someone will be asking them about their efforts to apply a planned strategy for change, they are more likely to persist in activities of change—or perhaps cancel the next appointment if embarrassed by their inactivity.

When you meet with family or significant others to demonstrate or discuss with them how to support and reinforce someone trying hard to develop new behaviors or attitudes, don't forget that these supporters may also need reinforcement and support if the client's behaviors outside of sessions are burdening or frustrating them.

SCOUTMASTER BEHAVIOR

Some clinicians approach the work with clients like a scoutmaster, with a fixed plan for each meeting once goals are set. They become anxious or concerned if the client spontaneously introduces unexpected material, worried that this will derail the schedule and take up time that had been allotted mentally for exploring a predetermined topic. They may cover a number of topics in a businesslike way, but never linger long enough to plumb the client's thoughts or reactions more than perfunctorily. The worker guides the focuses and keeps time precisely, with little left to chance. No matter where the client is when time for ending comes, the worker will say, "I'm afraid our time's up for today," and start to get up to leave.

Clients who like a businesslike approach to problem solving will appreciate such a worker's structure and guidance, and may feel very helped by the end of the contact. Those who like a warmer, more mutually evolved process may drop away with no explanation as to why, and are often unable to describe what didn't work for them, since the worker was courteous, focused, and determined to help.

EXPRESSING UPSETS WITH CLIENTS

When tired, stressed, or overburdened, we may build up or express impatience, anger, or judgments about clients' attitudes or behaviors that feel unfairly attacking or demeaning. To regain a professional stance of empathy and positive regard, a good step at such times is to identify these feelings with an instructor or consultant, blow off steam, whittle away at any identified counter-transference, and proceed in more helpful ways with the client.

On the other hand, there are types of worker distress that occur naturally in response to human events. For example, someone might suddenly call you out of a client meeting to tell you that a friend or family member has suddenly died or fallen ill—news that causes you to be openly tearful or distressed in other ways. *Clients understand that life happens,* and most will be completely understanding and sympathetic in such situations, just as you would be with them. If needed immediately elsewhere, you can return to the meeting to explain your need to exit and your wish to meet again once the demands of your situation are better resolved. Such occasions actually give clients the opportunity to express their own caring and support for us if they wish to.

> *I recall a time in psychiatric day treatment work when a man we'd all tried so hard to support through a psychotic period jumped to his death while on a group trip to explore a new commercial center downtown. We got this news during a meeting and we all began to cry in front of the clients, who seemed pretty scared and numbed by the event. I remember a highly medicated man coming over to touch the shoulder of the center director as she cried, and him standing there by her, shifting from one foot to the other, while she got herself together as we all were trying to do. We promptly called a community meeting and apologized for our getting so upset. We also thanked clients for their sympathy at this time, and everyone discussed our shared shock and grief at the loss of this man. The clients talked about how glad they were to see that we were human, too, and to see that we would feel a loss if something happened to them. Then they discussed their own worries and questions about why people kill themselves.*

NOT DEALING IN SUPERVISION WITH
FEELINGS ABOUT A CLIENT

A high-risk mistake is the experiencing of an unusual degree of feeling for or against a client, without talking these feelings out with an instructor or advisor who can offer constructive suggestions for resolving them. Feelings of attraction, dislike, apathy—even repulsion—can build up and affect the alliance and the work itself. Mehlman and Glickauf-Hughes (1994) describe the hateful feelings that can arise in mental health professionals when clients behave in extraordinarily demanding or dependent ways or as "help-rejecting complainers and martyrs" (pp. 145–146).

Bridges (1994) discusses the sexual and loving feelings that can arise between clients and therapists. She believes that the "psychic urgency" of these feelings often prompts an initial clinician response of denial, avoidance, or limit-setting (p. 425)—all the more reason to review such feelings with a trusted advisor in order to head off the possibility that thoughts will be converted into unwise or destructive actions.

"SHOULD" AND "OUGHT" STATEMENTS

Hepworth, Rooney, and Larsen (1997) regard "should" and "ought" statements as "sermonizing" and "moralizing," real barriers to communication, implying that workers have a knowledge or capacity to handle things superior to that of clients (p. 183). A worker might say to a client, "Well, of course that would not have happened if you'd done what you were supposed to . . . you should have called me before striking out like that," or "You shouldn't talk to me like that, it's not respectful"—both a lecture and a label ("not respectful").

We can fall back on these behaviors under stress. These behaviors fly in the face of ethical codes that ask us to remain accepting and nonjudgmental, regardless of circumstances. A patient, open-ended style of questioning would be a more productive response in reviewing behaviors troubling to the client or the worker: "What got in the way of sticking with your plan?" or "What do you make of that, looking back now?"

MISSPEAKING

Misspeaking can take many forms, but whatever the form, it throws the client and the conversation off and can make the worker seem inattentive or uncaring. We may accompany the client to another service or agency and misremember or misstate the problems to be conjointly addressed, forgetting how many people with disabilities there are in the home, or whether the client has temporary eye problems or chronic night blindness. We can also misstate agency policy too optimistically, as when we naïvely reassure clients that the agency can pretty much always find a way to keep important groups running, or can always reduce fees when people are out of work.

Additionally, we can misstate the causes or sources of agency or team decisions, as when saying to a teen, "I guess *they'll* all be meeting later to decide about your weekend pass," when we also will be at the meeting, but we're reluctant to take the heat for participating in decision making. When we misspeak, discomfort about doing so often shows in our detached facial expression, averted eyes, or hemming and hawing around as we become unresponsive and detached emotionally from customary frankness and authenticity. Once misspeaking is identified by either the clinician or the client, an acknowledgment and apology is extended.

ENDING SESSIONS EARLY
BECAUSE THE CLIENT IS SILENT

Uncomfortable with long silences, workers can try to justify stopping early in order to end their discomfort with "just sitting there." In so doing, they wrongly signal the client that silences are not productive, that the worker is intolerant of them and has better things to do, or that nothing significant can be made of a silence—all incorrect messages. The worker's invitation to stop can sound very cordial: "Well, about ready to wrap it up for today?" or "If there's no more to be said today, shall we finish and pick up here next time?"

If the worker is lucky, this invitation to stop may jumpstart the client to stay and react to the worker's abrupt ending, or say more about the silence. Otherwise, the client may pretend that this quick ending is fine with him or her when, actually, the client is unable to speak openly with the worker about what is going on at the moment. Much content and feeling can be missed this way, and some people's silences may be a test to see whether the worker can truly share control and leadership with clients as verbally touted along the way. Shulman (1999) regards the technique of "reaching inside of silences" as a crucial one in which the worker thinks of silence as communication about client fears and taboos, and moves to suggest and explore possible meanings within it (p. 152).

THE CLIENT IS TESTING
AND THE WORKER DOESN'T SEE

Sometimes clients who lack self-esteem, or who feel they are a burden to the worker, will unwittingly test for the worker's feelings about continuing with them by saying suddenly that they think they should come less often or stop the work for now. While such thoughts could be due to exigencies of daily life, often they are a form of checking for the degree of a worker's concern and wish to continue work with the client.

After an exploration as to why stopping would make sense at the moment, many of us have made the mistake of saying something like, "Well, if you feel strongly about it, I don't want to hold you back or try to make you come in," only to see disappointment flash across the client's face. Sometimes the issue of stopping comes up when the worker is taking a vacation or must be away for a conference or other duties, almost as an unconscious wish to beat the worker to leaving. It can also arise when clients are at a particularly painful place in their personal work and feel a need for respite. It's helpful to try to relate a client's sudden wish to stop to aforementioned possibilities, or current themes that might trigger a retreat from the relationship or work.

BLAMING CLIENTS FOR FAILURES
IN THE WORK

It seems easier for some workers to blame the client for unresolved problems in the work than to carry out a rigorous self-inventory and methodological review in order to determine where our own inadequacies, lack of knowledge or skill, or poor match with the client may play a role in bumps in the road or unanticipated endings of the work. Egan (1998) notes the difficulty clinicians can get into when they don't have an integrated theoretical perspective guiding their work and thus "fly by the seat of their pants," unable to tell clients what therapy is all about "because they themselves don't know what it's all about" (p. 57). The resulting work can feel unfocused, uncomfortable, grasping at straws—not convincing, engaging, or memorably helpful.

Instructors, supervisors, course learning, and consultation with senior colleagues can be helpful in carrying out concurrent and retrospective reviews of cases that can help clarify responsibilities when things aren't going well with clients, or when the work seems to have accomplished little or nothing. Smugly writing clients off as "unmotivated," "determined to fail," or "unable to use help appropriately" is rarely a useful reaction, since it avoids the very growth-producing process this book espouses: learning from mistakes in practice.

SERIOUS MISTAKES,
SERIOUS CONSEQUENCES

An increasing number of successful lawsuits and professional oversight committee actions against therapists testify to the many errors in judgment and behavior on the part of interns and professionals from all of the counseling disciplines. Knowledge of these errors can hopefully prevent or diminish their occurrence in people who start out in the professions agreeing to do their utmost to "do no harm" in work with clients.

BOUNDARY VIOLATIONS

Most clinical ethical codes and a number of professional licensing bodies stipulate that workers should not have sexual, financial, or other kinds of dual relationships with clients because of the fiduciary or trustee nature of the counseling relationship. Codes and laws stress the importance of maintaining sufficient detachment to be able to assess and respond to clients accurately, with no strings attached (Dorfman, 1996). Maintaining the professional relationship as a special, boundaried working alliance also allows clients ending work at this time to return in future as needed. Often after a quick warm-up, clients who do return can almost pick up where they left off, whereas if they require a new referral, they often have to detail many aspects of their stories all over again.

Simon (1992), an attorney, reminds workers considering friendships with clients during or after therapy that there continue to be "scores of lawsuits . . . in which extracurricular socializing culminated in some form of sexual relations" (p. 31). In addition, workers should always ask themselves why they have to look to clients to meet their social needs. We need to remember that such involvements often appear to outsiders to be the worker's attempts to meet his or her own narcissistic needs. More than that, when hearing that their therapist has become involved with a client, other clients of that therapist might assume either that they were not engaging enough to be chosen, or that while they were sharing intimate history in a heartfelt way, the clinician might have been thinking about a friendly or sexual relationship with them, too, instead of remaining fully attuned to what they were saying or feeling in the moment.

Dual relationships rarely turn out to be as balanced, mutual, and socially fulfilling as the client and worker imagine they will be. Green (1996), a counseling psychologist, courageously describes the process of boundary erosion and relationship damage she and her partner experienced at the hands of a self-styled "feminist therapist" exploiting her reputation as a local guru. Heyward (1993) elaborates her disillusionment as a theologian-counselor who felt encouraged by her therapist to expect extratherapeutic involvement, only to be rebuffed and distanced when Heyward began to explore such a possibility openly with her.

Most professional codes now explicitly forbid sexual relationships with clients. Some states have made such involvements an actionable offense, and even a felony, since clients may find it hard to refuse outside involvements with people they lionize or feel grateful towards. Sometimes unethical professionals target for exploitation the very clients they've assessed as more vulnerable due to isolation or longings for direction by someone else.

Sunny told me that in their first class together, her psychology professor had asked seminar members to recount their reasons for coming into psychology. A number, including herself, had shared personal stories of past exploitation or pain that had motivated them to want to become counselors and help others. She shared her own story of her mother's too-early death causing Sunny, hungry for mothering, to let herself be dominated by people with maternal qualities. As school progressed, her professor began to invite her for vaguely defined "discussions" over coffee, using these meetings gradually to tell Sunny about his own exploited past and failing marriage. Sunny felt drawn to his caring nature, and eventually entered into a sexual relationship with him played out at his country home on weekends. He promised to leave his wife and devote himself entirely to Sunny, but at the end of the summer, he dumped her, saying that the fall semester was approaching and, much as it pained him, it would be cruel to leave his ill wife, and inappropriate to be involved sexually with a student.

Many professionals believe that such a relationship can only be for the counselor's benefit, since transference feelings are longstanding and can color the client's ability to judge, respond, or refuse offers of intimacy. Vasquez (1991) observes that there are no known means of determining when a transference is resolved, nor any research that demonstrates that the transference *is* usually resolved. Hall (as cited in Brown, 1988), warns from long experience as a psychologist, supervisor, and teacher that "the half-life of transference is greater than that of plutonium" (p. 251). I have described the worker–client relationship as one of the last Western venues in which we try hard to restrain personal needs and wishes for the sake of another (1999), and to get these needs met elsewhere.

Boundaries can also be violated by sitting too close to clients, touching or holding them without their consent, or moving through their perimeter too quickly or in ways that threaten their sense of personal space or safety. Too much attention through scanning client physique or clothes can feel intrusive or offensive, and may be experienced as sexual harassment. Out-of-control workers can become obsessed with clients just as other people may develop obsessions, and may harass clients or colleagues by asking them out, stalking them, or leaving frequent, inappropriate phone messages for them. You should harbor no illusions that all people entering the human services are an ethical cut above others because of an avowed sense of purpose or mission.

Because of telephone Caller ID service, we were able to determine that a Residence Advisor for undergraduates—also an intern in our counseling program—was making obscene phone calls to women in nearby dormitories. He was arrested and tried, not without pleading that his own privacy had been violated by someone monitoring his phone calls! In another instance, background checks of students going into placements in children's centers or children's inpatient psych units uncovered two male students who had prior convictions for sexual offenses against children but had not disclosed these as required by our program's stated admissions procedures.

FUNNY MONEY:
IMPROPER FINANCIAL DEALINGS

Workers sometimes reduce their fees and then become resentful of clients because of it. Bridges (1993) writes of a therapist treating a fellow therapist who negotiated a very low fee out of empathy for his colleague's financial straits. Only much later did he learn from this client that the latter had inherited a great deal of money and had not disclosed this change in financial status to the therapist. To the therapist's dismay, the client then refused to renegotiate the fee, insisting that their initial agreement was binding. The therapist's outraged response would likely precipitate a speedy termination with the client, and perhaps even an ethical or legal complaint by the client.

Some workers have also accepted additional money, continuous or unduly expensive gifts, and things like inappropriate stock tips and financial assistance from clients. Clinicians who bill insurance companies for canceled sessions are billing for services not actually rendered. This practice violates legal statutes and insurance protocols and in some states may lead to loss of license and prosecution. Be careful in *all* financial dealings to avoid association with questionable organizations or practice partnerships whose consuming interest is profit, to the detriment of appropriate assessment and treatment of clients. Clients are greatly affected by real or symbolic behaviors that raise questions about a worker's judgment or trustworthiness.

WORKING WHILE IMPAIRED

Ethical codes forbid work under the influence of alcohol and other drugs, but because there will be some colleagues who practice while impaired, professions have created discreet emergency assessment and response committees who provide confidential triage, referrals, and treatment for those with substance abuse or other serious mental health or personal problems (Fewell, King, & Weinstein, 1993; Sherman, 1996). Such problems might include performing irregularly while severely depressed or subject to the distracting effects of an untreated bipolar disorder.

It may be that clinicians' experience with addictions or behavior problems in their own families have silenced them from speaking openly to colleagues about perceived problems that put others at risk (Fewell, King, & Weinstein, 1993; Hawkins & Hawkins, 1996). Staff discussions and professional conferences regarding problem identification and therapist rehabilitation educate professionals and students about how to address and assist colleagues around problem behaviors in a more timely and effective fashion. Remember that while impaired colleagues may respond defensively and insist that they have no problems, or that their problems are not affecting their clients, there is little "just-in-case" protection afforded their clients when clinical work occurs behind closed doors or in isolated settings where supervision and administrative oversight are minimal or nonexistent.

UNTRUTHFUL OR DEVIOUS BEHAVIORS

Untruthful communications to clients and colleagues are expressly forbidden by ethical codes, and yet they occur, frequently ending or seriously curtailing careers in the human services and sometimes causing loss of practice licenses and legal action. Common forms of lying include hiding, destroying, or alter-ing treatment or intervention documents so that these no longer exist or do not accurately represent what has ensued between clinician and client. These behaviors often occur when workers have made errors they fear will lead to legal action or punishment. Such instances can attract media attention when hospitals or government officials "lose" documents important in a trial, but lying also occurs when staff cover their own behaviors by blaming situations on clients when the staff itself is at fault.

> *A situation involving lying particularly disturbed me as I came up through the profession. A psychologist I'd admired actually destroyed his case notes and file on a couple he'd seen in intake because he "couldn't stand being manipulated by them." He had tried to pass both of them off to a family agency. They complained about the reception they got at our agency, but since no one could find any case file or schedule book notation on them (they were walk-ins), and no staff came forward, management could only respond that they had no proof that the couple had ever been seen.*

SEXUAL HARASSMENT
IN THE WORKPLACE

Workers can manifest sexual boundary problems with colleagues as well as with clients, relatives, and friends. In the human services workplace these problems can take the same form that they do in other work environments, but are more surprising coming from persons ostensibly committed to respect-ful and ethical treatment of all people (Jacobs, 1991). Workers can harass oth-ers through inappropriate sexual contact, remarks, jokes, and prolonged gazing at bodies or clothing. Colleagues can also be stressed by another person's pre-occupation with sexual topics, images, or fantasies. The degree of harassment experienced may vary by culture, region, gender, age, and family and spiritual upbringing. Most agencies today post harassment policies and have procedures in place for the reporting and processing of alleged harassment.

> *As a young woman in my twenties, I worked in a family agency where the unit supervisor was always telling me that the lives and dynamics of inner city clients had Freudian sexual overtones that I was missing. Genital longings were frequently proposed. I became very uncomfortable with this supervisor in a very short time, but since he was well-respected by people I respected, I thought something was just wrong with me. One day I mentioned this to a female colleague I liked, and she replied, "You, too?" She was from Greece, where she thought men to be flirty as part of a cultural style. She figured this was nothing new, yet it made her feel unusually nervous in supervision. So we asked around, and three other women on the large staff were feeling the same suspicion that there was something wrong about this sexual focus in our supervision. We didn't have the courage to face the man ourselves, but as a group, we reported our*

discomfort to our boss. It turned out that she had heard this complaint before, and now confronted the supervisor with it, moving him into an administrative position where no women reported to him. He later left.

RESPONDING TO EGREGIOUS BEHAVIORS

Egregious mistakes take time to figure out, because the clinicians involved often have serious emotional, character, or substance-use related problems that lend themselves to deceiving or manipulating people with some degree of ease and success.

A good first step is to talk with knowledgeable and trusted senior staff, reviewing troubling behaviors and sorting through action options (Strean, 1993).

As in the preceding example, others may have already either consulted together about an intervention or may have actually confronted the colleague about the behaviors. If the troubled individual is your supervisor or agency administrator, then discussion with a trusted instructor or professional consultant can be very helpful in clarifying next steps. However, Jacobs (1991), a social work intern, writes of the way she reported inappropriate supervisory behavior to her school liaison faculty, only to learn that that person was a close friend of the offender and found Jacobs' revelations hard to believe.

Thinking About Why Things Go Wrong

Kadushin and Kadushin (1997) wisely note that effective interviewers are asked to do "contradictory things simultaneously" (p. 404), a source of many errors. These contradictory things can include trying to join with the client while retaining an assessor's sufficient detachment, offering hunches and suggestions while retaining a not-knowing perspective that allows the client to be the expert, restraining personal reactions sometimes while expressing them at others, examining our inner process while ostensibly riveted on the client's story and feelings, using experience and judgment to form opinions and diagnostic impressions "without judging," and caring about and feeling close with clients without getting "too" close within the relational norms of widely varying cultures and communities.

A nourishing life outside work and a variety of supportive connections are crucial to our maintenance of esteem, energy, balance, empathy, and long-term centering on others' needs and well being. Egregious mistakes are sometimes made because people are stressed beyond their capacities to cope, or have unfulfilled needs. Sometimes problem behaviors involve personality difficulties, poor judgment, or unprofessional values. Like other professions, the human services attract many healthy, dedicated, highly ethical individuals; but they can also attract people whose aim is to use education and credentials chiefly to make money in private practice or to have authority over people and goods so as to exploit both for their own purposes.

Professions now have complaint and inquiry committees and procedures, and we must also identify knowledgeable and welcoming senior personnel in agencies and programs to whom interns and workers can turn safely when faced with ethical or practical problems too difficult to sort through alone. Good self-care, training about values and ethics in action, personal therapy, and clarity about one's own values offer some preparation of workers for the many complicated and stressful scenarios they will encounter as they go about their work.

CONCLUSION

Mistakes in the middle phase of work are not unlike mistakes that can be made in other phases, but they often surprise both worker and client, since both have become acclimated to the process following the initial period of adjustment and accommodation to each other's styles and pace. We need simply to remember that mistakes can never be completely eradicated, and in fact, may become more subtle, requiring more, not less, attention in order to catch and work on them with the client.

It's all too easy to attribute mistakes in the middle phase to transference or countertransference developments as relational problems manifest in both clients and clinicians. Mistakes can also happen because we aren't knowledgeable about certain matters; are tired, distracted, or not listening well due to personal concerns; or are just having an off day due to a combination of factors. Mistakes are particularly likely to occur when we're feeling rushed, unappreciated, overburdened, or unjustly criticized.

EXERCISES

1. *Reflection.* Reflect in your journal on mistakes you've made in the middle phase of work with one or two clients. Can you identify and discuss the sources of these errors? Were you later able to review your missteps with clients? If not, discuss why not. If you could, how did the discussion with them work out?

2. *Small Group Discussion.* In groups of three, prepare a role play in which you demonstrate a mistake in one of the following areas of middle-phase work: worker-client relationship, pace of work, a disappointed or sermonizing response to client behavior, or the interference in the moment of your own personal feelings. Rejoin as a large group and play these scenarios out in their mistaken and reconstructed forms, discussing their implications for your own learning and work.

3. *Class Discussion.* Talk together about the ways you stay fit and energized for the hard work of trying to help clients with their often complex and insufficiently resourced inner and outer lives. What things in the work or the workplace tend to throw you off or upset you, so that you have to be more watchful of mistakes?

4. *Instructor Activity.* Discuss with the class some egregious mistakes you have observed in your career, and what you learned from these. What guidance can you give them about responding to the impaired or calculating behaviors of colleagues? You may want to invite a guest speaker from your profession's Committee on Impairment to meet with the class to discuss some of the behavioral complaints that come before them and the options that are available in responding to complaints.

5. *Author Sharing for Further Discussion.* Starting out, I had a client I liked a lot, but who was very afraid to share personal business. I saw her at the end of the workday because she couldn't get off earlier from her job. She began to come ten, then fifteen, then thirty minutes late, and I didn't feel comfortable asking her about this, assuming that this was because of her discomfort with talking. As her arrivals got later and later, I'd end up in the agency all by myself waiting for her. My supervisor finally said with good humor, "She must wonder why you do all this waiting for her . . . why she is so important to you. Maybe your waiting so long makes her feel so guilty or so uneasy that she can't stand to come the whole time." I'd never considered these ideas, and just thought of myself as "being there for her." When I directly addressed her lateness with her, the client said she couldn't stand the focus so intensely on her revealing her inner feelings. She felt like she was betraying her hard-working parents by suggesting that anything had been wrong in her childhood. Then she said she felt like she would be betraying me if she stopped coming, because I always sat there waiting for her, like her mother did nights when she was out raising hell.

   For Class Discussion. If you were my supervisor, what advice would you give me as to how to respond to the client's explanations of her plight? What things might contribute to a worker's tolerance of so much lateness in a client? What are the client and worker missing out on when the worker doesn't raise the lateness as a focus of discussion?

RECOMMENDED READING

Bullis, R. K. (1995). *Clinical social worker misconduct: Law, ethics, and personal dynamics.* Chicago: Nelson-Hall.

Corey, G. (2001). Ethical issues in counseling practice. In *Theory and practice of counseling and psychotherapy* (pp. 42–63). Belmont, CA: Wadsworth.

Daniels, J., & D'Andrea, M. (1996). Ethnocentrism in counseling. In D. W. Sue, A. E. Ivey, & P. B. Pedersen (Eds.), *A theory of multicultural counseling and therapy* (pp. 155–173). Pacific Grove, CA: Brooks/Cole.

Dorfman, R. A. (1996). Things they don't teach you in professional school. In *Clinical social work: Definition, practice, and vision* (pp. 144–165). New York: Brunner/Mazel.

Groschi, W. N., & Olsen, D. (1994). *When healing starts to hurt: A new look at burnout among psychotherapists.* New York: Norton.

Haley, J. (1981). A quiz for young therapists. In *Reflections on therapy and other essays* (pp. 237–243). Chevy Chase, MD: The Family Therapy Institute of Washington, DC.

Jacobs, C. (1991). Violations of the supervisory relationship: An ethical and educational blind spot. *Social Work, 36,* 130–135.

Loewenberg, F. M., Dolgoff, R., & Harrington, D. (2000). The professional relationship: Limits, dilemmas, and problems. *Ethical decisions for social work practice* (pp. 148–172). Itasca, IL: Peacock.

Okun, B. F. (1997). Issues affecting helping. *Effective helping: Interviewing and counseling techniques* (pp. 250–284). Pacific Grove, CA: Brooks/Cole.

Regehr, C., & Glancy, G. (1995). Sexual exploitation of patients: Issues for colleagues. *American Journal of Orthopsychiatry, 65,* 194–202.

8

Common Mistakes
in Ending

Workers and clients end work together when goals have been accomplished reasonably well, and clients feel "ready enough" to tackle daily life and relationships without regular support from clinical work. Because of the caring, thought, time, and energy invested in the relationship and work, endings require careful thought and planning ahead of time so that finishing up feels like a natural next step in the client's development. We try to avoid abrupt endings or transitions that may undermine client confidence, or leave clients feeling pushed out or abandoned.

FACTORS INFLUENCING ENDING PROCESS

In planning ahead around endings or time-outs, we often consider the following factors that can greatly influence how endings will be experienced and structured.

Whether Ending Is Planned or Unplanned

Many endings today are planned well in advance, since clients are frequently seen in a specified number of home or office visits in which the limits on work are imposed by the service funding source. Time constraints are thus well known to all and serve as bookends for both the work and the degree of emotional attachment that workers and clients allow themselves to have within specific time parameters.

When initially contracting for work together, it helps to imagine a potential time frame for the work, and to talk together about what achievement of goals and consolidation of assets might look like in the client's everyday life. In brief interventions, workers should be particularly careful to frame time limits as realistic and helpful parameters that emphasize achievable goals and client capacities to work rapidly towards them. It's crucial that we communicate a belief that work doesn't have to be lengthy in order to be helpful, and that much can be learned and attained in a concerted and focused piece of work together.

> *Jyothi was moving to California for a better paying computer industry job, and contracted to meet with me in two two-hour sessions to review a poor relationship she was leaving "for her own mental health." She was embarrassed to cry in front of friends and family who were all celebrating her ending of what they thought of as an unhealthy relationship, so she told me she was "paying for a place to cry and let my worries all hang out." That's exactly what she did, as I guided her through a review of her past choices, her wisdom and strengths in ending these relationships, her current temptation to try one more time with someone not really supportive of her, and her worry that she would always be alone. She later wrote me from California to say how relieving the talks were, and how much she loved her new job and apartment. She missed the "moral support" of our talks and thought she might talk with a psychologist out there about her earlier habit of linking up with abusive men.*

Planned endings also include those that simply occur naturally when work accomplishes goals, and the worker and client agree that ending is appropriate. Both track goals and progress, and clients utilize and affirm their strengths in a process of further consolidation. At some point, either client or worker initiates discussion of the possibility of ending or of designing a trial period in which frequency of visits is reduced purposefully. This way, clients can experience themselves succeeding in their natural environments, checking for areas that may require further fine-tuning before stopping work entirely.

Unplanned endings are those necessitated by unexpected events or circumstances occurring in workers' or clients' lives. Agencies may close, clients or workers may have to move away unexpectedly or change their schedules to accommodate others, serious illness may disrupt care, or coverage may run out. Clients may decide suddenly to end clinical work temporarily and try things on their own, or decide that they prefer another provider or form of intervention. Such endings are usually more stressful, occurring within established relationships and in the midst of hard work.

Under such circumstances, we try to help clients make meaning of the contact, summarize and plan around any unfinished business, and express feelings about ending. It's okay for both worker and client to express concerns if they feel that work is ending unwisely, or that sufficient supports are not in place to sustain well-being.

Lorraine said she was happy with her new girlfriend and didn't need to come any more—she could talk everything over with Gina. I said I understood her longtime wish to have a family that could finally be there for her, but that it worried me that she'd only known Gina for a month, and things might feel differently over time. She asked if she could call me if there were problems like before, and I said that of course she could. I wondered if instead of that, we should cut back contacts now to once a month instead of stopping, to see how things would go over the weeks, but she was intent on stopping, so we did. Some time the next year she called to see me for another period of work, because, like her former lover, Gina had proved to be verbally abusive while drinking too much.

Quality and State of the Working Alliance

Some workers and clients who've had a contentious relationship or lived through a relational mismatch may actually experience some relief and eagerness to be done with each other as they think of an approaching ending, and that would be human. On the other hand, satisfying alliances and work are likely to leave participants with some normal feelings of sadness at ending, combined with feelings of pride of accomplishment and a readiness to move on. Mixed feelings characterize many forms of launching from familiar relationships, not just those between workers and clients.

The Nature and Intensity of the Work Done

Two meetings in which couples discuss the formation of an Elder Activities Club or the possibility of hosting teens from abroad during the summer are likely to wrap up more easily than two meetings in which families review the impact of a child's major mental illness on parents, or make decisions about whether an intermittently violent family member can be realistically lodged at home. Group meetings to prepare high school teens to make confident college or training applications will likely end with fewer reactions and complications around ending than group meetings in which teen moms discuss their loneliness and isolation in raising young children.

However, we can never take anything about endings for granted, and continuing assessment of current client capacities, needs, and outside supports is preferable to assuming that an ending process will be easy. Any piece of work can stir up a variety of human reactions that may indicate appropriate needs for additional support and work, either together or with another worker or agency.

Crisis Pileup

Clients may need additional support and a brief postponement of ending if major life events or crises arise to shake the foundations of coping. A sudden accident, health crisis, or major loss of employment or a loved one may call for more, not less, connection with the worker, in person or by phone if the client has to travel for an emergency or is hospitalized suddenly. Flexible timing and responsiveness are crucial in providing a platform of support if unexpected stress piles up.

If you work in a hospital or hospice, the time set to end work there may coincide with a client's dying. It's sometimes possible to continue to visit with the client and family by arranging returns to the site for the specific purpose of seeing families through the process of loss. Supervisory review and approval should precede any such activity, as you still represent the agency until you complete your contracted work. If your situation makes it impossible for you to continue to be available, a supervisor or colleague familiar with the situation and the client's capacities and needs can often step in to assist clients when you leave.

Unexpected diagnosis of a previously undetected serious illness in a patient about to be discharged from a medical unit also raises new issues about needs beyond discharge. The family may feel that they can discuss feelings and options more comfortably and frankly with their familiar inpatient worker rather than with an unknown outpatient worker to whom they've been referred at time of discharge. Patient and family may reasonably balk at having to switch workers who are a part of the same large care network, a transfer that feels arbitrary to them. The medical staff may wrongly assess the family's balking as a sign of personality problems or of making unreasonable demands. Here we can mediate with both the team and the family, clarifying with each the reasoning of the other. We can often work out a fair compromise that provides a good experience of support for patient and family at this time. Multiple interventions like these often prevent the later readmission of the patient for discharge-related stress, depression, and physical decline.

Degree of Client's Internalization
of Work Principles and Process

A goal of good endings is for the relationship and work to be internalized as a guiding and sustaining memory. Memory can then act as a repository of ideas and encouragements that endure inside individuals and systems, no matter where or how the worker is over time, so that dependence on agencies and workers diminishes, and reliance on natural and mutual helping systems gradually increases. As the work proceeds, the worker notes the extent to which clients are consolidating relational and work principles as working memory used between visits. Spontaneous first signs of internalization of the work can be observed in clients' descriptions of *picturing or envisioning the worker's support* in the form of an encouraging coach or supporter on one's shoulder, or a benign and helpful inner voice.

At a later point, clients *may begin to emulate the worker's language, special idioms, dress, or manner* as further evidence of beginning to take in helpful capacity. Frequent attendees of AA and other mutual aid groups often begin to quote slogans or watchwords from their programs, such as "live and let live"—a sign of internalization of new guidance and support systems for coping and changing. Still later, clients will mention *thinking about the worker* when a challenge arises, *deciding to try a strategy that the worker had suggested*—signs that choice and agency are developing within the client. Ultimately clients *spontaneously begin to say and do things learned through the work, without reference to the worker's image or voice.* Helpful elements of the process have now been transmuted into personal capacity to notice triggers, anticipate consequences, select a strategy that works better, and act on it, calling on friends and allies for support if needed. While some highly stressed or seriously impaired clients may never reach these levels of readiness to act without a professional's presence or guidance, many others can and do.

Client Coping Capacities

A reassessment of the client's internal and systemic coping resources at ending updates both worker and client on potentials and needs prior to finishing. The following questions can help to clarify current strengths, resourcefulness, and readiness to move ahead as planned.

- How easily and rapidly does the client bring resources and skills to bear when challenges and opportunities arise?
- How realistic and reliable are planning and follow-through relating to daily relationships, tasks, and pursuits?
- How positive and sustaining are the client's views of self, world, and prospects?
- What systems are in place for companionship, support, and emergencies?
- What other bits of evidence support the client's readiness to end or to taper visits down?

Actual Use of Supports

Ironically, when anticipating an ending, loss-sensitive people may quietly withdraw from the very friends and supports they need, not wishing to discuss with others their mixed reactions to ending their therapeutic work. Allies may cheer at the prospect of a friend's therapeutic work ending before that person can appreciate ending. Friendly encouragement about the client's apparent readiness to move on can sometimes leave him or her with some you–don't–understand feelings that briefly separate individuals from their best supporters. Review of the importance of relational support in coping can help clients move back towards those people who are most helpful at times of stress.

How People Interpret and Manage Change and Loss

The client's established style of dealing with change and loss is important to keep in mind when approaching an ending. We need to anticipate how much—and what kinds of—thinking, feeling, and action are likely to emerge when wrapping up. People typically more restrained or intellectualized around previous losses may repeat these behaviors during a current ending, just as people customarily deluged with feelings while trying to cope with losses and changes may manifest much upset during ending.

Hepworth, Rooney, and Larsen (1997) note that clients with histories of repeated rejections may mistakenly interpret termination as another rejection (p. 608)—a misinterpretation that requires sensitive exploration and the possible linking of current distortions with past unhappy experiences. Parting from the worker, no matter how welcome a sign of accomplishment and satisfaction, may still be experienced as a bittersweet loss evoking some sadness around which to do some additional grief work concerning unresolved prior losses. A good experience with ending can model for clients how leave taking can actually be a learning experience compared with prior separations full of unspoken sadness, hostility, or regrets.

Clients may surprise a worker (who no longer expects these earlier coping strategies to repeat) by returning to old impulsive behaviors briefly during ending. Sometimes people try out old behaviors one more time, as though to say goodbye to them or to see clearly that these behaviors are no longer viable options. Others may return to old behaviors because the degree of doubt or stress they're feeling is momentarily overwhelming the coping resources they can muster while thinking of ending.

Sometimes the return to older behaviors is like a cry for help or appeal to the worker to please reconsider the plan to end: "Hey, wait—I'm obviously not ready, how can you leave me when I'm feeling like this?" Usually clients who are really ready to end are as perplexed as the worker by the sudden return of old behaviors. It would be a mistake to become exasperated with or lose faith in the client during episodes of slippage in coping. When reviewed with clients compassionately, without judging, these episodes offer rich opportunities for further understanding of self and of responses to stress and loss.

The worker's experience, comfort, and skill in carrying out endings are pivotal in the process. Positive and hopeful attitudes about client readiness, coupled with a view of endings as inevitable and growth-producing human experiences, are important in good endings and are communicated by all that we say and do regarding the ending phase of work. Goodyear (1981) lists a number of conditions which make it hard for workers to end well with clients, including "worry about the client's capacities to function independently, guilt about not having done a more effective job, embarrassment when a client quits abruptly, loss of an important relationship or significant chance to learn, and problems with separation anxiety" (p. 138). We can also be affected by the number of goodbyes we have to say at one time. For example, workers may have to end with several clients, colleagues, and instructors at once, at the same time as they're going through a painful divorce or death in the family.

Endings are a time for taking special care of oneself, and of staying connected with allies and wise advisors for support and review of issues and reactions arising in work with clients. Proper diet, exercise, and spiritual replenishment are very important when grappling with one's own as well as others' changing feelings. This is also a time to make note of your own ending-related feelings and thoughts that may form an agenda for personal work in future.

Parallel Process in Endings

Current losses can stimulate feelings, memories, dreams, reminiscences, and symbolic actions related to unresolved past losses of both worker and client (Levinson, 1977). These reactions can lead to some stress–induced regressions in both workers' and clients' adaptive and expressive skills, depending on the understanding and capacities they bring to the tasks of managing loss and change. Instructors can help workers and interns identify and learn from their own reactions to endings, utilizing these as assets in appreciating and empathizing with client reactions at this time. Understanding the impact of change, rather than simply acting out old scenarios related to it, will help you become more specifically responsive, supportive, and informative with clients about how current reactions can contain elements of past experiences that need airing.

Endings often seem to trigger in both workers and clients an impulse to shortchange the process of ending in order to get on the other side of it without experiencing a lot of sadness. Shulman (1999) aptly describes a "farewell party syndrome" in which workers celebrate gains and focus on positives, sometimes with goodbye parties in the last meeting with a group or family, in order to detour around the sad aspects of ending important relationships (p. 618).

> *Twice when I was leaving placements as a student, I locked myself out of my apartment so that the fire department had to come with a ladder, climb in my window, and open the door from the inside. One of my friends forgot some client appointments, and another one lost her schedule book. In group supervision, our supervisor reviewed these occurrences as symbolic expressions of loss, and had us talk about what endings were like for us. I thought I was the only one having problems with it until then. Later on, when I was in therapy with a very skilled clinician, she double-booked me with another client and the two of us got up to go in when she opened her door. She was horrified— actually speechless—when she saw this, since it was to have been our last meeting. This delayed our ending, since she chose to have me come back the next week. I didn't know whether to feel special because she was delaying our ending, or to feel hurt because she had already booked my replacement!*

You may be able to end properly with clients, but have a hard time ending with supervisors and instructors, so that you "forget" class meetings, supervision, case notes, or other responsibilities during ending work, enacting your change stress in these ways, instead of meeting with clients. Just as workers and clients can forget appointments or detach from each other before ending, so can supervisors and instructors, who can also show sadness around endings when these trigger their own unresolved losses.

> *Our supervisor was widowed just before we came to practicum, and was grieving throughout the year, though very helpful in many, many ways. At ending time, though, she began to wear dark glasses during the day and in supervision, and would stress that "life is a series of losses," this being one more. We tried to protect her by talking about ending mostly among ourselves and outside the agency.*

It's no surprise that we all can make mistakes while ending that we thought we'd outgrown. For example, workers or supervisors who've loved having interns in the setting can suddenly become cranky and critical when having to take on the clients of the person leaving. Endings can affect everyone; course content and in-service presentations about endings, as well as skilled consultation from a colleague not involved in the endings at hand, can be very helpful in sorting out who is feeling what, as well as next steps with the client. During endings, knowledge, awareness, and carefulness are three of our best aids in heading off actions of ours that could undermine relationships or work together.

STEPS IN ENDING

When interventions are rushed or brief, workers may protest that they don't have the time or inclination to "deal with" ending, misunderstanding that such work has to take many weeks. In reality, time spent on ending work can range from several weeks to a few minutes at the end of one or a few meetings. People even wrap up by phone or letter when clients have intended to return for more meetings but now find this impractical or impossible due to realistic, unforeseen circumstances.

Once ending does become a central feature of the agenda, we make time to discuss a number of important topics that help clients digest and bring some closure to the experiences of relationship and work together.

Making Meaning of the Work

In summing up the work, workers should encourage clients to reflect on and articulate what they've learned, what they believe lies ahead for them, and the meanings they make of both their problems and potentials. Can they acknowledge and use their many personal contributions to the change process? Do they attribute their changes or progress to God or fate? To the worker's magic? Solely to a new medication? Some may be uncomfortable or unused to highlighting their own accomplishments, seeing such a focus as self-aggrandizing or lacking in humility. The worker may have to encourage this kind of self-honoring actively, emphasizing the importance of positive self-talk to future coping and growth.

Highlighting Gains and Achievements

A worker can highlight client strengths, gains, and enriched alliances with others by comparing where clients were at the outset of contact, with their current position, attained through hard work and determination. The worker accepts thanks for the help graciously, but then shifts focus back to the accomplishments of the client and the evidence of competencies that these provide.

Sometimes we can invite clients to look at initial contact forms or assessment notes as a reminder of what has been accomplished. This is a good time to let clients know that it's okay to acknowledge reactions to the work that they may not have shared previously. For example, a client might offer the good-natured critique: "I thought you would never stop asking me if I was going to finish junior college, and sometimes I felt like saying, hey, let up, will you?"

A worker might equally well offer a reflective observation about an aspect of the process: "We were both a little stubborn now and then, weren't we? But we worked it out." These moments of reflecting back together can be memorable experiences in clinical work, as the reciprocal nature of an effective work process crystallizes in an instructive way.

Expressing Thoughts and Feelings About Ending

Works should encourage clients to express richly their thoughts and feelings about ending a process that is both a relationship and a piece of work. It's helpful to ask clients about the ending styles they have grown up with or developed within their particular cultures, understanding that these styles will often play out with the worker during ending. Some clients will express sadness, anxiety, or nostalgia for the worker's continuing presence, and voice their idealization of the experience ("Nobody will ever be as good as you," or "I'll never forget you or what you've taught me").

Some clients have had very few people to idealize, and so need to idealize the worker now in order to feel like someone of worth by association with this good helper. Sometimes they haven't had the words or the encouragement to express gratitude, affection, and good wishes for the future to an important other person. If they struggle to do so, we help dignify such expressions with thanks and acknowledgment of all that the client has achieved in addition to anything we may have done.

Clients can also become uncharacteristically cranky, restless, or hard on themselves, not understanding that these feelings may well be related to ending with the worker. We can accept and discuss these reactions as expectable. Some clients may be tempted to breeze through the focus on goodbyes, skip appointments without calling, or end work precipitously in order to avoid feeling the feelings that can accompany endings. We can reach out to them by phone, letter, or visit, offering a tentative hunch that, by leaving before the last scheduled session, they may have hoped to short-circuit reactions that are likely to bubble up at some point anyway. An invitation to come back often helps a client stick with a more gradual disengagement process.

Once you've encouraged clients to express a range of feelings about working with and parting from you, you can respond by expressing your own sentiments about finishing up as well as any genuine appreciation you feel for what you've learned from them and keep from the work. We often thank them for things like their patience during an agency or worker slip up, or when services took much longer to arrange than they should have. You can also note any ways that feedback from them has improved your subsequent work with others.

Linking Current Reactions with Prior Experiences

If clients aren't aware that present reactions can be unusually strong because they contain residues of earlier losses, workers may want to suggest possible connections between present and past experience, providing opportunities for brief review of unresolved losses. While this tying together can help some clients get better closure on the past, others may prefer to let sleeping dogs lie. Sadness may occur especially if an ending with a cherished worker coincides with an anniversary of an important loss in the client's life or occurs at a particularly lonely time in a client's life. If the worker has kept detailed assessment notes, it's good to review these before saying goodbye, in order to keep possible anniversary reactions in mind at given times of the year, or at holidays.

Moving from Figure to Ground

As work wraps up, we briefly assume more leadership in educating clients about ending tasks and process and by helping them plan for the future. They are then encouraged anew to lead the process as often as possible—exactly the role envisioned for them in life ahead without a worker present. We can then intentionally ease the emotional process of ending by gradually transitioning from a more active or vocal foreground position to a less active, albeit clearly responsive, background stance in the work. This gradual stepping back expresses symbolically the ending to come, but doesn't at all call for worker silence or detachment. Rather, we encourage and support the client's initiative in talking, reacting, reflecting, and deciding as primary assets of this phase of work.

Reframing Ending as a Commencement

It's important that clients understand that stopping for now isn't the end of personal study and growth, which are the stuff of lifetime learning. Some people may worry that, without the worker, they won't be able to go on growing. These launching jitters ("What will I do without you? Can I call you if I need you?") are very common at ending, side by side with excitement about having done good work and being ready to move on. Many of the client's reactions at this time can be validated as natural and expected when transitioning from one way of being to another. You can sometimes ease client embarrassment around launching jitters by briefly sharing a transitional experience of your own to illustrate the universality of change anxieties.

Discussing Unfinished Business

It's not unusual for clinical work to end with unfinished business remaining in the client's life. Even when an ending occurs naturally after agreed upon goals are reached, people will still have complexities in their lives that they will be dealing with off and on over the life course. There are few illusions today that work of any length will neatly tidy up people's lives, provide high quality resources in great abundance, and leave clients with a brand new slate for the complete restorying of their lives. The work we do together can often alter patterns, relationships, and balances, but most clients realize that their lives will continue to have natural cycles of joy and sorrow, success and disappointment, and periods of stress throughout the life course.

Instead of reading the future for clients, we ask them to forecast ahead about what can be expected to go well, to stay about the same, or to change for the worse. We review resources that can help in future when challenges arise, including further contact with this agency or worker if feasible. Remember that discussion focused on other resources to be used in future can sometimes elicit renewed loss reactions, and that we shouldn't pretend to ourselves that we can push the adaptive process any faster than it will naturally go for each person.

Discussing How the Last Meeting Will Unfold

Talk of ending includes deciding on a date for closure. Along the way, we often plan with clients what form the final session will take. Some work ends with a review of what's ahead and a mutual offering of good wishes for the future. Following supervisory review, it may work well with some clients to take coffee or a meal together, or to eat a special meal of thanks with the family or group if work has been done through home, institutional, or residential visits. It can be very empowering for clients to be able to give something meaningful back to us, be it a small gift, treat, or personal creation like a poem or a culturally special dish. We can avoid Shulman's farewell party syndrome by making sure that important review, meaningful planning, and feeling exchange take place before or during ritual endings.

Being Friendly Without Being Friends

During endings, clients may ask you to become a friend after the work finishes, not wishing to relinquish what has been experienced as a special relationship. They may not be able to appreciate, as you do by virtue of your specialized education, that the worker-client relationship has both real and symbolic components that couldn't be duplicated in a friendship in which both participants would be real, not symbolic. What can't be duplicated in a friendship outside of the professional relationship is the unique and wonderful one-sidedness of the latter: the continuous, purposeful restraint of one person's frank expression of personal needs, unsettling feelings, or troubling life issues expressly for the benefit of the other person's development.

Since endings are an inevitable part of life, it's also important to help clients understand and develop skills in ending. They may have had few models of how to internalize the positive aspects of a good relationship in order to benefit from those good aspects without the other person being present. It takes confidence and skill to say goodbye and to cherish and utilize relational experience through use of memory. Learning to express satisfaction about shared experience, digest endings, and move on will add to client capacity in lasting ways that reach far beyond what a transitory friendship could offer. Any worker can be proud to help a client build these relational assets by means of a good ending. This is especially true with clients who've not yet experienced major losses through death or separations of great distance.

OTHER COMMON MISTAKES IN ENDING

Because they involve life review, loss reactions, new challenges, and the human tendency to avoid the painful, endings pose many opportunities to make mistakes as the clock runs out and time seems of the essence. Mistakes often become elephants in the room, enlarging until they squash process unless dealt with forthrightly. The following are some frequently observed errors during the ending phase of relating and working together.

Abrupt Ending: Little Warning or Preparation

Workers who know that a client has had severe reactions to loss sometimes try to delay bringing up the subject of leaving with them. The longer we wait to bring the subject up, the more we put the client in the position of having to end rather quickly because time is running out. It might seem to some that this will blunt the client's pain or expression of it, but the opposite is often true.

For example, a student may have told her client early on that she'll be leaving in spring, but doesn't follow up after winter break by exploring the impact on the client of this break or the way it can foreshadow for people the ending to come. A supervisor may have asked the student to devote time in several client sessions to review, ventilation, and preparation for the future. Yet the student puts off and puts off bringing up the subject of ending until there may be only one or two visits left for rushed discussion. Such an approach leaves clients little time to understand and deal with stunned reactions due to "forgetting you're leaving so soon."

Clinicians who haven't experienced major losses or haven't been shown how to manage loss and change well may have little sense of the impact of rushed goodbyes that don't allow expression of mixed feelings and mobilization of assets prior to ending. They may trivialize the ending process and simply keep the major focus on reassuring clients that they're ready to function without the worker or agency. Clients sometimes register silent protest by ending earlier than anticipated, or by disappearing from contact and ignoring subsequent outreach.

Whenever you wonder why someone who doesn't want to lose you might abruptly leave you behind, remember that disengagement, avoidance, flight, and denial are all widely exercised human strategies for limiting pain and stress. Additionally, some clients really do leave us because our handling of the ending process hurts more than it helps, and prompts a self-protective exit by the client.

Premature Disengagement from Clients and Work

We ourselves can detach too early from clients and setting, "forgetting" what occurred in meetings, forgetting process notes for supervision, coming late to client sessions, and the like. You may find yourself drifting and thinking about other things while interviewing around endings—mentally assembling your resumé, enjoying a reverie of an upcoming trip, or silently recalling endings that have touched you. You may even spot yourself focusing a lot on how ready and glad you are to leave, moving to the rear in meetings or joining colleagues less often for lunch.

Amazingly, workers have actually booked distant conferences or vacations during the last few weeks of work with clients. Avoid this behavior at all costs, because it is easily experienced by clients as indifference to their well being at a special time of wrapping up. Because of the feeling of safe anchorage that many clients enjoy in the relationship with a worker, it's important to keep this anchorage secure while ending the work. Leaving the client when in the midst of discussing the impact of leaving seems almost callous unless the worker is responding to an unavoidable emergency.

Once we can spot and own our own protective detachment maneuvers, it will be easier to spot and discuss clients' similar strategies with them as a part of the important learning that accompanies good endings. Discussion of premature detachment affirms the important relational principle of standing firm in commitments until an agreed upon ending is planned and enacted.

Practicing *remaining in place when anxious* also enhances this skill in both workers and clients.

Minimizing the Importance of the Relationship

Some workers may find it hard to explore meaningfully for a client's deeper reactions to ending with them, picturing that the client hasn't seemed that invested and may even be feeling relief about ending. If the work has seemed to founder or achieve little that the worker can see, it can be hard to believe that ending will matter. An offhanded or casual parting can miss client reactions that signal some aspect of the work or the relationship that the worker hasn't appreciated sufficiently before.

Learning can take place right up to and beyond the final moments of a contact, so our radar has to stay attuned for the possible and the unexpected. Clients have been known to call workers as soon as they get home from "ending" sessions to say things like, "I think I didn't say enough about how much you've helped me," or " I was so upset that I forgot to wish you luck in your new job." *Saying goodbye is an event, while ending is a process and can take time.*

In small villages or rural areas where workers and clients will see each other often by virtue of the institutions in which they all participate, there may be only a hint of goodbye—more likely, a "see you later," but with appreciation that future contacts will be for purposes other than therapy, and with a different feel and style to them. In churches or temples where spiritual leaders may also offer counseling and guidance to members of the faith community, ending talk may not contain a goodbye at all, as the participants have continued to experience each other regularly in their other roles as cocommunicants in faith practice, and usually continue to do so, unless some aspect of the work leads to ending of community membership.

Ignoring or Minimizing Signs of Risk

At ending, clients may bring up self-harming ideas or impulses that busy workers don't take seriously enough and don't explore with enough concern and detail. Lulled by the client's apparent readiness to end, we can sometimes hope or believe that people who haven't harmed themselves for some time—or ever—are surely not going to harm themselves here at the end. Such a belief can cause workers to refrain from introducing the topic of self-harm when the client hasn't mentioned it, for fear of insulting the client. This is a big mistake.

Every hint of self-harming must be explored for as long as the work goes on. It may be that the client has continued to experience impulses to hurt, but hasn't wanted to upset the worker with evidence of continuing difficulties. Sometimes impulses recede with expression of underlying feelings of vulnerability, anger, or loneliness, all of which must be assessed for the degree to which they are transitory in response to an identifiable stressor or to the ending of therapy, or are an ongoing aspect of core self that ebbs and flows in relation to situational factors.

Trying to Pack Everything In at the End

Sometimes when ending, we try to stuff too many topics into the conversation in a very short time. It's as though we want anything we haven't previously dealt with or focused on enough to get taken care of suddenly before finishing up. This vain hope leads to cluttering final contacts with too much rushed talking that ranges over too many different topics. It also leads to introducing new elements that would really require a level of exploration not possible in the amount of time left.

It's good to remember that many people and institutions support, educate, and assist clients every day, and that what hasn't made it onto the table in the present work will have many other opportunities to get settled through ongoing community experience. Unfinished business can also trigger a future request for help, provided the experience has been a good one. Patterson and Welfel (2000) observe that clients sometimes generate new agendas for work because of not wanting to leave the security of the relationship with the worker. If we suspect this may be so, we can broach this possibility with the client, perhaps eliciting a hesitation about ending that will respond well to further review of strengths.

Poor Case Management of Referrals and Transfers

The busy work of several endings at once can lead to workers forgetting the needs of various clients, forgetting to make needed calls and arrangements, and forgetting to apprise colleagues in other agencies of the client's emotional and action status at ending, so they know how to anticipate and plan for the client's arrival at their settings.

Whenever possible, we try to arrange for clients to visit a new worker before finishing with us, so that we can later reflect together on experiences with that new worker prior to our ending. Such arrangements are harder in busy settings, yet still often possible if workers are willing to put in the effort to arrange and follow up on transitional contacts. It's not unusual for the client to compare the new worker somewhat unfavorably to the old, urging that the first worker remain. It would be a mistake just to accept such criticisms and bask in the client's admiration rather than exploring the criticisms in some depth. A client's uneasiness about the new worker or agency may in fact signal worrisome deficits in the new agency or staff, or it may represent a simple longing not to change from the familiar.

A three-way meeting can be effective in giving workers a chance to discuss possibilities and questions, with the client chiming in as well. Sometimes a second referral is necessary if the first one doesn't take. The topic of transferring to other workers and agencies has to be broached with clients early enough to allow them to air their expectations, concerns, and any added regrets about having to transfer to another agency or worker. Ventilation helps to air and dilute some mixed feelings so that all of these need not be dumped into the new relationship.

Focusing Too Much on Self

Particularly at ending time, workers who've made lots of room for the client's voice and leadership can suddenly feel inner pressure to go on too long about things we have in common with the client, what we've gained from the work, who we picture the client becoming, and the like.

Some workers, feeling guilty about ending with clients when problems aren't all resolved, seem to want to give clients a gift of heightened spontaneity and self-disclosure. Others may have quietly bridled at having to be so self-contained as a clinician and now want at last to say more about who they are as people, perhaps thinking that clients will remember them more favorably after ending. Sometimes workers feeling sadness at ending may simply want to dispel some of that sadness through friendly chatting.

Talking a lot about oneself might be the right thing for someone with whom the worker has purposefully staged the work more casually, and the wrong thing for clients who specifically like a more formal and businesslike approach. Our talking also takes up a great deal of client time for our benefit just when the client's time to talk *and be heard* runs out. *Ending is not the time to be startlingly different,* or to try out startlingly different ideas and techniques on clients who are likely comfortable enough with things the way they have been.

Saving the Worst for Last

Some workers mistakenly believe that if they have bad news about anything to deliver to a client, they should save it for the last meeting so that the client isn't upset by it until other ending matters are covered. Usually there is a strong feeling that the news could damage either the client or the work, when what really damages a relationship is the afterthought, "Why didn't she tell me this sooner, while there was still time to talk it over and get my feelings out?"

Matters that may tempt us to delay till the last moment include the unexpected closing of the agency, pregnancy or serious illness in the worker (who's ending for that reason), or the worker taking a job just down the street but being unable to continue with the client there. One worker waited until their next-to-last session to tell a male client that she was moving to a distant town in order to partner with the man's best friend, a lesbian who'd also been keeping the relationship a secret from him—"not wanting to upset him any earlier than necessary."

Consideration shown to clients during endings is of the utmost importance, and signals clients about our real levels of understanding, human kindness, and skill. Leaving enough time to talk things out, express untidy feelings, and plan how to cope with what lies ahead trumps almost all other considerations in ending. Otherwise clients are left hanging with events or issues affecting them, now further burdened by a feeling that the worker did not trust them to be strong enough to deal adequately with whatever was at hand—a confusing blow, given the worker's ongoing commendation of client strengths.

Instructors can be very helpful in assessing and timing the tasks to be covered in the time available. They also help us think ahead about the importance to and effects on particular clients of any distressing material that must be introduced during ending time. Role play can also help us plan out the least harmful ways of presenting distressing material.

Bailing Out at the Last Moment

It's touching to see some students and workers carry out nice endings right up to the point of parting and then make important mistakes. One of these is to walk the client to the door, hug or shake hands while wishing each other well, and then break off mid-sentence when the phone rings, leaving the client in the lurch in order to take a call. Some clients just stand by, waiting to end again, while others may simply vanish, feeling small or dismissed.

We can make a similar mistake in trying to say goodbye while walking down a big street or corridor where others are likely to interrupt to say hello or chat with the worker or client, not realizing that, for this particular client, this is the last few seconds of a very special relationship. Better to say goodbye where the work has usually been done, so that both enact closure in familiar style and circumstances.

Have We Forgotten Anything in the Rush?

It's wise to check in with clients about any further business that needs to be covered before ending. Sometimes in the emotion and busy planning of the ending period, important things are forgotten: a letter or permission that needs signing, a green card hearing that needs a witness, or a call to a doctor about continuing to consult around medication side effects. At times the client tracks tasks more closely than the worker, but we have to learn to track well, too. It's wise to jot down a list of tasks to complete in the time allotted (which can range from a few minutes or hours to several weeks). The list can serve as a check-off guide to joint action towards ensuring that services needed by the client are properly developed and followed through on as time passes.

The Human Side of Goodbye

Many endearing human behaviors are witnessed during endings. A worker and client who have seen each other in home visits may say their appreciative goodbyes. The worker then leaves the home and goes on to three or four more appointments before remembering, startled, that she's left a stack of files in the client's kitchen, necessitating a return there and another goodbye. Another worker and client say goodbye at an agency and then bump into each other later in the local grocery store, the client bursting into tears.

A client in psychiatric day treatment comes to the last meeting with his worker wearing his motorcycle helmet, and says goodbye to her with the helmet visor down to hide his face. Another client lands up in a hospital room with her former welfare worker in the next bed. While driving past the agency, a client from years past calls on her cell phone to say cheerily, "I just wanted to hear your voice again and see if you're still there." A troubled man sends a restaurant napkin from Florida inscribed, "Don't forget me." These examples remind us that all endings are not equal and all aren't even true endings. In most cases, the process of ending, while touching us and requiring care and skill, need not be such a grave one, as the finality we imagine and react to may be an illusion.

CONCLUSION

"Termination" today often represents the client's ending a piece of brief or longer term work with a provider or agency, but by no means represents the end of personal or systems work towards the maximization of strengths, connections with others, and opportunities in life. "Ending for now" may thus be a more appropriate way to conceptualize the end of meetings with a particular worker at any given time. It may be only a matter of weeks or months before clients reach out again for services, or are mandated to participate in them.

Interestingly, endings call for use of the same engagement and assessment skills that beginnings do. Because a relationship has been built and maintained in order to facilitate work and growth, it needs careful attention and honoring at closure, too, as both the medium for the work and a valued experience between people. Memories of a good collaboration and a thoughtful ending can encourage and inform future help-seeking so that it occurs closer to stressful events and can be undertaken with more comfort, knowledge, and skill.

Some cultures ask that people suppress natural human feeling at parting so that those leaving don't feel held back by the reactions and needs of those remaining behind. By contrast, clinical practice cultures have traditions of utilizing the ending process to express feelings about the relationship and the work ending; to link past and present loss where appropriate; and to honor achievements, new relationships, and future directions. Good work and good endings go forward inside participants as lifelong assets to be cherished.

EXERCISES

1. *Reflection.* In your journal, reflect on some memorable endings you have had in your own life. Discuss your various reactions to these endings, and whether you did or didn't express a range of sentiments about what was happening and what the future would be like. What have important life transitions and endings taught you about the tasks and skills of ending? *Be prepared to discuss these last two questions in class.*

2. *Small Group Discussion.* In groups of four or five, discuss what you have learned about yourself and clients from ending work with them. Have any endings surprised you? Which are your solid ending skills now, and which still need work? Do you share any common needs for further learning about ending work?

3. *For Class Discussion.* Review as a class the major tasks and skills of ending. Contrast ending in a brief treatment, and ending after several months or years of work. Discuss your experiences with the ending customs of cultures different from your own. Pick a vignette or two to role-play in class, demonstrating mistakes in ending and some ways to reconstruct these.

4. *Instructor Activity.* Give examples of memorable experiences of your own around endings, or mistakes you learned from in ending work with clients. Explore what the big issues are for your class around endings with clients, responding to these issues after eliciting them.

5. *Author Sharing for Further Discussion.* Some years back, a client and I ended about twelve years of off-and-on work in which things went well and we developed a very warm alliance. She was able to partner and parent, and we gradually decided that couples work made more sense than individual work did. They found a good couples therapist in the area, and we parted cordially. I received cards from her from time to time, and saw her over the next few years when she would return to check in around a personal stumbling point or challenge. Gradually the cards and visits ceased as her life took its rightful shape and course. Driving past her area recently, I suddenly had the strongest urge to phone her, just to find out how she was, and how that son was who liked to wear girls' tutus. Would he be a dancer or a business major now? How was the dog whose pictures I'd seen so often, and what would have become of that hard-drinking older brother? My yearning to know about her surprised me, coming as it did from out of nowhere. I had passed her area many times without thinking about her, but I was definitely having a wish to know how she had turned out. I didn't

actually contact her—there was no real need. I just smiled to myself about it as I passed her area the next time.

For Class Discussion. Why might I have gotten the urge to find out how the client turned out after all these years? What are the factors in the client-worker relationship that can give it personal meaning even though the work remains thoroughly professional? For each of you personally, what factors make it easy to feel bonded and involved with some clients and less so with others? Discuss together the purpose and challenges of being friendly with clients without being friends.

RECOMMENDED READING

Fortune, A. E. (1987). Grief only? Client and social worker reactions to termination. *Clinical Social Work Journal, 15,* 159–171.

Murphy, B. C., & Dillon, C. (1998). Endings and transitions. In *Interviewing in action: Process and practice* (pp. 250–284). Pacific Grove, CA: Brooks/Cole.

Quintana, S. (1993). Toward an expanded and updated conceptualization of termination: Implications for short-term, individual psychotherapy. *Professional Psychology: Research and Practice, 24,* 426–432.

Shulman, L. (1990). Endings and transitions with groups. In *The skills of helping individuals, families, groups, and communities* (pp. 595–618). Itasca, IL: Peacock.

9

Epilogue

Developing Important Capacities, Allaying Common Concerns

There is no mistaking that a clinical practice career requires lifelong learning embedded in effective relationships with other people, whether they be clients, community members, instructors, or colleagues. This undertaking involves the continuous development and refinement of knowledge about self and about a great variety of people, cultures, and wide-ranging systems of support and influence. It involves seasoning through work within many different settings, modalities, and communities over the years.

QUESTIONS THAT HAUNT US ALL
FROM TIME TO TIME

Kottler and Blau (1989) believe that we all experience existential crises from time to time in our career-long development as clinicians. They suggest that the following "nagging questions" are a part of every clinician's professional and emotional world (p. 22):

- What if I don't have what it takes?
- What if I don't know what to do?
- What if my treatment harms a client?
- What if I'm caught making a mistake?

- What if I'm not really *doing* anything?
- What if my life's work doesn't really matter? (pp. 22–33)

Most of us have struggled with these questions at different points along our learning pathways. As you think about these questions and their implications, recognition dawns that you are not alone in any private agonies you may have about how well you are suited for clinical practice and how well it is suited for you. On the other hand, giving such questions too much power or free rein in your thinking can fuel excessive self-doubt and unwarranted anxieties about failing.

DEVELOPING IMPORTANT CAPACITIES

Seasoning through education, experience, and feedback helps to ease worries about competence and belonging in the world of clinical professionals. Seasoning also helps us develop capacities important to clinical practice. These capacities can't really be developed in isolation—a good thing, because in isolation we can't see our mistakes and rework them as well as we can in exchange with other frank and motivated learners. The capacities that follow must eventually manifest routinely as solid, reliable worker competencies. Instructors and mentors watch for evidence of these capabilities and often intentionally direct discussion towards their enrichment and consolidation.

Trust is the foundation stone of clinical practice and community collaborations. The very basis for the fiduciary or trustee nature of clinical roles and relationships is the trust accorded us by clients, regulatory bodies, and community observers who've experienced over many decades the reliability and helpfulness of most clinicians and clinical practice activities. We have to say what we mean, and mean what we say, demonstrating reliability and integrity in all that we undertake. Trustworthiness refers to how reliably we behave when no one else is around.

Without trust, clients wouldn't be able to meet with and reveal themselves to virtual strangers such as clinicians. Without trust in people and process, workers couldn't feel safe seeing clients outside of highly controlled work environments, since we wouldn't know who or what we might encounter. Responsible supervisors couldn't send inexperienced learners into clinical sessions without faith that both the learner and the client would emerge okay.

Authenticity, good will, and openness to others are expressed through warmth and genuineness in the work and by extending good humor, hopefulness, and welcome to clients and collaborators alike. Pretending is avoided, and workers leave people feeling respected and more at ease than may have been anticipated. The belief, encouragement, and positive regard extended to clients often stimulate hope and new initiatives from within them.

Empathy and nonjudgmental acceptance enable workers to align with clients' experience and perspectives with increasing accuracy and responsiveness, without forsaking our own core experience and perspectives in a destabilizing way. Relating with many different people and cultures increases familiarity and identification with their beliefs, values, expressive styles, and norms for relating, confiding, and working with outsiders. We seek consultation willingly when we experience unusually adverse or judgmental reactions to clients. We learn to accept people without necessarily approving of all of their behaviors, and are able to challenge destructive choices at times because we care about what happens to people. Personal work is used to expand our capacities for acceptance and empathy, especially when challenged or threatened.

Openness to new ideas and mentors allows for intensive study and the free exchange of new ideas and perspectives with colleagues and clients. Openness suggests vulnerability in its best sense: the opening up of old familiar ideas and ways to influence by the new, and accepting that there will be some pain involved in stretching. This openness inspires curiosity and the exploration of new venues for learning, as opposed to just accepting the minimum required and provided. Open learners take risks through case presentation and role play, understanding that frank feedback from colleagues regarding observed mistakes will advance practical knowledge and skill. We also come to value a not-knowing perspective, appreciating that there are many ambiguities in clinical practice and no one "right way" to understand and resolve problems.

Developing insight about self, others, and systems influences in client work involves learning to attend to multiple levels of influence at once. Since we can't help clients see or work on things that we haven't resolved or seen in our own lives, personal therapy is often undertaken to enhance calm, self-understanding, and accurate perception. Work on insight leads to more rapid and accurate identification and management of reactions in our work with a multitude of new people, systems, and cultures.

Another crucial aspect of insight is coming to terms with how privileged positions within our own respective cultures, neighborhoods, and institutions can lead us to favor some people and disempower others without awareness. Insight in these matters stimulates a wish to involve ourselves with many different cultures and to help institute social action to promote well being, rights, and opportunities for all people.

The ability to establish increasingly goal-directed and purposeful relationships with clients and others moves us from random, wandering interviewing to more focused and productive clinical conversation. We come to appreciate asking good questions, one at a time, restraining advice giving, excessive self-disclosure, and other intrusive behaviors that can detract from client time for self-exploration, expression, and reflection. We learn to work with silence and nonverbals communication, and to offer hunches aligned with the client's interests, pace, and understanding. We get better at purposely tracking time in sessions in order to leave adequate time for warm up, exploration and development of work themes and reactions, tapering down for ending, and anticipating next steps.

Developing an ethical stance towards people and work is another cornerstone of good clinical practice. Our conduct demonstrates the presence of a solid inner guidance system of values and standards that make us reliable to ourselves and others in spite of every temptation or pressure to the contrary. We put service to clients and their safety and well-being above other goals and concerns, and take action to protect, defend, and advocate for client rights and justice, even when these things are hard to do. We also expect to be treated ethically by colleagues and by the larger systems we work within, trying to hold them accountable when they think or behave in ways deemed harmful to employees, clients, or communities.

The capacity to establish and maintain productive boundaries and limits is one of the hardest assets to consolidate, since societies tend to swerve periodically between too numerous and too few limits, and between extremes of strict prohibitions and extraordinary lapses in guiding standards and structures. An old New England saying asserts that "good fences make good neighbors," and in clinical work, clarity about rules and boundaries often helps minimize confusion, ambiguity, and conflict over personal responsibilities, space, and rights. Without useful limits, environments can become chaotic and anxiety-ridden so that relaxation, constructive activities, and growth are more difficult. On rare occasions, we may have to stop working with people or settings that can't observe healthy boundaries.

WHERE TO FROM HERE?

Clinical work may feel like a calling or an avocation, but it's actually a demanding specialization affording all of the challenges, opportunities, and rewards of a discipline carried out with caring, concentration, high art, and good humor. Both the discipline and the art require years of personal stretching and acquisition of new knowledge and self-awareness. The humor and caring, while frequently indigenous to learners, are sustained through balancing and nurturing relationships and activities within and outside work.

Patience, persistence, a benign and informed learning environment, wise and caring mentors, and sufficient time for learning will all be required if clinical work is to work for clinicians as well as clients. If we're lucky, mistakes will remain our great teachers all along the way. That is a notion we can pass along very sympathetically to clients who, like us, will be learning from mistakes, as we all stretch and enrich familiar ways of knowing, being, and collaborating with others.

References

Akamatsu, N. N. (1998). The talking oppression blues: Including the experience of power/powerlessness in the teaching of "cultural sensitivity." In M. McGoldrick (Ed.), *Revisioning family therapy: Race, culture, and gender in clinical practice* (pp. 129–143). New York: Guilford.

Amodeo, M., & Jones, L. K. (1997). Viewing alcohol and other drug use cross-culturally: A cultural framework for practice. *Families in Society: The Journal of Contemporary Human Services, 227,* 240–254.

Angelou, M. (1986). *Mrs. Flowers.* Minneapolis, MN: Redpath.

Beck, J. S. (1995). *Cognitive therapy: Basics and beyond.* New York: Guilford.

Beck, A. T., Freeman, A., & Associates (1990). Theory of personality disorders. In *Cognitive therapy of personality disorders* (pp. 22–39). New York: Guilford.

Berlin, S. (1983). Cognitive-behavioral approaches. In A. Rosenblatt & D. Waldfogel (Eds.), *Handbook of clinical social work* (pp. 1095–1119). San Francisco: Jossey-Bass.

Berzoff, J., Flanagan, L. M., & Hertz, P. (1996). *Inside out and outside in: Psychodynamic clinical theory and practice in contemporary multicultural contexts.* Northvale, NJ: Jason Aronson.

Borysenko, J. (1987). *Minding the body, mending the mind.* New York: Bantam.

Brems, C. (2000). *Dealing with challenges in psychotherapy and counseling.* Belmont, CA: Wadsworth.

Briar-Lawson, K. (1998). Capacity building for integrated family-centered practice. *Social Work, 43,* 539–550.

Bricker-Jenkins, M. (1997). Hidden treasures: Unlocking strengths in the public social services. In D. Saleebey (Ed.), *The strengths perspective in social work practice* (pp. 133–150). White Plains, NY: Longman.

Bridges, N. (1993). Clinical dilemmas: Therapists treating therapists. *American Journal of Orthopsychiatry, 63,* 34–44.

Bridges, N. (1994). Meaning and management of attraction: Neglected aspects of psychotherapy training and practice. *Psychotherapy, 31,* 424–433.

Brown, L. (1988). Harmful effects of post-termination sexual and romantic relationships between therapists and their former clients. *Psychotherapy, 25,* 249–255.

Bullis, R. K. (1995). *Clinical social worker misconduct: Law, ethics, and personal dynamics.* Chicago: Nelson-Hall.

Burns, D. (1989). *Feeling good.* New York: Plume/Penguin.

Canda, E. R., & Phaobtong, T. (1992). Buddhism as a support system for Southeast Asian refugees. *Social Work, 37,* 61–67.

Cascio, T. (1998). Incorporating spirituality into social work practice: A review of what to do. *Families in Society: The Journal of Contemporary Human Services,* September/October, 523–531.

Chambon, A. (1989). Refugee families' experiences: Three family themes—family disruption, violent trauma, and acculturation. *Journal of Strategic and Systemic Therapies, 8,* 3–13.

Chao, C. (1992). The inner heart: Therapy with Southeast Asian families. In L. A. Vargas and J. D. Koss-Cionino (Eds.), *Working with culture: Psychotherapeutic interventions with ethnic minority children and adolescents* (pp. 157–181). San Francisco: Jossey-Bass.

Chu, J. (1991). The repetition compulsion revisited: Reliving dissociated trauma. *Psychotherapy, 28,* 327–332.

Coady, N., & Wolgien, C. (1996). Good therapists' views of how they are helpful. *Clinical Social Work Journal, 24,* 311–322.

Cobb, N. H., & Jordan, C. (1989). Students with questionable values or threatening behavior: Precedent and policy from discipline to dismissal. *Journal of Education for Social Work, 25,* 87–97.

Coleman, D. (2000). The therapeutic alliance in multicultural practice. *Psychoanalytic Social Work, 7,* 65–90.

Compton, B., & Galaway, B. R. (1994). *Social work processes.* Pacific Grove, CA: Brooks/Cole.

Corey, G. (1996). The counselor: Person and professional. In *Theory and practice of counseling and psychotherapy* (pp. 15–49). Pacific Grove, CA: Brooks/Cole.

Corey, G. (2000). *Theory and practice of group counseling* (6th ed.). Belmont, CA: Wadsworth.

Corey, G. (2001). *Theory and practice of counseling and psychotherapy* (pp. 42–63). Belmont, CA: Wadsworth.

Corey, G., & Corey, M. S. (1998). *Becoming a helper.* Pacific Grove, CA: Brooks/Cole.

Cormier, S., & Cormier, B. (1998). Knowing yourself as a counselor. In *Interviewing strategies for helpers* (pp. 11–34). Pacific Grove, CA: Brooks/Cole.

Corsini, R. J. (1991). *Five therapists and one client.* Itasca, IL: Peacock.

Cowger, C. (1997). Assessing client strengths: Assessing for client empowerment. In D. Saleebey (Ed.), *The strengths perspective in social work practice* (pp. 59–73). White Plains, NY: Longman.

Daniel, J. H. (2000). The courage to hear: African American women's memories of racial trauma. In L. C. Jackson & B. Greene (Eds.), *Psychotherapy with African American women* (pp. 126–144). New York: Guilford.

Daniels, J., & D'Andrea, M. (1996). Ethnocentrism in counseling. In D. W. Sue, A. E. Ivey, & P. B. Pedersen (Eds.), *A theory of multicultural counseling and therapy* (pp. 155–173). Pacific Grove, CA: Brooks/Cole.

DeJong, P., & Miller, S. D. (1995). How to interview for client strengths. *Social Work, 40,* 729–736.

Delgado, M. (1999). *Social work practice in nontraditional settings.* New York: Oxford.

Derubeis, R., & Beck, A. T. (1988). Cognitive therapy. In R. Derubeis & A. T. Beck (Eds.), *Cognitive therapies and research* (pp. 54–80). New York: Plenum.

de Shazer, S. (1988). *Clues: Investigating solutions in brief therapy.* New York: Norton.

Devore, W., & Schlesinger, E. G. (1996). *Ethnic-sensitive social work practice.* Needham Heights, MA: Allyn & Bacon.

Dillon, C. (1999). A relational perspective on mutuality and boundaries in clinical practice with lesbians. In J. Laird (Ed.), *Lesbians & lesbian families: Reflections on theory and practice* (pp. 283–303). New York: Columbia University Press.

Dorfman, R. A. (1996). Things they don't teach you in professional school. In *Clinical social work: Definition, practice, and vision* (pp. 144–165). New York: Brunner/Mazel.

Egan, G. (1998). *The skilled helper: A problem-management approach to helping.* Pacific Grove, CA: Brooks/Cole.

Feldman, L. B., & Feldman, S. L. (1997). Integrating psychotherapy and pharmacotherapy in the treatment of depression. *In Session: Psychotherapy in Practice, 3,* 23–38.

Fewell, C. H., King, B. L., & Weinstein, D. L. (1993). Alcohol and other drug abuse among social work colleagues and their families: Impact on practice. *Social Work, 38,* 565–570.

Fortune, A. E. (1987). Grief only? Client and social worker reactions to termination. *Clinical Social Work Journal, 15,* 159–171.

Gambrill, E. (1997). *Social work practice: A critical thinker's guide.* New York: Oxford.

Ganzer, C., & Ornstein, E. D. (1999). Beyond parallel process: Relational perspectives on field instruction. *Clinical Social Work Journal, 27,* 231–246.

Gardner, J. (1995). Supervision of trainees: Tending the professional self. *Clinical Social Work Journal, 25,* 271–286.

Garretson, D. J. (1993). Psychological misdiagnosis of African-Americans. *Journal of Multicultural Counseling and Development, 21,* 119–126.

Garvin, C. D., & Seabury, B. A. (1997). *Interpersonal practice in social work: Promoting competence and social justice.* Boston: Allyn & Bacon.

Gelman, S. R., Pollack, D., & Weiner, A. (1999). Confidentiality of social work records in the computer age. *Social Work, 44,* 243–252.

GlenMaye, L. (1998). Empowerment of women. In L. M. Gutierrez, R. J. Parsons, & E. O. Cox (Eds.), *Empowerment in social work practice: A sourcebook* (pp. 29–51). Pacific Grove, CA: Brooks/Cole.

Gluhoski, V. (1994). Misconceptions of cognitive therapy. *Psychotherapy, 4,* 594–600.

Goodyear, R. K. (1981). Termination as a loss experience for the counselor. *Personnel and Guidance Journal, 59,* 347–350.

Green, J. D. (1996). When a therapist breaks the rules. In N. D. Davis, E. Cole, & E. D. Rothblum (Eds.), *Lesbian therapists and their therapy* (pp. 1–10). Binghamton, NY: Harrington Park.

Groschi, W. N., & Olsen, D. (1994). *When healing starts to hurt: A new look at burnout among psychotherapists.* New York: Norton.

Gutierrez, L. M., DeLois, K. A., & GlenMaye, L. (1995). Understanding empowerment practice: Building on practitioner-based knowledge. *Families in Society, 76,* 534–542.

Gutierrez, L. M., Parsons, R. J., & Cox, E. O. (2000). *Empowerment in social work practice: A sourcebook.* Pacific Grove, CA: Brooks/Cole.

Haight, W. (1998). "Gathering the Spirit" at First Baptist Church: Spirituality as a protective factor in the lives of African American children. *Social Work, 43,* 213–221.

Haley, J. (1981). A quiz for young therapists. In *Reflections on therapy and other essays* (pp. 237–243). Chevy Chase, MD: The Family Therapy Institute of Washington, DC.

Hatch, M. L., & Paradis, C. (1993). Panic disorder with agoraphobia: A focus on group treatment with African Americans. *The Behavior Therapist* (October), 240–241.

Hawkins, C. A., & Hawkins, R. C. (1996). Alcoholism in the families of origin of MSW students: Estimating the prevalence of mental health problems using standardized measures. *Journal of Social Work Education, 32,* 127–134.

Heard, H. L., & Linehan, M. M. (1994). Dialectical behavior therapy: An integrative approach to the treatment of borderline personality disorder. *Journal of Psychotherapy Integration, 4,* 55–82.

Hepworth, D. H., Rooney, R. H., & Larsen, J. A. (1997, 2002). *Direct social work practice: Theory and skills.* Pacific Grove, CA: Brooks/Cole.

Herman, J. (1997). *Trauma and recovery.* New York: Basic Books.

Heyward, C. (1993). *When boundaries betray us: Beyond illusions of what is ethical in therapy and life.* New York: HarperCollins.

Holman, S. L., & Freed, P. (1987). Learning social work practice: A taxonomy. *The Clinical Supervisor, 5,* 3–21.

Holmes, G. E. (1997). The strengths perspective and the politics of clienthood. In D. Saleebey (Ed.), *The strengths perspective in social work practice* (pp. 151–164). White Plains, NY: Longman.

Jacobs, C. (1991). Violations of the supervisory relationship: An ethical and educational blind spot. *Social Work, 36,* 130–135.

Johanson, G., & Kurtz, R. (1991). *Grace unfolding: Psychotherapy in the spirit of the Tao-Te-Ching.* New York: Bell Tower/Crown.

Jordan, J. V. (1990). *Courage in connection: Conflict, compassion, creativity* (Work in Progress #45). Wellesley College, MA: Stone Center Working Paper Series.

Jordan, J. V. (1991). Empathy and self boundaries. In J. V. Jordan, A. G. Kaplan, J. B. Miller, I. P. Stiver, & J. L. Surrey (Eds.), *Women's growth in connection: Writings from the Stone Center,* (pp. 67–80). New York: Guilford.

Jordan, J. V. (1993). *Challenges to connection* (Work in Progress #60). Wellesley College, MA: Stone Center Working Paper Series.

Jordan, J. V. (Ed.). (1997). *Women's growth in diversity.* New York: Guilford.

Kadushin, A., & Kadushin, G. (1997). *The social work interview: A guide for human service professionals.* New York: Columbia University Press.

Kaufman, K. (1996). The therapist as self-object. *Clinical Social Work Journal, 24,* 285–298.

Kleinman, A. (1988). *Rethinking psychiatry: From cultural category to personal experience.* New York: Free Press.

Kottler, J. A. (Ed.). (1997). *Finding your way as a counselor.* Alexandria, VA: American Counseling Association.

Kottler, J. A., & Blau, D. S. (1989). *The imperfect therapist: Learning from failure in therapeutic practice.* San Francisco: Jossey-Bass.

Krupnick, J. L. (1997). Brief psychodynamic treatment of PTSD. *In Session: Psychotherapy in Practice, 3,* 75–89.

Laird, J. (1999). Gender and sexuality in lesbian relationships: Feminist and constructionist perspectives. In J. Laird, (Ed.), *Lesbians & lesbian families: Reflections on theory & practice* (pp. 47–89). New York: Columbia University Press.

Lee, C. C., & Armstrong, K. L. (1995). Indigenous models of mental health intervention: Lessons from traditional healers. In J. G. Ponterotto, J. M. Casas, L. A. Suzuki, & C. M. Alexander (Eds.), *Handbook of multicultural counseling.* New York: Sage.

Leigh, J. W. (1998). Assessment, negotiated consensus, treatment planning, and culturally relevant interventions and treatment. In *Communicating for cultural competence* (pp. 125–144). Needham Heights, MA: Allyn & Bacon.

Levinson, H. (1977). Termination of psychotherapy: Some salient issues. *Social Casework, 58,* 480–489.

Loewenberg, F. M., Dolgoff, R., & Harrington, D. (2000). The professional relationship: Limits, dilemmas, and problems. In *Ethical decisions for social work practice* (pp. 148–172). Itasca, IL: Peacock.

Lum, D. (2000). *Social work practice and people of color: A process-stage approach.* Belmont, CA: Wadsworth.

MacCluskie, K. C., & Ingersoll, R. E. (2001). *Becoming a 21st century agency counselor: Personal and professional explorations.* Belmont, CA: Wadsworth.

Madsen, W. (1999). *Collaborative therapy with multi-stressed families: From old problems to new futures.* New York: Guilford.

Malgady, R. G., & Zayas, L. H. (2001). Cultural and linguistic considerations in psychodiagnosis with Hispanics: The need for an empirically informed process model. *Social Work, 46,* 39–49.

McIntosh, P. (1989). White privilege: Unpacking the invisible knapsack. *Peace and Freedom* (July–August), 10–12.

McMillen, J. C. (1999). Better for it: How people benefit from adversity. *Social Work 44,* 455–468.

McQuaide, S. (1999). Using psychodynamic, cognitive-behavioral, and solution-focused questioning to co-construct a new narrative. *Clinical Social Work Journal, 27,* 339–353.

Mehlman, E., & Glickauf-Hughes, C. (1994). The underside of psychotherapy: Confronting hateful feelings towards clients. *Psychotherapy, 31,* 435–439.

Memmott, J., & Brennan, E. M. (1998). Learner-learning environment fit: An adult learning model for social work education. *Journal of Teaching in Social Work, 16,* 75–98.

Meyer, W. (1993). In defense of long-term treatment: On the vanishing holding environment. *Social Work, 38,* 571–578.

Miller, J. B., & Stiver, I. P. (1997). *The healing connection: How women form relationships in therapy and in life.* Boston: Beacon Press.

Miller, J. B., Jordan, J. V., Kaplan, A. G., Stiver, I. P., & Surrey, J. L. (1991). *Some misconceptions and reconceptions of a relational approach* (Work in Progress #49). Wellesley College, MA: Stone Center Working Paper Series.

Miller, W. R., & Rollnick, S. (1997). *Motivational interviewing: Preparing people to change addictive behavior.* New York: Guilford.

Mitchell, S. A., & Black, M. J. (1995). *Freud and beyond: A history of modern psychoanalytic thought.* New York: Basic Books.

Molidor, C. (1996). Female gang members: A profile of aggression and victimization. *Social Work, 41,* 251–257.

Mordecai, E. M. (1991). A classification of empathic failures for psychotherapists and supervisors. *Psychoanalytic Psychology, 8,* 251–262.

Mumm, A. M., & Kersting, R. C. (1997). Teaching critical thinking in social work practice courses. *Journal of Social Work Education, 33,* 75–84.

Murphy, B. C., & Dillon, C. (1998). *Interviewing in action: Process and practice.* Pacific Grove, CA: Brooks/Cole.

Nason, F. (1990). Diagnosing the hospital team. In K. W. Davidson & S. Clark (Eds.), *Social work in health care: A handbook for practice.* Binghamton, NY: Haworth.

Nicholson, B., & Kay, D. (1999). Group treatment of traumatized Cambodian women: A culture-specific approach. *Social Work, 44,* 470–479.

Okazaki, S. (2000). Treatment delay among Asian-American patients with severe mental illness. *American Journal of Orthopsychiatry, 70* (January), 58–64.

Okun, B. F. (1992). *Effective helping: Interviewing and counseling techniques.* Pacific Grove, CA: Brooks/Cole.

Okun, B. F. (1997). Issues affecting helping. In *Effective helping: Interviewing and counseling techniques* (pp. 250–284). Pacific Grove, CA: Brooks/Cole.

Okun, B. F., Fried, J., & Okun, M. L. (1999). *Understanding diversity: A learning-as-practice primer.* Pacific Grove, CA: Brooks/Cole.

Organista, K. C., Dwyer, E. V., & Azocar, F. (1993). Cognitive behavioral therapy with Latino outpatients. *The Behavior Therapist* (October), 229–233.

Patterson, L. E., & Welfel, E. R. (2000). *The counseling process.* Belmont, CA: Wadsworth.

Pearlman, L. A., & Saakvitne, K. W. (1995). *Treating therapists with vicarious traumatization and secondary traumatic stress disorders.* In C. Figley (Ed.), *Compassion fatigue: Coping with secondary traumatic stress disorder in those who treat the traumatized* (pp. 150–177). New York: Brunner/Mazel.

Pinderhughes, E. (1998). Black genealogy revisited: Restorying an African-American family (pp. 179–199). In M. McGoldrick (Ed.), *Re-visioning family therapy: Race, culture, and gender in clinical practice.* New York: Guilford.

Poindexter, C. C., & Linsk, N. L. (1999). "I'm just glad that I'm here": Stories of seven African-American HIV-affected grandmothers. *Journal of Gerontological Social Work, 32,* 63–81.

Poindexter, C. C., Valentine, D., & Conway, P. (1999). *Essential skills for human services.* Belmont, CA: Wadsworth.

Pope-Davis, D., & Constantine, M. G. (1996). Multicultural therapy theory and implications for practice. In D. W. Sue, A. E. Ivey, & P. B. Pedersen (Eds.), *A theory of multicultural counseling and therapy* (pp. 112–122). Pacific Grove, CA: Brooks/Cole.

Prochaska, J. O., Norcross, J. C., & DiClemente, C. C. (1994). *Changing for good.* New York: Morrow.

Ram, Dass, & Gorman, P. (1993). *How can I help?: Stories and reflections on service.* New York: Knopf.

Regehr, C., & Glancy, G. (1995). Sexual exploitation of patients: Issues for colleagues. *American Journal of Orthopsychiatry, 65,* 194–202.

Reynolds, B. C. (1942). *Learning and teaching in the practice of social work.* New York: Rinehart.

Rogers, C. (1967). The necessary and sufficient conditions of therapeutic personality change. *Journal of Consulting Psychology, 21,* 95–103.

Rollock, D., & Gordon, E. W. (2000). Racism and mental health into the 21st Century: Perspectives and parameters. *American Journal of Orthopsychiatry, 70,* 5–13.

Rooney, R. (1992). *Strategies for work with involuntary clients.* New York: Columbia University Press.

Rose, S. M. (2000). Reflections on empowerment-based practice, *Social Work, 45,* 403–412.

Saari, C. (1989). The process of learning in clinical social work. *Smith College Studies in Social Work, 60,* 35–49.

Sable, P. (1995). Pets, attachment, and well being across the life cycle. *Social Work, 40,* 334–341.

Saleebey, D. (1992). Biology's challenge to social work: Embodying the person-in-environment perspective. *Social Work, 37,* 112–118.

Saleebey, D. (1997). *The strengths perspective in social work practice.* White Plains, NY: Longman.

Schamess, G. (1999). Therapeutic love and its permutations. *Clinical Social Work Journal, 27,* 9–26.

Sharf, R. S. (2000). Comparison, critique, and integration. In *Theories of psychotherapy and counseling: Concepts and cases* (pp. 599–644). Belmont, CA: Wadsworth.

Sherman, M. D. (1996). Distress and professional impairment due to mental health problems among psychotherapists. *Clinical Psychology Review, 16,* 299–315.

Shulman, L. (1991). *Interactional social work practice: Toward an empirical theory.* Itasca, IL: Peacock.

Shulman, L. (1999). *The skills of helping individuals, families, groups, and communities.* Itasca, IL: Peacock.

Simon, R. (1992). *Clinical psychiatry and the law.* Washington, DC: American Psychiatric Press.

Strean, H. (1993). *Therapists who have sex with their patients: Treatment and recovery.* New York: Brunner/Mazel.

Sue, D. W., Ivey, A. E., & Pedersen, P. B. (Eds.). (1996). Basic assumptions of a theory of multicultural counseling and therapy. In *A theory of multicultural counseling & therapy* (pp. 13–29). Brooks/Cole.

Surrey, J. (1991). The self-in-relation: A theory of women's development. In J. V. Jordan, A. G. Kaplan, J. B. Miller, I. P. Stiver, & J. L. Surrey (Eds.), *Women's growth in connection: Writings from the Stone Center.* New York: Guilford.

Sussman, M. B. (1995). *A perilous calling: The hazards of psychotherapy practice.* New York: Wiley.

Swenson, C. R. (1998). Clinical social work's contribution to a social justice perspective. *Social Work, 43,* 527–537.

Swigonski, M. E. (1996). Challenging privilege through Africentric social work practice. *Social Work, 42,* 153–161.

Taylor, R. J., Ellison, C. G., Chatters, L. M., Levin, J. S., & Lincoln, K. D. (2000). Mental health services in faith communities: The role of clergy in black communities. *Social Work, 45,* 73–87.

Trachtman, R. (1999). The money taboo: Its effects in everyday life and in the practice of psychotherapy. *Clinical Social Work Journal, 27,* 275–288.

Urdang, E. (1979). In defence of process recording. *Smith College Studies in Social Work, 50*(1), 1–15.

Vasquez, M. (1991). Sexual intimacies with clients after termination: Should a prohibition be explicit? *Ethics and behavior, 1,* 45–61.

Weaver, H. N. (1999). Indigenous people and the social work profession: Defining culturally competent services. *Social Work, 44,* 217–225.

Webb, N. B. (1999). *Play therapy with children in crisis: Individual, group, and family treatment.* New York: Guilford.

Weingarten, K. (1992). A consideration of intimate and non-intimate interactions in therapy. *Family Process, 31,* 45–58.

White, M., & Epston, D. (1990). *Narrative means to therapeutic ends.* New York: Morrow.

Wolfson, E. R. (1999). The fee in social work: Ethical dilemmas for practitioners. *Social Work, 44,* 269–273.

Index

TO THE OWNER OF THIS BOOK:

We hope that you have found *Learning from Mistakes in Clinical Practice* useful. So that this book can be improved in a future edition, would you take the time to complete this sheet and return it? Thank you.

School and address: _____

Department: _____

Instructor's name: _____

1. What I like most about this book is: _____

_____

_____

2. What I like least about this book is: _____

_____

_____

3. My general reaction to this book is: _____

_____

4. The name of the course in which I used this book is: _____

_____

5. Were all of the chapters of the book assigned for you to read? _____

    If not, which ones weren't? _____

6. In the space below, or on a separate sheet of paper, please write specific suggestions for improving this book and anything else you'd care to share about your experience in using the book.

_____

_____

_____

_____

_____

Optional:

Your name: _____ Date: _____

May Brooks/Cole quote you, either in promotion for *Learning from Mistakes in Clinical Practice* or in future publishing ventures?

Yes: _____ No: _____

Sincerely,

Carolyn Dillon

Attention Professors:
Brooks/Cole is dedicated to publishing quality publications for education in the social work, counseling, and human services fields. If you are interested in learning more about our publications, please fill in your name and address and request our latest catalogue, using this prepaid mailer. Please choose one of the following:

☐ social work   ☐ counseling   ☐ human services

Name: _____

Street Address: _____

City, State, and Zip: _____

FOLD HERE

FOLD HERE